Quick!
Show Me
Your Value

A Trainer's Guide to:

- **Communicating Value**
- **Connecting Training and Performance to the Bottom Line**

Includes CD-ROM with
Ready-to-Use Templates

**ASTD
Press**

SOCIETY FOR
HUMAN
RESOURCE
MANAGEMENT

Theresa Seagraves

ASTD Press is an internationally renowned source of insightful and practical information on workplace learning and performance topics, including training basics, evaluation and return-on-investment (ROI), instructional systems development (ISD), e-learning, leadership, and career development.

The Society for Human Resource Management (SHRM) is the world's largest association devoted to human resource management. Representing more than 180,000 individual members, the Society's mission is to serve the needs of HR professionals by providing the most essential and comprehensive resources available. As an influential voice, the Society's mission is also to advance the human resource profession to ensure that HR is recognized as an essential partner in developing and executing organizational strategy. Founded in 1948, SHRM currently has more than 500 affiliated chapters within the United States and members in more than 100 countries. Visit SHRM online at www.shrm.org.

Ordering information: Books published by ASTD Press can be purchased by visiting our Website at store.astd.org or by calling 800.628.2783 or 703.683.8100. This book, other SHRM-published books, and a wide spectrum of books on business, management, and human resources can be ordered from SHRM by calling 800.444.5006, or via the Website at www.shrm.org/shrmstore.

Library of Congress Control Number: 2004101570

ISBN: 978-1-56286-365-4

Acquisitions and Development Editor: Mark Morrow
Copyeditor: Karen Eddleman
Interior Design and Production: Kathleen Schaner
Cover Design: Amy Waggoner
Cover Illustration: Eric Peterson

Printed by Victor Graphics, Inc., Baltimore, Maryland
www.victorgraphics.com

Table of Contents

Preface

It is widely accepted that the economics of the 21st century are driven by knowledge. It is the age of the knowledge-driven economy, which, according to the United Kingdom Department of Trade and Industry (1998), is " . . . one in which the generation and exploitation of knowledge play the predominant part in the creation of wealth." Competitive advantage is led by the capacity to gain knowledge and skill. Well-being, security, growth, and livelihoods are becoming more dependent on the talents and services of the knowledge worker. In short, people and, therefore, workplace learning and performance (WLP) matter more than ever before.

Our leaders recognize this fact. Industry studies (Sugrue, 2003) show that whether economic times are good or slow, many companies continue to increase spending on training as a percentage of their payroll. Top executives put their money on the recognition that the knowledge and productivity of their people equal the organization's success, but along with this recognition and spending comes increased responsibility.

Executives in all organizations—whether large or small, publicly or privately held, nonprofit, governmental, or academic—are the stewards of their people and the servants of their customers. The money available to their organizations is always finite, and in today's economic conditions there is nothing to spare. Funds must be spent in the wisest, most productive way possible.

Every day, executives must choose whether to allocate money to research, to technology, to infrastructure, to the refinancing of debt, to outside services, or to the development of their people. The more money that is spent in one area, the less there is to develop another. Every day is a balancing act. It is expected, even demanded, by governments, boards of directors, shareholders, and the people of the organization itself that executives be held accountable for their investments. For many executives, this accountability is stewardship. Stewardship is a call to courage and responsibility. Stewardship creates meaning and purpose in their lives. Money is the measure of their accountability. The language of their responsibility is finance.

As the stewards of their organizations, executives know that the performance of their people is of utmost importance, so they continue to spend on training. Yet every day, executives face the frustration of only being able to hope that their WLP solutions are creating significant financial value. As responsible servants, executives must allocate resources to where it is obvious that those resources can do the most good for all. If the value of WLP is not obvious to them, then these executives are honor-bound to uphold their duty and allocate more resources to those whose value they can understand. Even though people are becoming ever more critical to an organization's success, and some organizations do indeed continue to spend on learning and performance, the resources for WLP always seem to be on the edge of being reduced, shifted, or cut entirely.

To WLP professionals, people have always mattered. Many years of dedicated research, honed by hundreds of thousands of practitioners, have created a whole language around the improvement of human performance in organizations. There is a rich, deep body of knowledge of what works to improve knowledge, skill, productivity, and job satisfaction for workers around the world in an endless number of professions. This ability to improve the lives of others calls to the soul of the WLP professional. It creates meaning and a deep purpose in life. WLP professionals also carry the honor of accountability and responsibility. Evaluations are the measure of their accountability. The language of their responsibility is performance metrics.

WLP professionals do not spend their time hoping that their solutions will be effective. They can state with confidence, pride, and honor that they use their profession's vast knowledge of what works to meet the greatest call of all: service to others. Yet, every day WLP professionals face the frustration of being unable to communicate value in terms that others accept and understand. They can only hope that the value of what they bring to the table is obvious, but to their sorrow and sometimes deep personal loss, they discover that hope is simply not good enough. *For their own well-being and for the well-being of those whom they serve, they must move beyond hope.* In the fast-paced times of the knowledge economy, WLP professionals will be successful not only because of the quality of their solutions, but because of their ability to communicate their value in terms that executives understand.

The emergence of the knowledge economy has moved human talent and performance directly into the boardroom. Therefore, if investments in workplace learning and performance are to continue to increase, executives must understand—quickly, clearly, and decisively—the financial value they are receiving for those investments.

As a WLP professional, I've interacted daily with executives, colleagues, peers, and staff members. Early on, I struggled with and eventually became more adept at translating the impact of performance into the impact on finance. I also learned to translate the issues in finance into opportunities for performance. I couldn't help but notice, though, that this was not easy for me or for anyone else including executives, colleagues, peers, or staff members. Nevertheless, as the knowledge economy gains overwhelming strength, the need to make this communication easier and more transparent is getting more urgent.

This book helps clarify the connections between performance metrics and finance and helps WLP professionals and executives communicate with each other about the objectives for, the value of, and the results from WLP and human performance improvement programs.

Clarifying these connections is critically important. Great programs can get more support. More support can lead to even greater impact. Resources can be redirected for better service to the organization. Connecting performance metrics to finance can teach organizations what they do well and how to become even better at it. Connecting finance to performance can help an organization be more profitable or otherwise serve its customers, people, sponsors, and community more efficiently. Connecting performance to finance serves to make the resources available to improve performance and to help the organization fulfill its mission of service that all organizations ultimately have.

The primary purpose for this book is to move beyond hope when communicating the value of WLP solutions to executives; you, as a WLP professional, must be able to communicate the value of WLP solutions in a real and tangible way. But, there is another purpose for this book. Chances are that if you are a WLP professional, you didn't get into the field of learning and performance for the numbers. You got into WLP for the people. Telling a story of results and performance to the people who did the work is just as important as telling that story to the executives who manage them. People crave feedback. They need to know when they have done well. They need to know what they can do even better.

A story without numbers may be good, but a story with numbers can be incredibly powerful. Telling a group of people their own story, especially if it is a great achievement, can change their lives forever. Too often people really don't know what they've accomplished or how good they are. Putting their story into financial terms opens their eyes and gives them a reason to stand straighter, walk taller, and find meaning in their own lives. This knowledge ripples into their relationships and their marriages, into the examples they set for their children, and into their life ambitions.

I have seen the power of honest, believable numbers to transform a person's entire self-concept. Having the opportunity to tell a great story is like the privilege of playing Santa Claus for children when they are very young. The surprise, the excitement, the overwhelming feeling of wonder, pride, and joy that I see when people realize what they've accomplished creates deep satisfaction and a desire to give again.

I am always amazed at the power of understanding another's point of view and the power that numbers bring to the realization that a job has been well done. For me, understanding will forever be one of the greatest gifts that one can leave behind. May this book lead you to greater knowledge, greater compassion, greater communication, greater understanding, and greater service as stewards, leaders, and educators of people. If it has done so for even one, then I will be forever grateful for the gift of a life well spent in the service of another.

No book is possible without the support and guidance of many other people. First, I thank Cliff Lawley and Steven Wagner-Davis for their teamwork in the original presentation that became the genesis of this book. I gratefully acknowledge the work of Toni Hodges, the lead reviewer of this book and offer my thanks to Randall, the Deborahs, Bernice, Mitch, the Bills, Gary, Susan, Suzanne, Jim, Pauline, Dave, Sabine, John, Sarah, Lynne, Rick, Lane, Darnell, Marcela, and many more who have been very enthusiastic about these concepts and were willing to suggest, review, and apply. I thank my inspiring co-workers at TLSA: Mary Ann Seagraves, Andrea Moore, and Marita Peak. I thank my children, Kelly and Kevin, and, most of all, my wonderful husband, Bill.

Finally, I acknowledge the Divine Spirit who guides us all. Søren Kierkegaard said, "Life can only be understood backwards; but it must be lived forwards." I can't count how many times I wondered why I was living forward through something and yet when I look back, I think, "Of course! What else would have shaped me for how I needed to serve next?" I'm divinely cared for. How can one ever say thank you enough?

Theresa Seagraves
April 2004

Introduction

In the hectic pace of the knowledge economy, two things have become critical to every organization's success. The first is knowledge. The second is time. As a **workplace learning and performance (WLP)** professional, your role is to continuously improve the knowledge, skills, and performance of the people you serve. You've felt today's hectic, never-ending pressure to do more with less—less money, less time, and fewer people. And, it's not just you. Everyone around you is experiencing the same pressure as the knowledge economy speeds life up for us all.

When you finish this book, you'll have seen how to

◆ understand the basics of the executive language of finance
◆ search for and uncover hidden potential for value
◆ demonstrate your **value** with a solid program around the numbers
◆ leverage your most current business context
◆ get your point across quickly in today's fast-paced world.

Communicating Value Well—and Fast!

How can you communicate effectively in 30 seconds or less? Successful communicators rely on having a clear purpose; knowing their audience and their audience's immediate concerns; and organizing specific types of performance and financial information into simple, consistent formats so that they can rapidly communicate value. The key to their success is preparation.

This book will show you how to quickly and effectively communicate your financial value. **Value communication** is defined as clearly and succinctly describing the value of your WLP interventions in terms of the **financial**

measures that your audience is judged by. For example, if your chief financial officer is judged on a financial measure such as **return-on-assets**, showing how your WLP intervention has improved return on assets is a powerful way to gain approval and support.

Figure I-1 presents a concise model for identifying, positioning, delivering, measuring, and communicating your value.

Figure I-1. The flywheel of the financial value process.

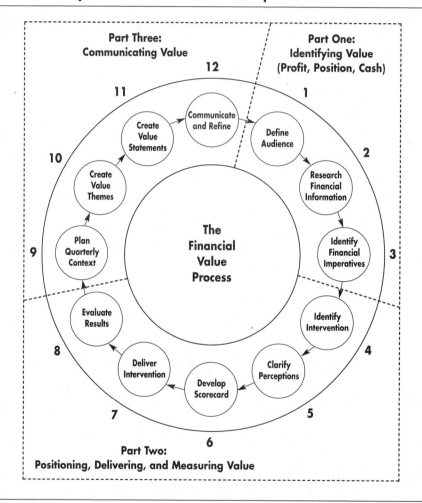

The groundbreaking book *Good to Great: Why Some Companies Make the Leap . . . and Others Don't* (Collins, 2001) describes building phenomenal business momentum as a process of turning a flywheel to generate power. The first few turns of the flywheel can seem slow and arduous, but the more turns that are completed, the faster the flywheel spins and the more momentum the business gains. Similarly, in figure I-1 the **financial value process** is depicted as a flywheel. Stick with the concepts in this book. The first few times you go through the process can seem slow and arduous. But the more people in your organization that you can get to push the flywheel and the more turns you complete, the more power, speed, and momentum you create for yourself and for your organization or your client's organization.

How Can This Book Help?

Excellent **value communication** starts with understanding what value is from your audience's perspective and how that value maps to your goals. Each layer of an organization perceives value differently. The definition of what will be valued and how much value there should be starts at the top where performance is measured in **financial metrics**. As responsibilities move down through an organization, financial metrics eventually become the required performance metrics of the individual contributor. Part One, "Identifying Value," explains value and helps you see how your value is interpreted by the people you are communicating with.

Not every reader will feel excited at the thought of using finance to communicate value. Some of you may even feel as if you've just been offered a trip to the dentist. But, in chapter 1 ("The Golden Key—Finance"), you'll find some compelling evidence about what executives expect as fundamental knowledge, skills, and abilities from WLP professionals.

Every organization has four basic layers of management and individual contribution. Even though the basic language is finance, specific financial measures are transformed as they move through these layers. This means that the way your value is perceived shifts, as well. In chapter 2 ("Decoding Value"), you'll look at step 1 of the financial value process: defining your audience. You'll examine these common layers, what the expectations and duties of people in these layers are, and how their measures are connected so that you can relate your value appropriately to each person you communicate with. In this chapter, and throughout this book, you'll find forms and exercises that will immediately help you apply what you've learned to your own organization or a top client's organization.

It's great to have a better understanding of how value must be translated to different levels of your audience, but that's not enough to gain true creditability. You have to know what issues your unique organization is grappling with right now, so that you can speak to real needs. In the financial value process, step 2 is research financial information. But, the first time through the flywheel, it's impossible to research when you don't yet know what you want.

Because the executives at the top of any organization determine what everyone else will focus on, it is important to first understand their perspective. Chapter 3 ("An Overview of What an Organization Will Value") defines the financial imperatives that keep your executives awake at night.

Step 3 of the financial value process is to identify financial imperatives. This step is covered in chapter 4 ("Profit"), chapter 5 ("Position"), and chapter 6 ("Cash"). You'll walk through explanations and examples of exactly how financial measures can be connected from the services you provide to the bottom line of your organization. You may find out that you are even more important to your organization's success than you realized. Or, you may find new opportunities for focusing your time and resources to bring even more value to your organization or your clients. Once again, you'll find exercises that you can use immediately in your organization.

Now, you are in the position to go back and address step 2 of the financial value process, researching financial information. In chapter 7 ("Business Intelligence: Researching What an Organization Will Value"), you'll learn why you want to get on the distribution list for reports you never thought you would be interested in. If you are a consultant who'd like to sell your services or a job seeker who would like to work for a new organization, you'll learn how to find out information from the outside looking in. Either way, you'll finish this chapter with a plan to find the information that describes the hidden (or not-so-hidden) value your executives need you to address.

At this point, you'll have learned a great deal. You'll know what's valuable to your executives. You know that you can create interventions that bring value, so you'll be ready to communicate, right? Not so fast. Even if you know the numbers behind the value and know that your intervention is what is needed, you must still deal with the perceptions of your audience. In Part Two, "Positioning, Delivering, and Measuring Value," you'll refine your **financial value chains** and value analysis through the lens of past history and future expectations. Every organization builds up conscious and unconscious expectations of what you do and how you do it. Part Two gives you insights on how these assumptions and realities affect how your value communication will be received and what you can do to make sure your value is positioned and measured appropriately.

Step 4 of the financial value process is to identify an intervention. Selecting the appropriate performance or learning intervention is an important step in creating value. But wait! Before you do the work of delivering your intervention, you need to perform step 5 of the financial value process: clarify perceptions. As a WLP professional, there is a great deal that you do every day that is taken for granted. Other things that you do would delight your audience if they only knew about them! You don't want to confuse the two situations because each dramatically affects your ability to be heard. Chapter 8 ("What Have You Done for Me Lately?") reveals a model for dealing with the obvious and hidden assumptions about your value.

Now that you've dealt with the conscious and unconscious assumptions about what you do or are offering to do, you still need to relate your value to what's happening right now with your audience. Chapter 9 ("The Financial Imperatives Scorecard") will show you how to plan and track your value so that you'll know what types of numbers you are delivering and can show how much value you bring to your audiences' financial value measurements. This chapter helps you complete step 6 of the financial value process: develop scorecard.

Step 7 in the financial value process is to deliver the intervention. This is a step that many WLP professionals are very comfortable in performing. It is Step 8 of the financial value process, evaluating results, that is often missing when communicating financial value. It's possible to make a claim that you will provide a certain amount of value within a specific timeframe, but eventually you have to prove your claim or lose your creditability. Chapter 10 ("Value and the Levels of Evaluation") shows you how levels of evaluation map to the four layers of an organization and what level of evaluation data is the minimum needed at each layer. But, because no one's evaluation data ever seems to be ideal, you'll get some ideas on how to make the best use of the data you have.

Anyone can get numbers, but if you can't communicate your value quickly, you'll lose your chance to have your executives understand how valuable you are. Part Three, "Communicating Value," describes how to put all the information you have gathered into an accessible, concise format so that your value can be heard.

Every audience you communicate with has its own hectic workload of tasks to manage. Step 9 of the financial value process is to plan quarterly context. This step is covered in chapter 11 ("Building Your Context Plan"). This chapter shows how to predict what tasks your audience will need help with throughout the year. If you've never looked at how the natural lifecycle of a business drives the activities of executives, and how they prioritize and filter your communication, this chapter will help. When you finish this chapter, you'll not only know what value to focus on, but when it's best to communicate about it.

Great negotiators recommend picking a central theme and sticking to it when convincing others of the value of what they offer. In chapter 12 ("Your Communication Base: Value Themes"), you'll learn how to create performance-based value themes that allow you to focus your communication.

This chapter covers step 10, which involves creating themes for your **financial value**.

In chapter 13 ("Creating Financial Value Statements"), you take all of your planning and pull it together into great communication! The average executive gives you 30 seconds or less to get your point across. Creating statements is the goal of step 11 of the financial value process. This chapter introduces a quick, concise format to communicate your value and shows you how to polish just what you'll say in your 30 seconds. You'll get hints on different ways to use your financial value statements. The way you look at communicating value will never be the same again.

Finally! All that preparation is going to pay off. Step 12 is communicate and refine. Chapter 14 ("Putting It All Together") refines all the exercises, examples, and forms that you'll have worked so hard to complete throughout this book. You'll see a summary of how the financial value process can work to generate momentum and power in your value communication. And, because your insights will have grown as you've worked through the book, you'll have a chance to review your questions, data, and statements so that your value will really shine.

But, if executives believe you should be able to do these things now, they'll expect even more in the future. Executives need professionals who not only know what is valuable and when it's valuable, they need people who can help them move faster and faster to stay ahead of their competition and meet the needs of the people they serve. For these goals, hope is not a strategy. In chapter 15 ("Conclusion: The Courage to Begin"), you'll look again at the difference between the WLP professional's focus on the goal of the job and your executive's focus on the goal behind the job. In the end, the difference between the two is the courage to lead others from an understanding of the numbers to an understanding of the power of workplace learning and performance.

Perhaps this seems like a great deal of work. Well, it is. After all, the knowledge and skill of an organization's people is one of the most important competitive advantages in today's global marketplace. Retaining and building the best talent is an urgent topic in the executive boardroom.

It may seem unreasonable to have to work this much to get your value across in 30 seconds or less, but remember: You only have one chance to make a good first impression. First impressions are important to your momentum. If you haven't been communicating financial value well in the past, it can be hard to get your flywheel started. Nevertheless, the rewards can be phenomenal. Once your flywheel is turning, it will rapidly pick up power and speed. The strongest flywheels will feel like an unstoppable force in the service of your people.

Help Navigating This Book

To make this journey to financial know-how easier, this book uses a series of icons that you can use along your roadmap to success. These icons serve as signposts and can tell you what is important to remember, point out key facts along the way, and let you know when it is time to try something on your own. Here are the icons you can expect to see:

 In This Chapter: Look for this icon to tell you what will be found in each of the book's chapters. This signpost is especially important because this book builds from general business information to specific application about communicating your value.

 Here's the Point: One of the special features of this book is that it speaks directly to WLP professionals. Just so that the point of discussion about reading financial statements does not get lost, look for this icon to tell you concisely why understanding a concept is important.

 ABC MediCompany Case Study: One of the ways that this book explains its concepts is through the use of a fictional organization called the ABC MediCompany. You can follow the progress of the WLP professionals working with this company by following the icons throughout the book.

 Let's Review: At the end of each chapter you'll find a set of bullets informing you about the key learning you should have gained in the chapter and providing you with a financial learning challenge.

 Website: In many of the chapters, you'll find one or more exercises that will help you apply the concepts in this book to your own work. These exercises may be easier for you to complete if you can print larger versions or multiple copies. When you see the Website/CD icon, you will be able to find a downloadable version of the exercise at www.astd.org/astd/publications. For your convenience we have included a CD-ROM at the back of this book with the same set of exercises just in case an Internet connection is not immediately available.

Quick! Show Me Your Value offers two other tools to aid you in your quest for a seat at the executive table. First, you'll notice that key words are highlighted in bold type throughout the book. You may consult the glossary at the back of the book to look up their meaning. Second, there is an Additional Resources section, organized in a fashion to help you pinpoint sources of supplementary information.

The Monster Under the Bed

Workplace learning and performance professionals have long believed that they should have a seat at the executive table. Yet, other types of executives are never promoted to the table without the knowledge and skills addressed in this book. Executives do not accept people without these skills as their equals or trusted advisors. By expressing dislike or even fear of finance and numbers, WLP professionals must bear much of the responsibility for the challenges we face stemming from a lack of respect from executives, absence of influence within the organization, unreasonable budget constraints for WLP programs, and no seat at the table.

Simply put, WLP professionals do not communicate their value. WLP professionals have not been equipped to communicate their value. And, because executives cannot perceive WLP professionals' value, it simply does not exist for the executives.

A fear of finance is like the monster that children think might be under their beds. One day, when they are brave enough to look, they realize that the monster doesn't really exist at all. The concepts in this book may seem big and scary, but once they are explored and learned, you'll wonder what you were really so afraid of. You'll be free of the monster! You'll be able to explore the new possibilities available to you when you really understand the value you bring to your organization and when that value is recognized, accepted, and applauded by your peers at the table.

Part One

Identifying Value

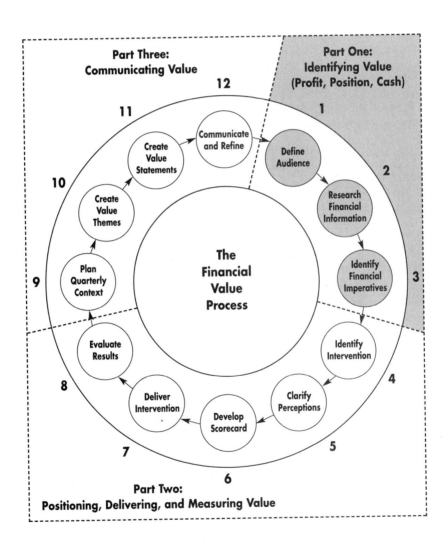

Part Three:
Communicating Value

12

11

10

9

Part One:
Identifying Value
(Profit, Position, Cash)

1

2

3

Communicate and Refine

Create Value Statements

Define Audience

Research Financial Information

Create Value Themes

Identify Financial Imperatives

Plan Quarterly Context

The Financial Value Process

Identify Intervention

Evaluate Results

Clarify Perceptions

Deliver Intervention

Develop Scorecard

8

7

6

5

4

Part Two:
Positioning, Delivering, and Measuring Value

Communicating your value starts with identifying the audience you would like to address with your communication and what that audience will value in financial terms. The first part of this book will cover the first three steps in the financial value process:

- ◆ Step 1: Define Audience
- ◆ Step 2: Research Financial Information
- ◆ Step 3: Identify Financial Imperatives.

In the seven chapters of Part One, you will

- ◆ learn why executives are requiring WLP professionals to speak the language of finance
- ◆ be introduced to a simple structure for translating value from the measures of your senior executives into the learning and performance measures of your WLP solutions and back again
- ◆ discover how to recognize opportunities for communicating value by reading the same reports your executives read: income statements, balance sheets, and cash flow statements
- ◆ perform business intelligence research that will show you exactly where to find the data you need.

The Golden Key—Finance

 IN THIS CHAPTER:

- An example of communicating value
- The importance of quick connections to what is valuable
- What knowledge and skills executives require for the new workplace learning and performance professional
- How financial communication increases sales and funding
- How financial communication improves job search success
- Why communicating financial value is as important to the participants in your programs as it is to executives.

So, you want a seat at the table. This book offers you some practical and, in some ways, easy steps that can get you out of the position of feeling like you are an expendable part of the organization and into a position of being in control of your destiny. How? By knowing a few facts about what is important to those who sign the checks (yours included) and how to present what you do to these decision makers in an understandable and bottom-line-driven manner.

Take a look at the following statement regarding an inventory management performance solution:

"Five months after implementing our inventory management performance initiative, spoilage decreased by 30 percent, thereby reducing our cost of goods sold by $475,000. The result is a significant increase in our gross profit and available cash. This improvement in cash flow means that our company can implement our aggressive new market strategy in the first quarter with substantially less risk from short-term debt."

How do you think your senior management would react if you walked into a meeting and presented a version of this statement for a program you had delivered? Do you think it could help you gain a seat at the table and more respect for yourself or your department?

If you are reading this book, the answer is probably yes. The purpose of this book is to show you how to think about your own organization in these terms; how to create your own unique **value statements**; and, ultimately, how to develop a solid plan to constantly communicate value up the ranks to the most senior levels of your organization or your client's organization.

As you might guess, being able to make these kinds of statements is the result of some work on your part and a little knowledge. As you go through this book, you will build the knowledge and confidence to develop your own plan, but to create your plan you will have to understand some basic concepts.

Stick with it. This book tells you just what you need to know and nothing more. In addition, you will be advised all along the way why these concepts are important to **workplace learning and performance (WLP)** professionals. As you work through this book, you will find easy to follow worksheets and exercises that simplify the process of connecting your WLP solutions to the financial value your senior executives are looking for.

Shouldn't the Value of WLP Be Obvious?

During this, the information age being driven by the knowledge economy, it is more apparent than ever that the knowledge, skills, and abilities of an organization's people drive its effectiveness, competitiveness, and bottom-line value. It would seem that your **value** as a WLP professional, who builds and nurtures an organization's people, would be amazingly obvious. Communicating your value should be easy, effective, even fun.

Such is not the case, however. Many WLP professionals are baffled that what seems obvious to them is not so obvious to others.

There's no doubt about it: Clearly understanding your value and helping others to see that value is one of the most important things you can do. It makes a difference in your own life, helps you support or manage your department, and earns recognition and support for the departments you serve or for your customers. Unfocused communication wastes everyone's time.

There is also no doubt about this fact: Building and retaining talent has become an urgent topic in the boardroom. Executives can no longer assume that their WLP programs or other key interventions are paying off. They need frequent, clear communication about their employees' performance improvement. If your value as a WLP professional is not obvious, the problem must not be the importance of the message. So where's the problem?

The Eye of the Beholder

If ever there were a loaded word, *value* would be it. One person may believe your value as a WLP professional is fantastic, but another may scoff in disbelief. There are good reasons why each person perceives the value of WLP professionals so differently. The first and most important one is how the measures—especially **financial measures**—of an organization affect audience perspective.

In an organization, each individual's value is determined by how well they meet the **financial metrics** or financial measures of their job. Therefore, people value what helps them meet their measures more easily; for example, fewer customer complaints about their helpdesk technical advice or what helps them improve the level of the measures they pay attention to every day (a smaller cost of goods sold). People are people, no matter what level or job title they hold. The fact that people manage their behavior to meet their measurement objectives holds true, whether you're talking about individual contributors or the top officers of the largest multinational organizations.

The recognition that people manage their behavior based on how they are measured and that they value what helps them with those measures has been well known for decades. The issue in communicating value does not lie in whether you are moving the bar on people's metrics; it lies in your audience's ability to quickly (in 30 seconds or less) make the connection between what you are doing and their own personal benefit. Most of the time, that connection is very hard to make without help.

Because this point cannot be overemphasized, this book offers stories of WLP professionals just like you who have dealt with the challenge of making the financial value connection.

Michael's Story

Michael (not his real name) has just been promoted to corporate training manager for a large manufacturing company. But just two years ago, he was thought to be failing miserably in his former position of field training manager.

At that time, Michael's job was to oversee training in his company's manufacturing plants. Michael says that he dramatically turned around the perception that he was failing by making only one change: He started reporting the progress of his trainees in a way that underscored the financial gain to his corporation and the connection to the measures of each of the plant managers.

Michael became a hero by doing nothing differently other than communicating value in a way that helped his plant managers see connections that were simply not obvious in their fast-paced environment.

But, I HATE Numbers!

You probably didn't go into organization development, people development, or any other "development" for the numbers. You got into your profession because you love people. Even if you don't hate numbers, practitioners in WLP have not focused nearly as much attention on financial numbers as line managers do in other parts of a business. If you don't know why you would want to focus on finances and numbers, then consider the following studies.

Twin Cities Study

In 2001, members of the Twin Cities (Minneapolis and Saint Paul, Minnesota) Human Resource Association, ASTD, and the Organization Development Network came together to identify what kept human asset professionals away from the leadership table (Kindley, 2001).

The group invited business leaders to a workshop to clarify their expectations and how human asset professionals could meet their expectations. The workshop participants listed several knowledge, skills, and abilities necessary for a human asset professional to gain access to and respect in executive circles (table 1-1).

Table 1-1. Knowledge, skills, and abilities required of executives (Kindley, 2001).

Knowledge About:	Skills to:	Ability to Think Like a:
Competitive environment (sales, cost, profit)	Write a business plan	General manager
Executive team and their roles	Write and present a business case	Sales manager (internal and external)
	Manage a budget Read financial statements	Marketer
	Ask higher-level questions Sell Think strategically rather than tactically	Independent contractor or free agent

Reprinted with permission from Randall Kindley and HR.com.

Notice that planning, developing, or running any type of WLP program is not even mentioned in this list. WLP proficiency was simply taken for granted by these executives. Clearly, in order to gain creditability and respect, these executives are expecting an expanded and financially oriented perspective from practitioners in the human asset professions.

Sales Skills Return-on-Investment Study

In 2002, a major technology firm commissioned a **return-on-investment (ROI)** study to determine the effectiveness of a financial selling skills course (Seagraves, 2003). The course taught salespeople to read **financial statements** to understand the issues that an organization was facing and then to show the value of their solutions to the executives within that organization. In other words, just as was shown in the Twin Cities study, this class taught salespeople to read financial statements and to think strategically, rather than tactically.

One of the most significant findings of the study was that when salespeople used the concepts and techniques taught in this class in a deal, those salespeople reported that they were more than 30 percent more likely to win those deals than they were before they took the class.

During debriefing interviews, several salespeople in the study insisted that their use of a financial value approach was the only reason they had won some of their deals during the tough economic conditions of 2002. These salespeople stated that they had gained more respect and trust from executives because those executives believed the salespeople understood their business and could effectively communicate the value of the solution they were offering. The salespeople had earned a seat at the table as trusted advisors to their clients.

Notice that the executives in the Twin Cities study expected human asset professionals to have the ability to read financial statements, to present a business case, and to sell. In the Sales Skills ROI Study, being able to communicate value in financial terms was a critical skill set to master in order to gain respect and a competitive edge.

Job Search Success Stories

If the requirements of the Twin Cities executives and the success of salespeople using financial based strategies don't appeal to you, then consider the success of WLP job seekers using these techniques.

Job seekers who discuss the value of their skills in terms of the financial benefits those skills could bring to their potential employers report getting further in highly competitive interviews and having shorter job search cycles.

In a very successful case, during the tough job market of late 2002, the president of one of the chapters of the International Society for Performance Improvement (ISPI) cold-called a company and landed a job just a day after hearing a presentation on the concepts in this book. She credits her success to what she learned from the presentation. Apparently, her hiring manager agreed with the executives from the Twin Cities: Speaking the language of finance makes a dramatic difference in communicating value.

If Not for Yourself, Then for Those You Serve

There is another important reason for understanding and communicating value in terms of financial numbers. As noted in the preface, telling a story of results and performance to the people who generated those results is just as important as telling that story to the executives who manage them.

Familiar, Comfortable, Confident

Human resource management and development is starting to move into the executive boardroom. If you want to gain more recognition, respect, resources, or ability to help the people you serve, you cannot avoid numbers. The answer lies in becoming more familiar, comfortable, and confident in using numbers to understand, identify, demonstrate, and communicate value.

 LET'S REVIEW: ───────────────────

- Communicating value depends on a command of financial terms and a clear, concise structure that summarizes the most important points in 30 seconds or less.
- The terms used to communicate value must correspond to the measures that the audience pays attention to every day.
- A seat at the table will only be gained if the WLP professional acquires the ability to think like a general manager or salesperson, to think strategically and not tactically, to understand financial statements, and to sell.
- Financially based communication has been shown to significantly increase persuasiveness, sales, and job search success.
- Understanding how much their performance improvements have improved the bottom line can be just as important to participants as it is to their executives.

In the next chapter, you'll uncover one of the most important keys to communicating comfortably and confidently with numbers. That key unlocks the secret code behind the numbers and measures that make up value.

2

Decoding Value

 IN THIS CHAPTER:

- ◆ Step 1 of the financial value process: define audience
- ◆ How to play the game and break the ROI code
- ◆ How cascading metrics create financial value chains
- ◆ How to translate from the language of performance to the language of finance and back again
- ◆ Why you must make the translation clear for your audience
- ◆ Why understanding your audience's ROI timeframe makes a difference in getting them to pay attention to your value statements.

"What is my return-on-investment for this program?" This question is one of the most frustrating questions today's WLP professional can face. Even if you, as a WLP professional, give what you think is a good answer, you may often get the sinking feeling that your audience is thinking politely that you just don't get it. Even if you've gone to the effort to determine a return-on-investment answer of, for example, 125 percent, you may still be left with the sense that you didn't answer the real question and that you've blown it, but you don't know why. What went wrong?

How the ROI Game Works

When people say "my return-on-investment" or "my ROI" or "my value" for a program, sometimes they are asking for a number such as 125 percent, but more often, they are not. They are using ROI as a codeword—a codeword that means something different for each person who uses it. To see how fast the definition of value changes and why it is important to be able to connect your answer to what is meant by each individual person, let's reminisce about a childhood game of communication called "Rumor."

Children usually play "Rumor" with eight to 10 people. The players sit in a chain, and someone volunteers to go first. The first person makes up a rumor: the more fantastic, the better. He or she then whispers the rumor into the ear of the next person, who in turn whispers it to the next person, and so on. When the rumor reaches the last person, he or she announces what he or she heard. Then the first person in the chain shares the original rumor, which usually bears little resemblance to the rumor after it's been passed along by all the children in the chain.

> *Understanding value in an organization works much the same way as the game of "Rumor." What is described as valuable in an organization changes as it moves from the beginning of the chain (a senior executive) to the end (the individual performer). What's different in an organization is that the change in how value is described is much more predictable than in a simple game of "Rumor." That predictability is the key to breaking the ROI codeword.*

Using the principle of cascading metrics, the financial measures at the top (profit, liquidity ratios, cash flows) are always broken down into more specific measures for the next layer of management. That management layer breaks the metrics down again. Eventually, what began as the financial measures of the top officers becomes the performance metrics of the individual contributor.

Cascading Metrics

Just as it is well known that people manage their behavior to meet their performance metrics, the idea that organizations have cascading metrics is not new. This concept has been described in such famous business management methodologies as the Japanese **Hoshin process** (Kenyon, 1997) introduced in the 1970s and 1980s and in the **balanced scorecard movement** (Kaplan and Norton, 1996) of the 1990s and 2000s. If it seems sometimes that you just do not understand what your audience is asking, it may be a signal to take a step back and reexamine what you know.

This chapter takes you back to the fundamentals and looks at the movement of finance, metrics, and value through an organization from a fresh perspective. This process will help you complete step 1 of the **financial value process:** define your audience.

The Financial Value Chain

Figure 2-1 shows the layers of people in an organization as a **financial value chain.** For simplicity's sake, four levels are used to describe the movement of value through any organization. Depending on the size of the organization you work with, there may be more or fewer actual levels in your organization. No matter how many organizational layers you really have, the people in these layers tend to operate like one of the four levels in this model.

Figure 2-1. The financial value chain.

Individual Performer

The first level (shown at the far right in figure 2-1) is the level of the Individual performer. This is the level that WLP professionals are most comfortable with simply because this is where most of the people in an organization reside and where the majority of the WLP professional's work is focused. WLP professionals know how to "talk" at this level because they often think of the success of their WLP programs in terms of performance objectives—in other words, in terms of the Individual performer's metrics.

First-Level Management/Operations

The second level is the First-Level Management/Operations (1st/Ops, pronounced *first ops*) layer. This is a tactical layer comprising first-level supervisors and high-level operations contributors who have a great deal of influence over the financial performance in other jobs. An example of a 1st/Ops person is a lead buyer in a purchasing department. This person may be an individual contributor but, depending on the business, would need to be highly positioned to work closely with other 1st and Mid-level managers in manufacturing, distribution, or marketing units.

Middle Management

Moving to the left in figure 2-1, the next level in the financial value chain is the Middle management (Mid) layer. These are the managers of managers. These people operate at a strategic level. They are, however, still required to stay within the budgets they have been assigned. They must still follow the directions of the final, or Senior level.

Senior Level

You will recognize the Senior level (at the far left in figure 2-1) by the use of certain words in their titles. Chief anything (chief executive officer, chief financial officer, chief information technology officer, and so forth) is a tip-off that a person occupies the Senior layer.

The word senior or executive coupled with a title is another clue. For example, many corporations use several levels of vice presidents. Senior executive vice president is a typical senior title. In other organizations, such as the government, there can be many levels of directors. Senior executive director is a higher form of the title of director and is more likely to be used at the top of the organization. The focus of the Senior layer is to create the vision, direction, and pace for the rest of the organization. This layer has the most discretion in moving funds across the organization and the most clout in supporting key initiatives that get time, resources, and attention.

Translating Value Through the Chain

Communicating **value** seems difficult because it is invisible. If the terms for value at each layer become visible, then understanding the code for value suddenly becomes easier to do. Figure 2-2 is a sample financial value chain that shows how the definition of value changes as measures move through the four layers of an organization. A financial value chain is defined as a cascading, linked set of measures where the left-most measure is a broad, financially based measure of a Senior executive and the right-most measure is a specific, performance-based measure of an Individual contributor.

In the example shown in figure 2-2, Senior management is concerned about the organization's **contribution profit margin (CPM).** The contribution profit margin represents the difference between how much money comes in and how much money it costs to create and deliver products or services,

Figure 2-2. A sample financial value chain.

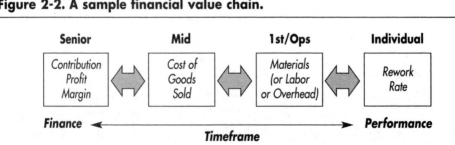

before one worries about things like being able to spend money on new research and development (R&D), pay fixed expenses, make loan payments, pay taxes, or announce dividends.

Most organizations operate on much slimmer margins than many people realize. If production costs creep up faster than revenue comes in, the contribution profit margin slips. The business is headed for trouble. Eventually, there may not be enough money to invest in crucial R&D, make payroll, or take advantage of new **market** opportunities. As stewards of their organizations, Senior managers know what it means not to be able to keep ahead of their competitors or not make payroll, loans, or taxes. It means layoffs, restructurings, and other unpleasant situations to have to deal with. You can bet that the contribution profit margin keeps many Senior managers awake at night.

Senior managers share their sleeplessness with others. They assign each of their Mid managers a portion of the organization's costs to control or revenue to generate. In the case illustrated in figure 2-2, Mid manufacturing management is concerned about the growing **cost of goods sold (COGS)** and how that affects the contribution profit margin. The cost of goods sold is defined as the total of the **material costs,** labor costs, and overhead costs required to make or buy the products that an organization sells. Organizational insomnia gets worse as Mid managers tighten their focus on COGS. With all this lack of sleep, is it any wonder that your audiences have such short attention spans when you are trying to communicate your value?

Now, Mid managers will not go it alone either. COGS is made up of material costs, labor costs, and overhead costs. In this case, the focus is on material costs. Since people will manage to their measures, 1st/Ops-level managers are completely focused on getting material costs under control. In figure 2-2, contribution profit margins, COGS, and material costs finally make it down to the Individual contributor in the form of improving **rework rates.** The rework rate is defined as the percentage of goods or actions that are defective or of such low quality that they must have additional material or labor added to them before they can be sold or accepted.

Most WLP professionals focus on the Individual layer. The language of this profession is the language of performance objectives. WLP professionals must ask themselves questions such as: "How can we best train our manufacturing workers to minimize the rework rate in plant seven?" At the Senior level, though, the language is the language of finance. Senior managers ask themselves questions such as: "How can we improve our contribution profit margin?" At the beginning of this chapter, it was noted that many WLP professionals feel as though they just did not get it when they were asked, "What is my return-on-investment for this program?" To get it when communicating value, WLP professionals must be able to make the connections in the financial value chain visible so that they understand the perspective of their audience.

How to Translate Value

Each level of manager in each separate department, division, or unit has more or less responsibility and, therefore, smaller or broader measures depending on his or her level. This is one part of going back to the basics.

Another part of the basics that many of WLP professionals miss is that each level of your audience will not make the translation for you of what, say, a change in rework rates means to material costs, COGS, or contribution profit margin. Because many WLP professionals are not comfortable with the language of financial measures or skilled in mapping financial value chains, it is easy to fall into the trap of hoping it will be obvious how valuable they are if they speak the language of performance.

In the Information Age, people have no time. They are completely focused on value in the terms that they know it by. They simply will not translate for you what you are trying to say. Your Senior managers want you to act like a salesperson. A key reason is that salespeople know it is their job to make that translation because no one will give five minutes of their time to translate for them.

A personal story may help illustrate this point. I once worked for a high-level sales manager who had a short attention span and a blunt communication style. I interviewed him as part of a research study on how executives viewed the value of **human performance technology (HPT)**. During that interview, I asked this manager what he believed the value of HPT to be. His response was that it was not his job to tell me what the value of HPT was. It was my job to tell him. He had people approaching him every day telling him exactly why and how they could help him accomplish his goals. If I could not tell him why HPT was valuable to him, then I was wasting my time and his.

Translating value is your job. If you force others to make a translation for you, they will either assume there is no value, or they will draw their own conclusion. Just as in the game of "Rumor," their conclusions may not bear any resemblance to what you wanted them to hear. That can be disastrous to making a sale. It is also disastrous in communicating value. If you are being looked at as though you didn't get the ROI code-word, the first thing to determine is whether you stated your value in terms that matched their level in their measures.

Financial Value Timeframes

Even if you are giving people information at their level and in their terms, you may still be overlooking another basic piece of the puzzle. In figure 2-2, the final piece of the picture is the timeframe that each audience is interested in. Knowing the timeframe of each level's measures is important when you are showing that you can follow the value story down the chain and that you get the code.

Timeframes are dynamic. What the levels of management care about depends very much on how the economy is doing. In a poor economy, urgency goes up and time gets even shorter. All measurement timeframes compress. Table 2-1 offers some guidelines about the effect of the economy overall.

Table 2-1. The effect of the economic climate on financial measure timeframes.

Financial Value Chain Level	Good Economy	Poor Economy
Senior	Manages financial measures to meet the goals of a three- to five-year period	Wants to know what you can do for them in a year
Mid	Works to achieve goals within a one- to three-year period	Wants to hear about results you can achieve in this quarter
1st/Ops	Manages in a timeframe of one quarter to one year	Needs information that will help them in four to six weeks
Individual	Works in one-week to one-quarter periods	Needs immediate daily or weekly help from your program

You not only need to match your value to the terms of the audience, but you must also acknowledge the timeframe the audience needs to have results delivered in.

Building Financial Value Chains

If you have never built a financial value chain, your next question might be, "Where do I start?" The answer is anywhere. Start at the bottom and build up, at the top and build down, or in the middle and build out. Start with whatever you know.

If your target organization or the organization that you want to communicate value to is a megacorporation, you may never communicate directly with the CEO or CFO, but the management layers you work with often do. You need to be able to communicate value directly to your immediate audience. You also need to help the audience communicate value to the next level and up.

This is a good time to get started on your financial value chains. Exercise 2-1 asks you to define the names and titles of your audience and the timeframes that it needs to see results in.

No matter how much you think an audience ought to care about the value you are communicating, the fact remains that people only have so much time and attention to spend. They will focus on results that solve their most pressing priorities, as they understand them from their managers. You will go a long way in being perceived as "getting it" if you communicate value that way, too.

 LET'S REVIEW:

- This chapter addressed step 1 of the financial value process: define audience.
- ROI should not always be taken literally. It is frequently used as a codeword. The term ROI is often used when a person would like you to tell them the value of your interventions in terms that matter to him or her.
- What is valued within in an organization is always defined at the top of the organization. The terms that the value is referred to transform themselves as measures are taken from a broad to a narrowly defined state. This linkage of measures can be described in a financial value chain.
- The broad, high-level measures of the Senior level are described using financial terms or in the language of finance. The narrow, specific measures of the Individual level are described in performance terms or in the language of performance. By demonstrating a direct causal link from broad to narrow measures, the WLP professional can translate value into any point along the financial value chain.
- It is critical to make the translations for your audience so that you draw them to the conclusions that you would like them to reach. If you leave the translation for your audience to do, the audience either will not do it or will draw an incomplete or incorrect conclusion.

Exercise 2-1. Define your audience and its timeframe for results.

 Directions: Complete the following steps for this exercise. If you prefer not to write in this book, go to the companion Website (www.astd.org/astd /publications) to download a PowerPoint file for this exercise.

1. Fill in the names and titles for each of the four boxes displayed under one of the levels of your audience.
2. Fill in the timeframes you believe each audience may be most focused on demonstrating results.
3. If you don't know the names, titles, or timeframes for one or more of your audiences, you may put a question mark in the box or the timeframe. This will be a reminder to you that you have some research to complete as you read about performing business intelligence research in chapter 7.

Step 1: Define Audience

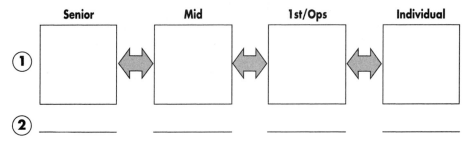

Example:

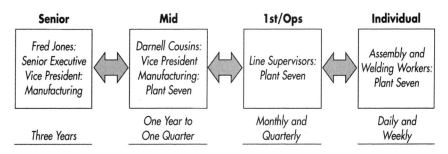

◆ Understanding the timeframe in which each level of your audience needs to hear about results is as important as being able to describe results in terms the audience recognizes. If results are not available in the appropriate timeframe, your audience will not see the value of your interventions.

◆ Connecting your value communication to the highest priorities of the Senior level will gain you more time and respect.

No matter where you decide to start, there is one more fundamental that should not be overlooked: You must be certain that the financial value chain you are communicating about is connected to the top priorities of the Senior-level managers.

The next chapter will describe the broad categories of financial value that your WLP intervention can provide. Whether you work inside or outside your target organization, the chapters after that will show you how to analyze an organization to discover its most pressing financial priorities. Matching the value of your intervention to what is valued by the organization is a critical connection.

3

An Overview of What an Organization Will Value

 IN THIS CHAPTER:

- An introduction to step 3 of the financial value process: identify financial imperatives
- Basic assumptions underlying the financial examples used in this book
- The keys to what executives value: profit, position, and cash
- An introduction to ABC MediCompany.

You know that numbers are important, but many WLP professionals have not paid much attention to financial numbers. You may be facing the daunting task of figuring out both where to find the numbers you need and how each individual number connects to the larger scheme of things.

By understanding the three fundamental types of financial priorities, as well as the balance that exists among them, you will be able to translate financial measures down through each level of the value chain. As you learn more about financial priorities in this chapter and in chapters 4, 5, and 6, you will be able to complete step 3 of the financial value process. After you understand what you are looking for, you'll be ready for chapter 7, which addresses step 2 of the financial value process (research financial information).

A Note About the Financial Examples

There are many, many types of organizations around the world. Organizations may be publicly held (that is, they sell stock, or portions of ownership, to the general public), or they may be privately held. They may be gigantic or very small, for profit or nonprofit. Organizations may be within the government, provide education, or sell commercial products or other services.

The industries that these organizations serve are equally varied. The organization may be a manufacturing company, but what it manufactures can vary from food to automobiles. It may provide services, but those services may be as different as computer repair services or dry cleaning.

In the United States, accountants are required to follow **generally accepted accounting principles (GAAP)** when preparing financial statements, but, even so, this book cannot provide a complete understanding of all of the variations possible for every organization.

The goal of these examples is to introduce you to the language, framework, and the most common types of financial issues that senior managers face. These examples can impart an understanding of how you, as a WLP professional, help drive the desired financial outcomes within a organization. This book relies upon basic examples suitable for either a simple manufacturing or service situation. As you read these examples, allow your creativity to play with how the same concepts can be applied for your unique organization. You can learn more about basic finance by reading the finance books listed in the Additional Resources section in the back of this book.

Depth of Detail

The depth of financial information available to you will differ depending on whether you are internal or external to your target organization. Other than what is required by law to be published, financial information is usually treated very confidentially. Many readers, such as OD directors, instructional designers, or on-staff instructors, have access to internal memos, white papers, intranets, and management financial reports. Management financial reports are more detailed versions of public financial reports, plus additional reports that allow managers within an organization to monitor their daily operations and take informed action. Financial statements prepared for external publication are less detailed on the theory that it is best not to tell your competition too much about how you are running your day-to-day operations.

Readers who are external consultants, training vendors, or job seekers may benefit by understanding the financial statements and value chain examples presented in the next few chapters. Your strategy for researching financial value chains will differ in that you will need to rely more heavily on additional external sources of information, networking, and a sound strategy for asking excellent questions during sales calls or interviews.

Beginning the Chain: Financial Imperatives

Because Senior-level managers drive the measures of everyone else in the organization, it is important to start by understanding the three financial imperatives, or yardsticks, by which Senior managers are ultimately measured. These imperatives are **profit, position**, and **cash.**

Maintaining a daily balance of profit, position, and cash is the role of every Senior-level manager. Figure 3-1 draws a picture of these imperatives and the balance among them.

Profit

The starting point in this analysis of value is the organization's profit performance. Profit is measured by adding incoming revenue and subtracting outgoing expenses within a specified period of time. Profit is shown on a report known as the **income statement** or the **profit and loss statement.**

Many people believe that if an organization is making a profit, it must be doing well. Not necessarily! An organization may be making a profit, but how it does so defines the stability of its business position. The dot.com bubble taught many people the value of managing position.

Figure 3-1. The financial imperatives and their measures.

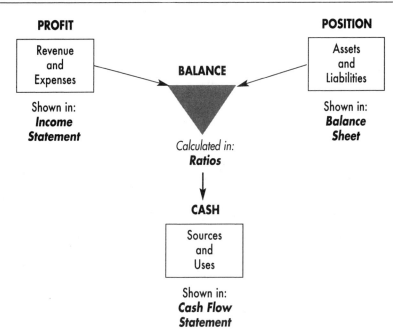

Position

Position is the mix of the assets and liabilities of an organization. An organization that is too heavily in debt, versus other methods of funding to make a profit, is at a high risk of being unable to withstand adverse business conditions. Such an organization is said to be highly **leveraged**, that is, to be carrying far too much debt versus the amount of assets on hand available to pay back that debt if it should suddenly need to do so, given a greatly reduced revenue stream.

Individuals know that if they have reached the limit on their credit cards and then lose their job, they could be forced into bankruptcy to resolve money problems. Such individuals have borrowed a great deal, assuming that future income would cover their debt. Unfortunately, because of the loss of a job, they are unable to pay the debt back or to get more debt to cover expenses.

Organizations can get into the same situation. **Managing position** means maintaining the appropriate mix of the assets, liabilities, and owner's equity of the organization. **Assets** are items such as cash or things that can be converted to cash in the short or long term. **Liabilities** are short- and long-term debts. **Owner's equity**, also known as **shareholder's equity**, is the ownership claims to the value of the assets in an organization. An organization's position is shown on its **balance sheet.**

Cash

Profit and position define the third imperative: cash. Every manager and every WLP professional who wants a seat at the table must understand that *profit does not equal cash.* An organization may be making a profit, but the actual cash from that profit may be tied up in forms that are not easy to spend. The cash may be tied up in what is known as **accounts receivable,** or the payments owed to the organization by its customers for what they have purchased. Or, the cash may be tied up in the form of **inventory**, the stock on hand that's ready to deliver as soon as a sale is made.

Senior managers must always ensure that the organization has enough real cash on hand at all times to cover its payroll, expenses, and loan payments. The sources and uses of cash come from continuous changes in the net income, assets, and liabilities. These changes are documented in the **cash flow statement.**

A Balancing Act

Managing profit, position, and cash is a constant balancing act. The final part of knowing what keeps Senior-level managers (and, therefore, everybody else) awake at night requires that you understand how the organization maintains an optimal balance among these three imperatives. Senior managers monitor balance by using ratios. **Ratios** are a comparison of how large one type of profit, position, or cash measure is in relation to another. Examples of common ratios are inventory turnover ratio, return-on-assets (ROA), and **contribution profit margin ratio.**

Ratios consist of two types: **operating ratios** and **financial ratios.** Operating ratios tell a Senior manager if the organization's day-to-day activities are staying within acceptable boundaries. Financial ratios tell a Senior manager if the organization is maintaining the appropriate returns for its efforts.

Creating value chains that reach from the language of performance to the language of finance requires a connection to profit, position, cash, as well as the balance that must be maintained among these three imperatives.

Making the connection between what WLP professionals do and what those who manage the financial side of organization do during the week is sometimes not easy to see. To help you see the connection, this book uses a fictitious medical manufacturing and services company: ABC MediCompany. ABC manufactures a line of products, offers some services related to its products, and has an established customer base. In the next three chapters, you will see sample financial statements and ratios for ABC. You will learn how to use measures from these statements to communicate your value to ABC's Senior managers, Mid managers, 1st/Ops managers and Individual contributors.

LET'S REVIEW:

- ◆ Financial information is often treated very confidentially. The amount of data you may have access to will vary depending on whether you are internal or external to an organization.
- ◆ In general, executives value three broad categories of financial impact. These categories are their financial imperatives: profit, position, and cash.
- ◆ It is important to know the basic types of financial statements and what they describe, so that you can explain what you are looking for when researching financial data. Profit is shown in the income statement, position is shown in the balance sheet, and cash is shown in the cash flow statement.

◆ Executives value solutions that can be shown to help maintain or improve the balance among their financial imperatives. In the language of finance, balance is described in the form of ratios. There are two types of ratios: operating ratios and financial ratios.

◆ This book uses a hypothetical case involving a hypothetical company—ABC MediCompany—to help explain financial value concepts and demonstrate financial value communication.

In the next chapter, you'll take a closer look at tying the value of WLP interventions to the first financial imperative: profit.

4

---------------------------→

Profit

 IN THIS CHAPTER: ─────────────

- ◆ The profit component of step 3 in the financial value process: identify financial imperatives
- ◆ How to read an income statement
- ◆ Why revenue and sales mix are so important
- ◆ The four key profit lines in an income statement
- ◆ Examples of financial value chains connected directly to revenues, expenses, and profit lines
- ◆ Some important profit ratios.

Profit (or loss) is where the analysis of financial performance begins. Examining profit begins your work on step 3 of the financial value process: identify financial imperatives. Accounting terminology is not standardized for the report that depicts an organization's profit and loss. This report may have such titles as profit and loss statement, **statement of operations**, income statement, or a similar name. This discussion sticks with the widely recognized term *income statement*.

The Income Statement

On the income statement, information about revenues (incoming funds) and expenses (outgoing costs of doing business) are added and subtracted.

33

Ultimately, the addition and subtraction creates what is known as the bottom line, or the **net profit** (or loss) for the organization.

 Figure 4-1 displays the income statement for the fictitious company ABC MediCompany.

Figure 4-1. A sample income statement for ABC MediCompany.

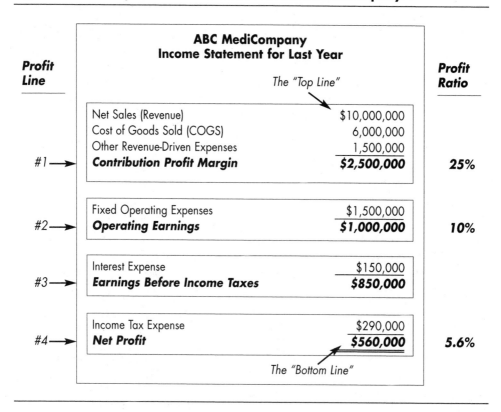

Notice that the income statement is split into four parts. Each part reflects a separate profit line that must be carefully managed in order for the organization to thrive. Table 4-1 explains the four profit lines.

Both the top line (net sales or revenue) and each of the subsequent three profit lines must be constantly monitored by Senior managers to ensure that the organization meets its goal for the **bottom line**—the fourth profit line (net profit or loss). On the right-hand side are three profit ratios, or a calculation of how big that profit line is compared to the size of the top line of net sales (revenue).

Table 4-1. The four profit lines that appear on an income statement.

Profit Line	Calculation
Contribution Profit Margin	Net sales (revenue) minus COGS and other revenue-driven expenses
Operating Earnings	Contribution profit margin minus fixed operating expenses
Earnings Before Income Taxes	Operating earnings minus interest expense
Net Profit (or Loss)	Earnings before income tax minus income taxes

For companies that are publicly traded, there is a great deal of attention paid to the profit margins, with investment gurus such as David and Tom Gardner of "The Motley Fool" (www.fool.com) recommending that they prefer to see margins that stay even or slightly and consistently rise as one of the key indicators of good stock performance (Gardner and Gardner, 1996). This puts a great deal of pressure on Senior managers.

A Picture Is Worth a Thousand Words
Many WLP professionals find a list of numbers, even one as simple as ABC's sample income statement, difficult to relate to. Because revenue, **profit lines**, and **profit ratios** are so important in communicating value, let's put the income statement into a picture. Figure 4-2 paints a picture of how ABC's Senior management did within the analogy of a profit yardstick.

What These Numbers Mean
The first thing to notice in the bars in figure 4-2 (or if you prefer, in the numbers in figure 4-1) is that what started as a large amount of revenue at the top ended as a rather small sliver of remaining net profit. Many people believe that for-profit businesses keep a huge percentage of their revenues as profit. This is rarely the case. A few exceptional organizations can manage to keep as much as 10 percent of their revenues as net profit. The majority of businesses, though, are closer to the 5 to 7 percent net profit range (Tracy, 1996).

In ABC's case, the net profit is 5.6 percent, or $560,000 of the original $10 million. Is this a good net profit for ABC? It's hard to say without comparing ABC to its competitors. Given current conditions in ABC's industry, making 5.6 percent profit is very respectable. Still, with a net profit of

Figure 4-2. Sample revenue and profit line chart.

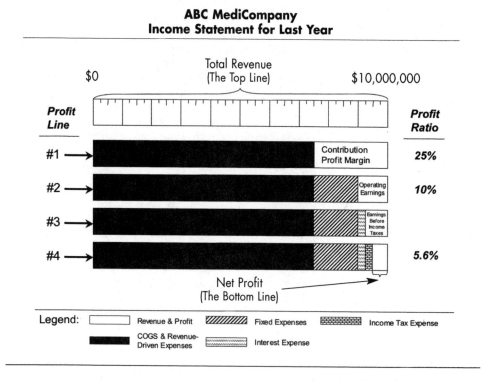

this size, there's not much room for error. If ABC keeps its revenues the same next year, the rising cost of inflation alone would eat approximately 2 percent of ABC's net profits next year. If there were a sudden shortage of a key material or an aggressive new competitor in ABC's market, it would not take much to push ABC into a net loss instead of a net profit. For successful Senior managers, there is no time when they can reduce their diligence about the bottom line. For the struggling Senior management team, there is even less rest for the weary.

The next thing to notice is how large some of the expense bars are in relation to others. Senior managers must manage every profit line, but they will spend their time and attention in proportion to the size of each expense bar in order to make sure that the entire organization is managed well.

Senior managers will spend their time and attention with you in the same way. If it is possible for you to do so, prioritize your value communication to make the most connections to where you already know your Senior managers will be focusing large portions of their time.

The Top Line: Revenue

The first bar to at look in figure 4-2 is the top revenue line. Bringing in sufficient revenue is crucial. Without enough revenue to start with, Senior managers will have to take drastic steps by cutting expenses elsewhere.

But, not all revenue is created equal. Senior managers and high-level sales and marketing managers spend a great deal of time making sure that they have the right **sales mix** of products and services, price and volume. In a manufacturing business, too high a price for a product drives customers to the competition. Too low a price raises volumes but will also raise the corresponding expenses needed to produce that volume. The lower price may bring in more volume, but that volume may also raise expenses to the point where the business loses money on every sale.

The appropriate sales mix is also critical in maintaining or improving the very important measure of **market share.** The organization with the largest share of the total market for an industry enjoys considerable power within that industry. Many companies are very concerned about any slip in market share and will constantly adjust their sales mix to protect or improve their market share position.

Every WLP professional needs to understand the revenue of his or her target organization because so much of the rest of the financial language around profit is discussed in terms of how much of the original revenue the organization gets to keep for its efforts. If you are a WLP professional working with sales or marketing, it is also critical to understand the desired sales mix to make sure the correct knowledge and behaviors are supported by your interventions. A small miscalculation in behaviors can create a big difference in final profit. Move behavior to the optimum mix, and you enhance revenue at minimal cost. Encourage suboptimal behavior, and the organization may struggle mightily with controlling costs and maintaining market share. Struggle too long or too much and the organization no longer exists.

For further discussion of the advantages and disadvantages of various sales mix scenarios for product or service businesses, see John Tracy's book *Budgeting à La Carte: Essential Tools for Harried Business Managers.* It's listed in the Additional Resources section of this book.

Another way in which revenue is not created equally is when the organization records revenue from a one-time transaction such as the sale of a large asset or division of the company. For this discussion in communicating the value of WLP interventions, the focus is on renewable revenue generated by ongoing sales or other continuing activities.

To see how revenue breaks into cascading measures through an organization and how those measures can be translated into value chains, take a look at figure 4-3.

 To help draw a visual link from the financial value chain to WLP interventions, the financial value chains in this and subsequent profit, position, and cash examples have possible WLP interventions depicted.

Where to Place Your Value. In the top half of figure 4-3, starting on the left-hand side, are examples of revenue measures for each type of audience, ending on the right with examples of WLP interventions that may improve those measures.

The closer you get to the Individual level of your audience the longer and more varied the list of possible measures and interventions becomes. The list of measures and possible interventions in this example are not restricted to what our fictitious ABC MediCompany might use. The list of measures and possible interventions is also by no means exhaustive in covering every type of organization in every industry. The point of the example in figure 4-3 is not to give you an exhaustive list, but rather to show you how such a list can be created so that you can use this format to build a list ideally suited to your target organization.

Figure 4-3. Revenue measures and a sample financial value chain.

Possible Revenue Measures:

Senior	Mid	1st/Ops	Individual	Intervention
Contribution Profit Margin	Revenue Examples: Net Sales, Rents, License Fees, Royalties	Revenue Measures Examples: Region, District or Store Quota; Average Deal Size for Territory; Average Discount Rate; Promotion Response Rates; Rebates; Coupons; Returns	Revenue Measures Examples: Sales Rep Quota; Daily Sales; Average Deal Size; Average Discount Rate; Renewal Rate; Orders per Week; Percentage Returns per Store	Examples: Basic or Advanced Sales Skills; Negotiation Skills; Presentation Skills; Proposal Writing; Account Management Process; Customer Courtesy; Product Training; Cash Register/Point-of-Sales Training; Consulting Skills; Compensation and Incentives

Sample Revenue-Based Value Chain:

Senior	Mid	1st/Ops	Individual	Intervention
Contribution Profit Margin	Net Sales	Average Discount per Deal for Region	Average Discount per Deal	Negotiation Skills

Finding Your Value. Note that at the bottom of figure 4-3 is an example of how one set of revenue measures has been formed into a chain that links the development of negotiation skills to revenue and a very important profit margin—the contribution profit margin.

In the ABC MediCompany example, let's assume that the salespeople are negotiating discounts that exceed the industry average and that ABC is in danger of losing too much profit if this trend continues. The sales training manager for ABC has done an excellent job of determining the root cause of the problem. An investigation has determined that the company's salespeople lack confidence in their sales skills and jump to offering a discount much too quickly in order to get the sale. This issue is widely spread across ABC's sales regions. The practice is bringing down the total net sales for the company. Negotiation skills training with a subsequent reinforcement program is the selected intervention.

The connection from negotiation skills to revenue and the contribution profit margin may seem a little too obvious for some. But, using an easy example allows you to focus on the format of the example itself.

Profit Line #1: Contribution Profit Margin

When managers refer to their profit margin, the contribution profit margin line is the one they are usually talking about. Contribution profit margin is calculated by adding together all of the incoming net revenues for a organization and subtracting out the

◆ costs of the materials or labor used to make the products, otherwise known as the cost of goods sold (COGS)
◆ operating expenses that are dependent on and driven primarily by revenue-generating activities.

If you want to calculate what is known as the gross profit, take net sales and subtract out only COGS. Looking back at figure 4-1, you can see that the CPM for ABC would have been calculated by taking net sales ($10,000,000) and subtracting COGS ($6,000,000) leaving a remainder or gross profit of $4,000,000. Then, taking gross profit ($4,000,000) and subtracting other revenue-driven expenses ($1,500,000) leaves a CPM of $2,500,000.

Once again, different types of organizations subtract different types of expenses from their revenue to determine CPM. Service organizations, for example, may not have a line called cost of goods sold.

Take a look at figure 4-4 to see what savvy WLP professionals might suggest for measures involving COGS.

Figure 4-4. Cost of goods sold measures and a sample financial value chain.

Possible Cost of Goods Sold (COGS) Measures:

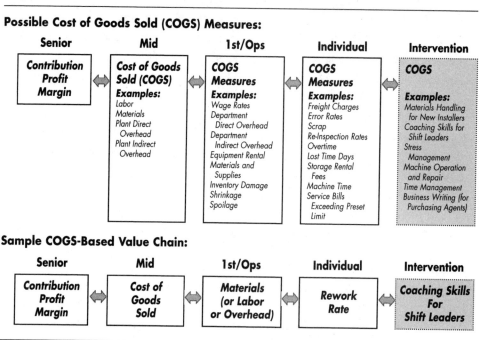

Sample COGS-Based Value Chain:

In figure 4-4, some possible measures for cost of goods sold have been listed. Exactly where a measure falls between the Mid, 1st/Ops, and Individual levels may shift depending on the size of your organization. As you create your own charts for your unique organization, where you place your measures will depend on your experience, your research, your best judgment, and the advice of others. There is rarely one right answer.

ABC MediCompany spends 60 percent of its revenue, or $60 million dollars, on COGS. Another 15 percent, or $15 million, is spent on other revenue-driven expenses. In other words, a total of 75 percent of the revenue is required to fund the goods produced and the cost to sell those goods. This calculation demonstrates the first financial ratio shown in figure 4-1, the contribution profit margin ratio:

(Contribution Profit Margin ÷ Net Sales) × 100 = CPM Ratio
$2,500,000 ÷ $10,000,000 × 100 = 25%

Dividing CPM by net sales leaves a CPM ratio of only 25% of revenue to fund the rest of the company's expenses and to retain a net profit. Look at figure 4-2 and you can see how large COGS and other sales-driven expenses are in relation to everything else on the income statement.

The COGS financial value chain in figure 4-4 draws the links between rework rate issues and the contribution profit margin. In this version, however, the recommended intervention is coaching skills for shift leaders.

At ABC MediCompany, the production line managers have been with the company for several years. They all worked their way up from doing the production jobs themselves. The line managers were very skeptical of the premise that teaching shift leaders to stop, take time, and make sure that new hires learned better techniques would actually lower rework rates in the long term. To them it only looked like a waste of time on unproductive talk. It slowed the production lines, not only because the new hires were taking time out for demonstrations, but also because the shift leaders were the most skilled and fastest workers on the line. To convince the plant managers to incorporate the training, the manufacturing performance director had to work out the business case of how much rework—particularly on the part of new hires—was costing the company in its profit margins and then convince Senior- and Mid-level management that this method would help fix the problem. Did it work? Yes. This example is based on a number of successful coaching programs offered by a company that specializes in this area.

Other Sales-Driven Measures. Depending on the type of organization that is being managed, other sales-driven expenses can vary greatly. Look at figure 4-5.

In the last year, ABC MediCompany has moved from a single-person sales strategy to a team sales strategy, but ABC's salespeople are having a difficult time adjusting to this change. They have been encouraged to be such fierce competitors with each other for so long that they are now having a very difficult time trusting each other as team members. The proposed intervention in figure 4-5 is a team-building event. Some sales managers may immediately dismiss such a recommendation as too expensive, risky, and emotionally awkward. The sales training director has done his homework on the effects of the lack of teamwork on poor communication, mistakes, and longer-than-average sales cycle times. Sales cycle time is defined as the average length of time it takes for a salesperson or sales team to close a sale. Longer sales cycle times result in higher sales-driven costs such as allocated salesperson

Figure 4-5. Other sales-driven expense measures and a sample financial value chain.

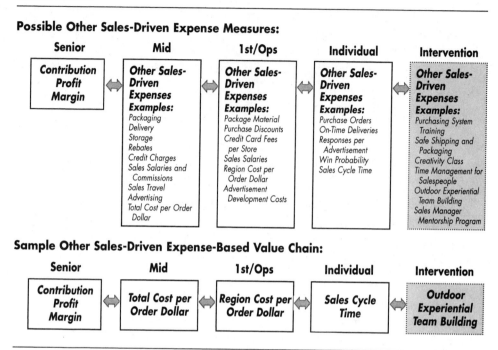

Possible Other Sales-Driven Expense Measures:

Senior	Mid	1st/Ops	Individual	Intervention
Contribution Profit Margin	**Other Sales-Driven Expenses Examples:** Packaging, Delivery, Storage, Rebates, Credit Charges, Sales Salaries and Commissions, Sales Travel, Advertising, Total Cost per Order Dollar	**Other Sales-Driven Expenses Examples:** Package Material, Purchase Discounts, Credit Card Fees per Store, Sales Salaries, Region Cost per Order Dollar, Advertisement Development Costs	**Other Sales-Driven Expenses Examples:** Purchase Orders, On-Time Deliveries, Responses per Advertisement, Win Probability, Sales Cycle Time	**Other Sales-Driven Expenses Examples:** Purchasing System Training, Safe Shipping and Packaging, Creativity Class, Time Management for Salespeople, Outdoor Experiential Team Building, Sales Manager Mentorship Program

Sample Other Sales-Driven Expense-Based Value Chain:

Senior	Mid	1st/Ops	Individual	Intervention
Contribution Profit Margin	**Total Cost per Order Dollar**	**Region Cost per Order Dollar**	**Sales Cycle Time**	**Outdoor Experiential Team Building**

salary per sale, extra administrative support, additional travel for customer meetings, and time spent making corrections in formal proposals. The teamwork issues were creating more cost to bring in the same level of order dollars or what is sometimes called the **cost per order dollar (CPOD).**

Is this sales training director going to be able to convince skeptical sales managers who hate potentially emotional events to fund an outdoor experiential team-building program based only on the financial numbers? Perhaps not. Using financial numbers is not a panacea for getting everything that you want. Remember that the salespeople who participated in the ROI study cited in chapter 1 said they were 30 percent more likely to win their deals, not 100 percent more likely to win everything. Still, 30 percent is a huge leap in creditability in sales terms, and the sales training director will definitely gain more respect by presenting his proposal with a clear financial connection. By creating a financial value chain, he leaves himself in a better position to propose alternative interventions if necessary or to come back later with the same proposal.

Profit Line #2: Operating Earnings Margin

As shown in figures 4-1 and 4-2, the next largest type of expense on the income statement is **fixed operating expenses.** Subtracting fixed operating expenses from the CPM yields the **operating earnings** profit line. The operating earnings profit line cannot be neglected. Senior management may have done an excellent job in managing the CPM only to blow it on fixed operating expenses.

 In the ABC MediCompany example, operating earnings is calculated as follows:

Contribution Profit Margin − Fixed Operating Expenses = Operating Earnings

$$\$2,500,000 - \$1,500,000 = \$1,000,000$$

Fixed operating expenses, or fixed expenses as they are often called, are more difficult to control or change in the short term. Fixed expenses can be adjusted, but at considerable effort, additional expense, and negative impacts on long-term working relationships. Once adjusted, the investments to reinstate necessary contracts, licenses, facilities, or equipment can be quite expensive to bear.

When operating earnings are being squeezed too thin, one of the first areas that can be cut is money for research and development (R&D). As every CEO knows, if R&D money is cut, eventually the life of the company could be in jeopardy. If a company cannot keep up with its competitors, then it can enter in a downward spiral of smaller **operating margins** and then even less money for R&D. Many stock investors recommend watching the percentage that an organization continues to spend on R&D year after year. If this figure takes a sudden drop, this could be an indication that the company is experiencing problems with revenue or expense control.

 As a WLP professional, in addition to pointing out your value in controlling fixed expenses, you may also want to keep an eye on R&D expenditures. If they are being squeezed, you can look for even more ways to help the company increase revenue or reduce costs.

 ABC MediCompany's operating earnings profit ratio is 10 percent. This means that after COGS, other sales-driven expenses, and fixed expenses are removed from revenue, only 10 percent of the revenue is left.

Figure 4-6 provides some examples of possible fixed expense measures and interventions to address training issues in managing fixed expenses. Once again, this is not an exhaustive list, merely a sampling of the types of measurement cascades you will find related to operating earnings and fixed expenses.

Figure 4-6. Operating earnings measures and sample financial value chain.

Possible Operating Earnings Measures:

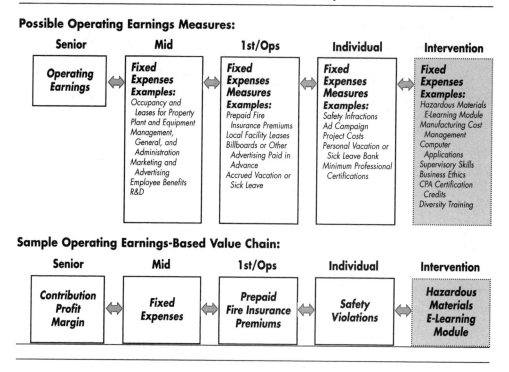

Sample Operating Earnings-Based Value Chain:

In the operating earnings sample value chain, the recommended intervention is an e-learning module on handling hazardous materials.

At ABC MediCompany, management has mandated that every manager must find a way to reduce fixed expenses. Legally, the plant training staff must deliver a certain level of hazardous material training to every employee in each plant every year. The manufacturing performance director was having a hard time convincing Senior managers to invest in what they saw as an extra expense in moving to on-demand e-learning based solely on making more efficient use of instructors. By connecting the new format to cuts in a fixed expense (prepaid fire insurance premiums), the manufacturing performance director was able to make a stronger case that the e-learning module reduced costs while still meeting legal (and insurance company) requirements.

Profit Line #3: Earnings Before Income Taxes

The next profit line is known as **earnings before income taxes.**

For ABC MediCompany, interest charges are now removed from operating earnings. ABC's interest charges are an aggregate of all of the various interest rates that ABC is paying for its different types of loans or other debt. ABC had $150,000 of interest charges. Senior managers must closely watch this line to ensure that they are getting the best use of the money for the cost of any debt they incur. CEOs value any reductions in interest charges. One of the most overlooked areas that can have a huge impact on these expenses is the **cost of capital** or the finance charges an organization must pay to get the cash to cover payroll, seasonal fluctuations between revenues and expenses, or other extraordinary items.

As a WLP professional, if you can show how your WLP interventions reduce the cost of capital for an organization, you have a great story to tell when communicating your value. CEOs and CFOs value programs that cut costs or raise revenues not only for the obvious effect on profit margins, but also because these interventions save interest charges that the organization does not have to pay. It improves the overall credit rating of the organization if it does not have to rely on as much credit! When calculating the value of your interventions, services, or programs, don't overlook the cascading effects of cutting costs or raising revenues on other parts of managing an organization.

In reality, there are also often accounting changes or other adjustments that also need to be accounted for. This is also sometimes referred to as **earnings before interest, taxes, depreciation, and amortization (EBITDA)**. It is calculated just as the name implies, by looking at earnings after COGS, other sales-driven expenses, and fixed operating expenses have been removed from revenue, but before interest, taxes, depreciation, and amortization are taken into account.

Calculating EBITDA is especially helpful when a company has a large amount of depreciation, such as for machinery-intensive manufacturing organizations, or a large amount of amortization, such as for purchases of patent rights or other intangible assets. Removing depreciation and amortization reduces the distortion of these numbers and allows creditors, investors, and industry analysts to compare within and across industries. EBITDA is more likely to be used in large companies with significant assets or debt financing (Investorwords.com, 2003). EBITDA may be a term you hear used by senior executives. A WLP manager at a large company reported that when his firm was bought by outside investors, EBITDA became the new buzzword. Everyone's measures were aligned to improve EBITDA.

Profit Line #4: Net Profit (or Loss)

The final profit line is known as net profit (or loss). This is the proverbial bottom line on the income statement. Net profit is calculated by removing income taxes from earnings before income tax. Income taxes will vary depending on where a company is headquartered and where it operates facilities or sales offices, especially if it is based in multiple countries.

ABC MediCompany has only $560,000 in revenue from the original $10 million in revenues. The net profit ratio is calculated by dividing the net profit by net sales and multiplying the result by 100. In this case, the net profit ratio is 5.6 percent:

(Net Profit ÷ Net Sale) × 100 = Net Profit Ratio

($560,000 ÷ $10,000,000) × 100 = 5.6%

Knowing how to calculate ratios can be important when you are communicating value. Executives sometimes use the ratios as a quick way to discuss whether the business is in or out of balance. If ratios are frequently used in your target organization, you can sometimes use a value chain that references the ratio instead of the profit line itself.

Create Your Own Value Chain

Creating your own profit chart and profit financial value chain for your (or your target) organization may be hard at first. Don't expect to be able to fill out everything on the first try. The most important part of exercise 4-1 is to start defining what you *do* know. Then, examine the rest of what you need and take the opportunity to do your research, networking, and financial exploration. Completing this exercise moves you forward in completing Step 3 of the financial value process: identify financial imperatives.

 LET'S REVIEW: ─────────────────────────────

- This chapter provides details for the profit component of Step 3: identify financial imperatives in the financial value process.
- An income statement is where the organization tracks how well it is doing in meeting the financial imperative of profit. Income statements can go by several different names, but they all display the same basic information about a company's profit picture.
- Revenue (or the top line) of the income statement is an important piece of information for the WLP professional to know because so much of the rest of the income statement is judged in terms of how much revenue is left at certain points in the calculations on the statement.
- For WLP professionals who support sales or marketing functions, understanding the goals of the sales mix is critical to understanding the appropriate goals for WLP interventions.
- The four key profit lines on an income statement are the contribution profit margin, the operating margin, earnings before income tax, and

Exercise 4-1. Your profit measures and financial value chain.

Directions: Complete the following steps for this exercise. If you prefer not to write in this book, go to the companion Website (www.astd.org/astd /publications) to download a PowerPoint file for this exercise.

1. Fill in the names of as many measures as you can for the four audience levels that you identified in exercise 2-1 in which you defined your audience. Don't worry if you have them exactly right. Treat this as a brainstorming exercise or a rough draft that you can use as an aid for later research into more complete lists of measures.
2. Use some of your measures to complete a financial value chain. Take this chain to some of your co-workers or customers for their insights on this or other value chains.
3. Make sure to take note of research you need to complete or questions that you would like to ask your boss or a mentor. There are so many intriguing questions that can come up, it's easy to lose track of some while you are pursuing the answers to others. Chapter 7 will give you hints on how to find more business intelligence about your organization or your target organization.

Step 3: Identify Financial Imperatives

Profit Measures:

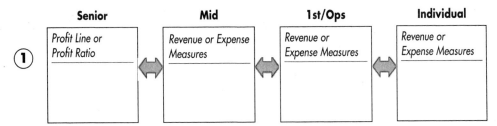

Profit Value Chain:

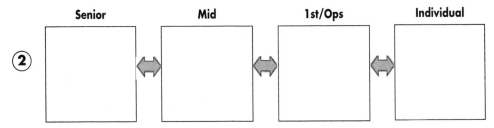

Profit Research Notes:

③ _____

_____

_____

net profit. Executives will spend their time proportionately to the impact each of these profit lines has on the health of the organization.

♦ Financial value chains can be drawn for every line on the income statement. Examples in this chapter include financial value chains for revenue, cost of goods sold, other sales-driven expenses, and fixed operating expenses.

♦ Knowing how to calculate profit ratios such as the contribution profit margin ratio or the net profit ratio is important because executives may sometimes refer to the ratios of the numbers instead of directly to the profit lines on the income statement. You may want to draw financial value chains that point to ratios instead of to profit lines.

This next chapter introduces the second financial imperative for Senior managers: position.

5

→

Position

 IN THIS CHAPTER: ——————————————

- ◆ The position component of step 3 of the financial value process: identify financial imperatives
- ◆ How to read a balance sheet
- ◆ Why the proportion or the size of each asset or liability matters so much to the position of an organization
- ◆ Important operating and financial ratios that can point you to what your executives will value in improved learning or workplace performance
- ◆ Examples of financial value chains connected directly to assets and liabilities.

In this chapter, you'll continue the connections to financial statements and work on step 3 of the financial value process by examining balance sheets. Balance sheets reflect the distribution of an organization's assets, liabilities, and owner's equity. This distribution describes the organization's financial position. Assets are things that are owned by an organization and that are to be used to generate future income. Liabilities are obligations for which the organization is expected to pay others. After the liabilities are paid, what's left is known as the owner's equity.

Balance Sheet Versus Income Statement

A balance sheet differs from an income statement in terms of what it describes. An income statement covers a range or period of time such as a month or a year. An income statement describes how much money came into an organization during a period of time, how much went out as expenses, and what was left at the end of the period. A balance sheet is usually generated to show a snapshot of what an organization owns or owes on the last day of the period covered by the income statement. The balance sheet describes what the organization owns or owes to keep making or paying money during the next period of time covered by the next income statement.

As an analogy, say that two individuals tracked how much salary each brought in during the year and what expenses each had during that year. At the end of the year, these individuals find that they started with exactly the same salary, had exactly the same amount of money go out as expenses, and had exactly the same amount of money left as a net profit or loss at the end of the year. If you were to examine their balance sheets, however, you would find two very different pictures. Much more of the first person's expenses went toward buying stocks, bonds, and real estate. The second person's expenses went to into buying the latest fashions and taking lavish vacations. At the end of the year, the first person's investments paid off, consequently, he or she has much more in personal assets than in debts. The second person has less in assets and much more in debt.

The types of things that each person owns and owes are very different. Likewise, the proportion (or balance) of the amount each owns versus the amount each owes is very different. Finally, the first person is in a better position to make even more money in the next time period because his or her investments should help generate even more revenue. The second person is not in as good a position to bring in as much money next year. If the first person becomes unemployed, there is a cushion (some assets) to fall back on—at least for a little while! The second person would be in a tough spot if he or she were laid off because there is no asset "cushion" to weather a period of unemployment.

In essence, the income statement tells you how much money came in and how much went out. The balance sheet tells you what the money turned into. The statements are related but different. A good manager or a good WLP professional must understand both.

 Figure 5-1 displays the financial position for the fictitious company, ABC MediCompany.

Figure 5-1. Sample balance sheet.

ABC MediCompany Balance Sheet			
Assets:	**This Year**	**Last Year**	**Change**
Cash	$1,420,000	$720,000	$700,000
Accounts Receivable	1,100,000	960,000	140,000
Inventory	750,000	990,000	(240,000)
Prepaid Expenses	200,000	160,000	40,000
Property, Plant & Equipment (PPE)	2,900,000	2,415,000	485,000
Accumulated Depreciation	(300,000)	(245,000)	(55,000)
Total Assets	**$6,070,000**	**$5,000,000**	
Liabilities and Owner's Equity:			
Accounts Payable	820,000	$775,000	$45,000
Accrued Expenses	185,000	170,000	15,000
Long-Term Liabilities	1,035,000	585,000	450,000
Owner's Equity	4,030,000	3,470,000	560,000
Total Liabilities and Owner's Equity	**$6,070,000**	**$5,000,000**	

Dissecting a Balance Sheet

On a balance sheet, the total amount of assets must always equal the total amount of liabilities and owner's equity. The balance sheet changes constantly. Money flows in and out of an organization as it receives payments, purchases goods, and makes other daily transactions. For this reason, the balance sheet is considered a snapshot of the mix of assets, liabilities, and owner's equity on a single specified date.

The balance sheet shown in figure 5-1 is an extremely simplified one, used to describe the concepts involved in managing financial position. In reality, there can be many unique types of assets and liabilities that an organization can use to produce income. Senior managers must manage the relative proportion of each type of asset, liability, and owner's equity within the balance sheet and between the balance sheet and the income statement. Whether the organization is maintaining the appropriate proportions, or balance, is tracked by calculating ratios of how big one item is relative to another.

To make the concept of proportions easier within the balance sheet, let's redraw a portion of the balance sheet as a graph, as shown in figure 5-2. This way, you can visualize the balance sheet as a yardstick.

Figure 5-2. Sample balance sheet chart.

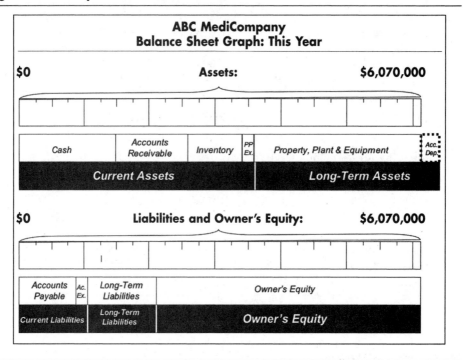

The amount of assets must always equal the amount of liabilities and owner's equity. Figure 5-2 takes the amounts shown in "This Year's" column in Figure 5-1 and lays them out side-by-side for assets and side-by-side for liabilities and owner's equity. This arrangement allows you to more easily see the relative size of each item on the balance sheet in proportion to the others.

When communicating value, it is important to know that every item on a balance sheet has an optimal range for its size. What that optimum is varies depending on the organization and its industry norms. It will be important for you to discover the appropriate proportions for your target organization because anything that is out of proportion may signal a financial problem. If you can offer interventions that create better proportions, you will get the attention of your audience.

On a balance sheet, assets that will be converted into cash within a year are known as **current assets**. Other assets that will not be converted into cash within a year are known as **long-term assets.** One special case for cash in assets is **accumulated depreciation,** which will be covered in more detail later in this chapter.

> A common example of a long-term asset is a manufacturing plant. ABC MediCompany's manufacturing plants are included under the item known as "property, plant, and equipment." Liabilities that will be paid within a year are known as **current liabilities.** Liabilities that will not be paid within a year are known as **long-term liabilities.**

The items on a balance sheet can be listed in any order. For assets, cash is often at the top of the list. Some accountants list items in order of their size. Others list assets in the order in which they can be most easily converted to cash, with cash being at the top of the list. Converting an asset into cash is called making the asset liquid. The easier it is to turn something into cash, the more **liquidity** the item has. Liabilities can be listed in the same way, with the items needing the most immediate use of cash listed first. Other liabilities and then the owner's equity may follow in descending order of their need for cash.

Examining Assets

Let's examine the proportion of each type of item on the balance sheet so that you can see how you can communicate your value in helping your organization maintain its optimum balance or financial position. This section deals with assets, but the first item under assets—cash—will be addressed in the next chapter.

Accounts Receivable

After cash, accounts receivable (AR) is the next most liquid item on the balance sheet. Accounts receivable is what is owed to an organization by its customers.

> Maintaining the appropriate amount in AR means that ABC MediCompany does not hassle its customers too early for what it allowed them to purchase on credit, yet it does collect payment quickly when it is due. If ABC does not do a good job of collecting payments when they are due, then ABC loses the opportunity to use the cash from those payments to pay its own bills or to make other necessary investments. The longer ABC is unable to collect what it is owed, the more costs it incurs to get its money and the less likely ABC is to get full payment from a customer.

Growth in AR should approximate growth in net sales. If AR is growing faster than net sales, then a company may not be able to convert AR into cash quickly enough to pay its other expenses. The proportion, or balance, of AR to net sales will get out of balance. This proportion is an example of how an operating ratio can be translated into a monitoring tool. In this case, the monitoring tool is known as the **accounts receivable collection period**. Figure 5-3 shows how the AR collection period is calculated.

ABC MediCompany's AR collection period is 40.2 days—not bad within ABC's industry—but ABC's Seniors are concerned because they know that the AR collection period was 38.4 days at this same time last year. ABC's collection period has crept up by 1.8 days. Without more information, it is impossible to know if this trend indicates a great job by ABC's collection group in getting payments during a poor economy or if it is an indication of performance or other problems within the collections department. Either way, the AR collection period is a number that ABC's Senior management team needs to watch closely to ensure that this trend does not continue. Smart stock investors will also be watching this number to ensure that the organization does not run into trouble. Workplace learning and performance managers or vendors should watch the AR collection period in case they want to offer a intervention that will help ABC improve its cash flow.

Inventory

The next asset to examine and the next operating ratio monitoring tool to look at is inventory in figures 5-1 and 5-3. Like accounts receivable, the general rule is that growth in inventory should approximate growth in net sales and for the same reason. If inventory grows faster than net sales, precious cash will be tied up in inventory and unavailable to pay other expenses of the organization.

Figure 5-3. Sample operating ratios.

ABC MediCompany
Operating Ratios

Accounts Receivable Collection Period

$$\frac{\text{Accounts Receivable}}{\text{Net Sales}} = \frac{\$1,100,000}{\$10,000,000} \times 365 \text{ Days} = 40.2 \text{ Days}$$

Days Inventory Supply

$$\frac{\text{Inventory}}{\text{Cost of Goods Sold (COGS)}} = \frac{750,000}{\$6,000,000} \times 365 \text{ Days} = 45.6 \text{ Days}$$

ABC's inventory on this year's balance sheet is $750,000. Now examine inventory for this same time last year. It was $990,000. Let's say that for some time, ABC's growth in inventory had been faster than its growth in net sales. In one year, however, the amount of inventory on hand has decreased by $240,000, freeing up a large amount of cash.

Inventory This Year – Inventory Last Year = Inventory Increase (or Decrease)
$750,000 – $990,000 = ($240,000)

In the last year, ABC has made some significant investments in **just-in-time (JIT) inventory management**. The **days inventory supply** has dropped to an average of 45.6 days. This is much more in line with ABC's industry average. ABC has made a great improvement by decreasing the size of this non-cash asset relative to others on the company's balance sheet. ABC's management team hopes to reduce that number even further in the coming year. Stock investors would be happy to see this change.

How long an organization should be holding its inventory varies greatly by its industry. For retail establishments, inventory is the goods offered for sale to the public.

If the days inventory supply is growing faster than sales, Senior executives may have trouble generating enough cash to cover expenses. They may then have to lower prices—possibly to an unprofitable level—or borrow at more expensive interest rates and levels of risk on the belief that future revenue is forthcoming. Customer satisfaction, employee efficiency, purchasing excellence, and information-technology-based process improvements are just a few of the things that can affect inventory and just a few of the areas WLP may be able to influence. Senior management at many organizations would be happy to hear how your WLP interventions helped decrease the amount of cash tied up in inventory.

This discussion of inventory demonstrates an important aspect of the balance sheet displayed in figure 5-1: Balance sheets are published with two columns of numbers for comparison purposes. This format allows the amount of change in an item to be easily calculated. These changes figure into the cash flow statement, which will be addressed in the next chapter.

Prepaid Expenses

After inventory, the next asset on the balance sheet is **prepaid expenses**. Prepaid expenses are those that must be paid for in advance of their use. Common examples include fire insurance premiums, advertising contracts such as for a year of magazine or billboard space, or quarterly machine maintenance agreements.

Like AR and inventory, prepaid expenses tie up cash. These expenses need to stay in line with what is reasonable within the industry. ABC's prepaid expenses are $200,000 and have grown from last year's amount. Given some of ABC's investments in property, plant, and equipment, increases in prepaid expenses for maintenance contracts are reasonable to expect.

Property, Plant, and Equipment

The next asset on the balance sheet is long-term assets, which, in ABC's case, consist only of property, plant, and equipment (PPE, sometimes referred to as fixed assets).

ABC MediCompany has made some significant investments in PPE (fixed assets) last year. If last year's balance sheet numbers were put into a bar graph, such as the one in figure 5-2, you would see that the size of the bar for PPE is much larger this year relative to ABC's other assets. In fact, this is what is shown in figure 5-4.

Accumulated Depreciation

On the balance sheet shown in figure 5-1, you can see a line for another asset—accumulated depreciation—which follows PPE. Accumulated depreciation is different from other assets in that it is a write-off of a certain percentage of value from the organization's PPE assets.

Long-term assets age and eventually must be replaced. Organizations pledge their long-term assets as collateral for loans. If the organization never adjusts the amount that a long-term asset is worth, then the value of the asset, or the organization's borrowing basis, is artificially inflated. The organization would be pledging assets that were not really worth as much as the original purchase price. Depreciation allows the organization to reduce the value of the asset on their books in order to reflect a fair borrowing basis to their lenders. In figure 5-4, you can see accumulated depreciation outlined as a dotted area at the end of long-term assets. The dotted area is subtracted from the book value of PPE so that the amount of PPE is more fairly represented.

Examining Liabilities and Owner's Equity

Now turn your attention to the other half of the balance sheet, the half that describes liabilities and owner's equity. Just as we did with assets, we will examine the proportion of each type of item under liabilities and owner's equity so that you can see how you can communicate your value in helping your organization maintain its optimum balance or financial position.

Figure 5-4. Year-to-year asset comparison.

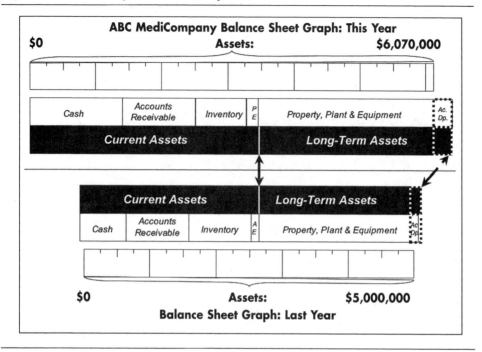

Accounts Payable

On the liabilities and owner's equity half of the balance sheet (figure 5-1), you can see that accounts payable and accrued expenses are the current liabilities. **Accounts payable** consists of purchases required for ABC to manufacture its goods, create its inventory, and run its daily operations. **Accrued expenses** consist of expenses such as property taxes that accrue every day that an organization owns a piece of property, but which will be paid on a specified future date. Pay due to employees can also accrue each day but will be paid only at specified times during a month.

> ABC MediCompany's balance sheet (figure 5-1) does not break out under the entry for long-term liabilities the types of long-term liabilities ABC has incurred in the last year. You can see from the balance sheet that ABC has significantly increased its long-term liabilities. In the last year ABC management has decided that it needs to renovate, improve processes, and expand some of its marketing efforts in order to stay competitive. For this reason, ABC chose to take on additional long-term debt.

Owner's Equity

The remainder of the balance sheet (figure 5-1) is shown as owner's equity. In a corporation, owner's equity is called shareholder's equity. There can be a number of items that make up owner's or shareholder's equity. Owner's equity can be built through contributed **capital** or through retained earnings or the net profit that the organization kept for itself. In corporations, shareholders can obtain equity by purchasing common or preferred stock. For additional information on balance sheets, please take a look at the books listed in the Additional Resources section at the back of this book.

Checking the Balance: Ratios

Now that you have a basic understanding of the items contained in the income statement (from the previous chapter) and contained in the balance sheet, it is time to compare the size or proportion of different items to each other. This comparison is known as checking the balance, or the ratios, of an organization. Ratios tell Senior managers and savvy WLP professionals where problems exist and can hint at what interventions might create the most value by bringing the items back into balance.

Current and Quick Ratios

The goal for any company is to keep its ratios of assets to liabilities above one, or, in other words, to have more assets than liabilities such that there are no restrictions in normal business activities due to a shortage of cash and no embarrassment of having to put off creditors. These proportions are often expressed as the **current ratio** or the **quick**, or **liquidity**, **ratio.**

Lenders like to see more assets than liabilities because that means that the organization can find a way to repay its loans. To derive the current ratio, current assets are divided by current liabilities.

The quick (or liquidity) ratio is an even harsher test of whether a company can pay back its loans. This ratio excludes inventory from the total amount of current assets and then divides by current liabilities. Inventory can sometimes be very difficult to sell. An example of hard-to-sell inventory is trendy fashions that suddenly go out of style.

Was ABC MediCompany in a good position to have taken on the additional long-term debt to renovate, improve processes, and expand some of its marketing efforts? Even with the new debt, ABC has enough assets to pay its obligations. To see how this works out, let's look at some financial ratios. Figure 5-5 shows five financial ratios for ABC.

The current ratio and the quick ratio demonstrate the balance between ABC's most liquid assets (current assets) and ABC's debts or obligations that must be paid the most quickly (current liabilities). With a current ratio of 3.45, ABC has nearly three and a half times the number of current assets as it does current liabilities. Even when applying a more stringent criterion, it appears that with a quick ratio of 2.71 that ABC still has nearly two and three-quarters more assets than liabilities and could pay off its current debt.

Ratios are important to understand because they offer a shortcut to knowing what your Senior executives will value. Sometimes your executives will align management incentives and performance programs to improve a specific ratio. If you understand which two items are being measured against each other, you will know where to direct your WLP interventions and how to connect the value of what you bring to the table directly to the items in the ratio.

Knowing a company's current and quick ratios is only half of the story. Knowing what is reasonable and customary within a company's industry is the other half. Let's get a little more specific about the industry ABC MediCompany operates in.

If you were to go to www.bizminer.com, select "Health Care," and ask for a financial analysis profile for electromedical equipment, you would be able to find an industry financial analysis report that summarizes how other firms

Figure 5-5. Sample financial ratios.

ABC MediCompany Financial Ratios				
Current Ratio:			*Factor*	*Percentage*
Current Assets / Current Liabilities	=	$3,470,000 / $1,005,000	= **3.45**	
Quick or Liquidity Ratio:				
Current Assets − Inventory / Current Liabilities	=	$2,720,000 / $1,005,000	= **2.71**	
Return-on-Assets (ROA)				
Net Profit / Total Assets	=	$560,000 / $6,070,000	= **0.09** × 100	= **9%**
Return-on-Equity (ROE)				
Net Profit / Owner's Equity	=	$560,000 / $4,030,000	= **0.14** × 100	= **14%**
Leverage or Debt-to-Equity Ratio:				
Total Liabilities / Owner's Equity	=	$2,040,000 / $4,030,000	= **0.51** × 100	= **51%**

in this industry are doing. These profiles are not free, so keep in mind that there are other ways to find this information. This example just gives you a brief idea of what kinds of data you can find about an industry from existing financial data services.

In the year ending July 2002 for the electromedical equipment industry, the average company maintained a current ratio of slightly over three (3.2) and a quick ratio of just over one and a half (1.6). Comparatively speaking, ABC is doing as well or better than its competitors.

Because ABC seems to be in relatively good shape in its current ratio and quick ratio, would Senior executives pay as much attention to a proposal for how WLP could improve the ratio even more? If ABC were considering taking on even more debt the answer might be yes. If ABC were not considering more debt, then Senior executives may pay attention to other ratios first. Senior executives might rather want to know if they are getting enough value from the assets they already have. This leads to another ratio, **return-on-assets (ROA).**

Return-on-Assets

Return-on-assets describes how much profit a company generated for each dollar in assets. It is also an excellent indicator of **asset intensity**—how much is required in the way of big and expensive assets to generate profit for an organization. Companies can be asset-intensive (the ROA is less than 5 percent) or asset-light (the ROA is greater than 20 percent). A railroad, for example, is asset-intensive. An advertising company is asset-light (beginnersinvest.about.com, 2003a).

The ROA is calculated by dividing net profit by total assets. It is often expressed as a percentage, thus:

$$\text{Net Profit} \div \text{Total Assets} \times 100 = \text{ROA}$$

As you can see in figure 5-5, ABC MediCompany has an ROA of 0.09 or 9%. The Bizminer report for electromedical equipment reveals that the last three years have been very difficult in this industry. The average net profit is negative, so the average industry ROA is negative as well. For ABC to have a positive ROA of 9 percent, it must have a very special niche or be doing something to sell more asset-light services to offset the costs of its manufacturing operations.

You'll see in a subsequent chapter on business intelligence research how a knowledge management consultant used her insights about ABC MediCompany's ROA to ask questions about how ABC was maintaining a competitive advantage and how an investment in her knowledge management services could protect or enhance this competitive advantage.

Return-on-Equity

Return-on-equity (ROE) is another common ratio that investors and Senior executives will watch. It is an indicator of how well the company is reinvesting its capital. For most of the 20th century, the Standard & Poor's 500 averaged ROEs of 10 to 15 percent, with ROEs moving up into the 20 percent range for part of the 1990s. The 20 percent range has not been sustained during the economic downturn of the early '00 decade (beginnersinvest.about.com, 2003b).

The ROE is calculated by dividing net profit by the amount of owner's equity and multiplying the result by 100. ABC MediCompany's ROE is 14 percent, as you can see in figure 5-5. Is this ROE good for ABC? The minimum benchmark for ROE is the percentage yield on 30-year U.S. government bonds. A source to look up rates on 30-year U.S. bonds is http://www.marketvector.com/interest-rate/30-yr-t-bond.htm. ABC's ROE should be substantially higher than what is available from what is considered the standard for risk-free investment because if it's not, ABC management would do better to just put the company's money there rather than trying to run the business (Bing, 2002). But, as the Bizminer report shows, most of ABC's industry has produced negative ROEs for the last three years. ABC is doing well in comparison to the minimum standard and to comparable companies.

Leverage or Debt-to-Equity Ratio

The **leverage ratio**, often called the debt-to-equity ratio, is the final ratio that will be covered in this book. The leverage ratio, which is often expressed as a percentage, shows how much owner's equity there is in the company versus the combination of all of the liabilities. From a lender's point of view, the smaller the number is the better. According to Drake and Dingler (2001) any number under 0.5 (50 percent) is favorable.

Figure 5-5 shows that at ABC MediCompany, the leverage ratio is 0.51 (51 percent). Even though it is doing well compared to its industry, ABC appears to have reached the limit of the debt it can hold without being considered high risk. ABC will now have to look at ways to cut costs, raise revenues, or generally make better use of its assets to fund any additional investments it would like to make in its business. As a WLP practitioner at ABC, it would be important for you to target your interventions over the next one to three years to improve the leverage ratio to keep your organization out of the high-risk category.

Help! I'm Overwhelmed!

All of this discussion about ratios can seem daunting, but don't get discouraged. As a WLP professional and former mathematics teacher pointed out to me, all her math students became discouraged about midway through the school year. They also felt better about what they were learning as time went on and they became more comfortable and confident. The important thing is not to give up. Familiarity, comfort, and confidence with ratios and financial statements make all the difference in helping your audience understand your value.

Examples of Asset Financial Value Chains

How can you use this information about balance sheets and ratios to communicate your value? To see how assets break into cascading measures through an organization and how those measures can be translated into value chains, take a look at figure 5-6. To help draw a visual link from the financial value chain to WLP interventions, the financial value chains have possible WLP interventions depicted.

In the top half of figure 5-6, starting on the left-hand side, are examples of asset measures for each type of audience, ending on the right with examples of WLP interventions that may improve those measures. The closer you get to the Individual level of your audience, the longer and more varied the list of possible measures and interventions becomes. The list of measures and possible interventions in this example are not restricted to what ABC MediCompany might use and are by no means exhaustive in covering every type of organization in every industry.

In figure 5-6, examples of current and long-term asset measures are combined. The interesting thing to note is that although the terms have changed at the Senior or possibly the Mid-level, many of the same measures can appear for the 1st/Ops and Individual audiences as were on the income statement.

The same intervention can sometimes positively affect profit, position, and cash all at the same time. You can keep your value communication fresh and more powerful by understanding how to point out the impact of your interventions in terms of more than one financial statement.

The sample asset-based value chain in figure 5-6 selects current assets as the Senior-level measure and AR as the Mid-level measure. To help with monthly and weekly collections, employees are receiving training and reinforcement coaching in effective telephone techniques when asking for payment.

Examples of Liability Financial Value Chains

A similar set of measures and a sample financial value chain are shown on figure 5-7.

Figure 5-6. Asset measure and sample financial value chain.

Possible Asset Measures:

Senior	Mid	1st/Ops	Individual	Intervention
Current or Long-Term Assets	**Asset Measures** *Examples:* Cash; Marketable Securities; Accounts Receivable; Inventory; Plant, Property, and Equipment; Intangible Assets (e.g., Patents); Goodwill; Accumulated Depreciation	**Asset Measures** *Examples:* Monthly Collections; Inventory Shrinkage; Facilities Maintenance Budget; Patents Filed; Customer Survey Scores	**Asset Measures** *Examples:* Weekly Collections; Inventory Counts; Facilities Repair Records; Number of Research and Development Experiments Completed; Customer Complaints or Compliments	**Asset Measures** *Examples:* Effective Telephone Techniques; JIT Inventory Management Procedures; C++ Programming; Simple Statistical Analysis; Customer Service Skills

Sample Asset-Based Value Chain:

Senior	Mid	1st/Ops	Individual	Intervention
Current Assets	Accounts Receivable	Monthly Collections	Weekly Collections	**Effective Telephone Techniques**

Figure 5-7. Liability measures and sample financial value chain.

Possible Liability Measures:

Senior	Mid	1st/Ops	Individual	Intervention
Current or Long-Term Liabilities	**Liability Measures** *Examples:* Accounts Payable; Accrued Expenses; Current Portion of Long-Term Debt (Interest Payable); Long-Term Bonds or Loans	**Liability Measures** *Examples:* Raw Material Costs; Labor Subcontract Rates; Total Office Supplies; Utility Bills	**Liability Measures** *Examples:* Purchasing Contract Margins; Time Cards; Personal Office Budget; Station Water Usage	**Liability Measures** *Examples:* Purchasing Total Quality Process; Negotiation Skills for Parts Buyers; Monthly Lunch-and-Learn; Office Management for Administrative Assistants; Budgeting Basics for New Supervisors

Sample Liability-Based Value Chain:

Senior	Mid	1st/Ops	Individual	Intervention
Current Liabilities	Accounts Payable	Total Office Supplies	Personal Office Budget	**Office Management for Administrative Assistants**

In this case, administrative assistants are required to attend monthly lunch-and-learn sessions. The cost of these sessions is being questioned. The value of the sessions is being linked to a number of profit, position, and cash measures. This sample value chain lists just one: helping to control the expenses for office supplies. In reality, any number of chains could be drawn to show how a WLP professional helps to reduce current liabilities such as the expenses in accounts payable. Chains could also be drawn to show how a WLP intervention reduces the need for short- or long-term debt by cutting costs, conserving cash, or generating additional revenue that could be used to fund expenses without the need for more debt.

 Because ratios compare such items as assets, liabilities, equity, revenue, costs, and profit, you can also point out how any of the financial value chains improve the ratios that the Senior executive measures are a part of.

Create Your Own Value Chain

Now it's time to complete a position chart and position value chain for your target organization (exercise 5-1). This exercise may have been difficult to fill out completely when you did it in the last chapter for your profit chart and profit value chains. The same holds true when working on position measures and chains. Don't expect to be able to fill out everything on the first try.

The most important part of this exercise is to start defining what you do know. Then examine the rest of what you need, and take the opportunity to make more notes for your research, networking, and financial exploration.

 If you need a little incentive to do this exercise again for position, here's a special tip: Doing this kind of work can really distinguish you from your competition during a job interview. Very few interviewees have the ability to demonstrate their value in financial terms and even fewer are able to show their potential new manager how he or she can explain his or her value in the same way. For those readers who aren't looking for a job, isn't it true that some people just seem to get lucky and get offers without even knowing they were being considered? As the old saying goes, luck favors the prepared. If you are a consultant, translate "job interview" into "consulting sales call."

 LET'S REVIEW: ―――――――――――――――――

- ◆ This chapter provides details for the position component of Step 3: identify financial imperatives.
- ◆ A balance sheet is where the organization tracks the amounts of assets, liabilities, and owner's equity it has. Because money is always flowing

Exercise 5-1. Your position measures and financial value chain.

Directions: Complete the following steps for this exercise. If you prefer not to write in this book, go to the companion Website (www.astd.org/astd /publications) to download a PowerPoint file for this exercise.

1. Fill in the names of as many measures as you can for the four audience levels that you identified in exercise 2-1 in which you defined your audience. Don't worry if you have them exactly right. Treat this as a brainstorming exercise or a rough draft that you can use as an aid for later research into more complete lists of measures.
2. Use some of your measures to complete a financial value chain. Take this chain to some of your co-workers or customers for their insights on this or other value chains.
3. Make sure to take note of research you need to complete or questions that you would like to ask your boss or a mentor. Add these to the questions you had for research into profit measures. Chapter 7 will give you hints on how to unearth more business intelligence about your organization or your target organization.

Step 3: Identify Financial Imperatives

Position Measures:

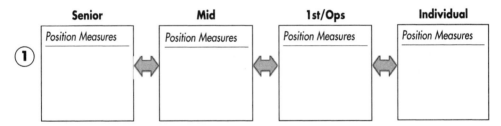

Position Value Chain:

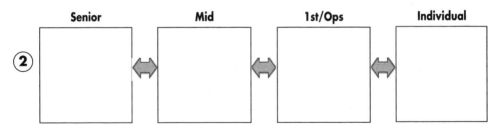

Position Research Notes:

③ _____

in and out of an organization as a result of sales and purchases, the balance sheet is a snapshot of one point in time. The balance sheet reflects the position or financial health of the organization on a specific date.

◆ The proportion, or size of each asset or liability in relation to others, is what is meant by the position of an organization. Too many liabilities versus assets can be a very risky and high-cost situation for the executives of an organization to manage. Likewise, lack of attention to assets such as accounts receivable or inventory can cause serious cash flow problems for the organization.

◆ Operating ratios (such as days inventory outstanding) or financial ratios (such as return-on-assets) can give the WLP professional a quick idea of problems in the organization and, therefore, what executives will value from WLP interventions.

◆ Examples of financial value chains were shown connecting WLP interventions to assets and liabilities. Chains could also have been drawn using operating or financial ratios as the leftmost Senior executive measure.

◆ Because assets and liabilities are tied to the income and expenses that generated them, the same WLP intervention can be shown to affect financial imperatives for both profit and position. This is good news for the WLP professional, as this situation creates more options in communicating value.

The next chapter looks at the third financial imperative for Senior-level managers: cash.

6

Cash

 IN THIS CHAPTER:

- The cash component of step 3 of the financial value process: identify financial imperatives
- Why cash is not the same as profit
- Why executives must manage cash in addition to profit and position
- How to read a cash flow statement
- How changes in net profit (or loss) and changes in the balance sheet increase or decrease cash flow
- Examples of financial value chains connected directly to cash flow.

In this chapter, you'll finish making connections to financial statements and work on step 3 of the financial value process by examining cash flow statements. Cash flow statements go by various names such as **statement of utilization of funds, source and application of funds,** or some equivalent title.

Cash flow statements track the sources and uses of an organization's cash to ensure that the organization is maintaining enough actual cash to pay the organization's expenses on time. As you examined the balance sheet in chapter 5, you saw that profit from the income statement did not equal cash on hand. Much of the organization's profit can be tied up in non-cash assets such as accounts receivable or inventory. If too much cash is tied up in these types of assets, the organization cannot pay its employees or its suppliers. Not being able to pay your employees or creditors is a very unpleasant situation to be in.

Because shortages of actual cash can stop the organization from running, Senior managers must ensure that sufficient supplies of cash are available at all times.

As a WLP professional, if you know what is causing cash flow problems, when having enough cash on hand is likely to be an issue for your organization, and how your solutions help Senior executives manage cash, then you have a valuable story to tell.

Figure 6-1 depicts the cash flow for ABC MediCompany. Numbers from the income statement and the balance sheet are used to reflect the changes in cash that our fictitious company, ABC MediCompany, has experienced.

Figure 6-1. ABC MediCompany's cash flow statement.

ABC MediCompany
Cash Flow Statement

Cash Flows from Operating Activities:

Net Profit	$560,000
Accumulated Depreciation	55,000
Accounts Receivable	(140,000)
Inventory	240,000
Prepaid Expenses	(40,000)
Accounts Payable	45,000
Accrued Expenses	15,000
Cash Flow from Operating Activities ("Free Cash")	**$735,000**

Cash Flows from Investing Activities:

Purchases/Additions to Property, Plant & Equipment	**$(485,000)**

Cash Flows from Financing Activities:

Debt Borrowings	500,000
Debt Repayments	(50,000)
Cash Flow from Financing Activities	**$450,000**

Net Cash Increase	**$700,000**

As you can see, the cash flow statement is split into three parts:

1. cash flows from **operating activities**
2. cash flows from **investing activities**
3. cash flows from **financing activities.**

The Reverse Flip

Everything on the cash flow statement comes from either the income statement or the balance sheet. But, searching through each kind of statement to try to figure out how they are linked can be rather confusing. To make the explanation of where each number comes from easier, try looking at the cash flow statement in another way. Figure 6-2 displays the cash flow statement as you would normally see it on the left. On the right-hand side of the figure, the numbers are listed first.

Figure 6-2. Normal (left) and reversed cash flow (right) statements.

NORMAL LAYOUT

ABC MediCompany
Cash Flow Statement

Cash Flows from Operating Activities:

Net Profit	$ 560,000
Accumulated Depreciation	55,000
Accounts Receivable	(140,000)
Inventory	240,000
Prepaid Expenses	(40,000)
Accounts Payable	45,000
Accrued Expenses	15,000
Cash Flow from Operating Activities $	735,000

Cash Flows from Investing Activities:

Purchases/Additions to Property, Plant & Equipment	$ (485,000)

Cash Flows from Financing Activities:

Debt Borrowings	500,000
Debt Repayments	(50,000)
Cash Flow from Financing Activities $	450,000
Net Cash Increase	**$ 700,000**

REVERSE LAYOUT

ABC MediCompany
Cash Flow Statement

Cash Flows from Operating Activities:

$ 560,000	Net Profit
55,000	Accumulated Depreciation
(140,000)	Accounts Receivable
240,000	Inventory
(40,000)	Prepaid Expenses
45,000	Accounts Payable
15,000	Accrued Expenses
$ 735,000	Cash Flow from Operating Activities

Cash Flows from Investing Activities:

$ (485,000)	Purchases/Additions to Property, Plant & Equipment

Cash Flows from Financing Activities:

500,000	Debt Borrowings
(50,000)	Debt Repayments
$ 450,000	Cash Flow from Financing Activities
$ 700,000	**Net Cash Increase**

As you can see, all the information is the same on these two views of the cash flow statement. The only difference is their format. Now, use the reverse format to compare the cash flow statement to the other two financial imperative statements: the income statement and the balance sheet.

What Comes From the Income Statement?

The first line on the cash flow statement is net profit. The number on this line came from the bottom line of the income statement. In figure 6-3, you can see exactly where an accountant would get the first line of the cash flow statement.

Figure 6-3. Income statement and cash flow statement connection.

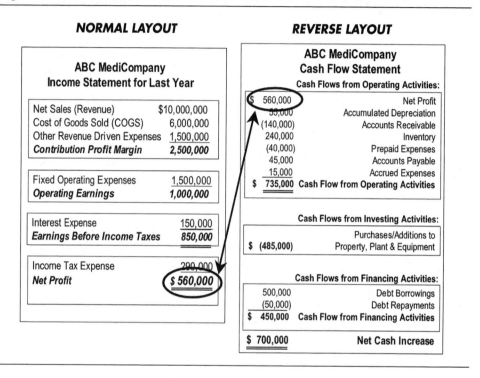

What Comes From Assets on the Balance Sheet?

All other items on the cash flow statement come from the column of changes between last year's figures on the balance sheet and this year's figures on the balance sheet. The impact on cash flow from assets is different than the impact from cash flow from liabilities and owner's equity.

The rules for cash flow from assets will be discussed first. Figure 6-4 shows the movement of cash relative to assets.

The rule for the changes in cash caused by non-cash assets is that cash flow moves opposite to changes in non-cash assets. If a non-cash asset such as AR increases, that is a use of cash. In other words, this means that the organization is not getting paid for its goods or services by its customers. Therefore, the amount of the increase is subtracted from the cash flow statement. If a

Figure 6-4. Movement of cash and assets.

non-cash asset, such as inventory, decreases, that is a source of cash. Therefore, the amount of the decrease is added to the cash flow.

Depreciation is a different type of expense in that it does not take any actual cash from the organization. Depreciation is added back as a source of cash in the operating section of the cash flow statement.

 ABC MediCompany's cash flow statement demonstrates this reciprocal relationship between non-cash assets and cash, as shown in figure 6-5.

Figure 6-5. Balance sheet assets and cash flow connection.

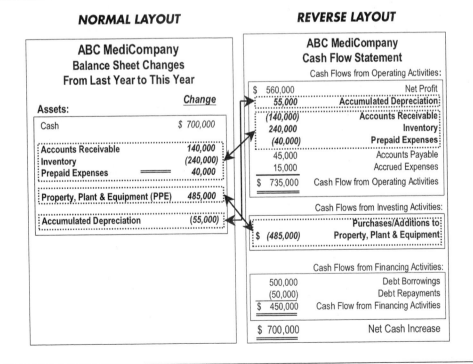

You can see how each change in an asset corresponds to a line on the cash flow statement. In this case, the changes in ABC's current assets (AR, inventory, and prepaid expenses) and long-term assets (property, PPE, and accumulated depreciation) are highlighted on the left-hand side in the order in which they were displayed on the balance sheet. These same items are highlighted on the right-hand side in the order in which they are displayed on the cash flow statement. There is no one correct order to list the same assets on the balance sheet in relation to the cash flow statement.

You can see that cash moves in the opposite direction as non-cash assets from the way that the same numbers are displayed as either positive or negative on the balance sheet and cash flow statement. For example, on the changes in the balance sheet, the increased investment in PPE is shown as a positive number of $485,000. But, to get that increase in PPE shown on the balance sheet, ABC MediCompany had to pay out some cash. That's why the same number for Purchases/Additions to Property, Plant and Equipment is shown as a negative number, or ($485,000), on the cash flow statement. Cash had to go down by that much for the asset to go up.

What Comes From Liabilities and Owner's Equity on the Balance Sheet?

Liability or owner's equity has an effect opposite to that of an asset on the cash flow statement. In this case, a positive change on the balance sheet carries over to a positive change on the cash flow statement (figure 6-6).

Why would this be? If an organization is delaying payment of a liability, such as accounts payable or accrued expenses, then they are conserving their

---

Figure 6-6. Movement of cash, liabilities, and owner's equity.

Cash Flow for Liabilities and Owner's Equity

IF	THEN
Liabilities or Equity Increase	*Cash Increases*
⬆	⬆
IF	THEN
Liabilities or Equity Decrease	*Cash Decreases*
⬇	⬇

cash by doing so. Of course, an organization cannot refuse to pay their bills forever without making their suppliers very angry. Delays in payment might help the organization negotiate some immediate cash flow problems, but this situation negatively affects the organization's future credit and ability to purchase additional goods or services to keep the organization running. Therefore, any rise in cash flow due to delays in payments is a serious trend that must be quickly caught by Senior management.

Likewise, if new liabilities or equity are created by adding long-term debt or by issuing additional stock in a company, these changes to liabilities or owner's equity are also additions to an organization's cash flow. On the other hand, if the organization pays its bills, it reduces its cash. The liability goes down, and the cash goes down.

 In figure 6-7, you can see how cash moves in the same direction as liabilities and owner's equity for ABC MediCompany.

Figure 6-7. Balance sheet liabilities, owner's equity, and cash flow connection.

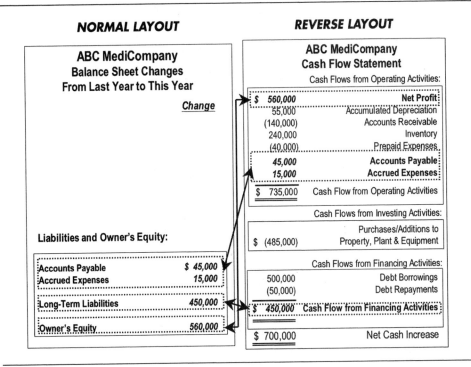

The current liabilities, accounts payable, and accrued expenses are shown as positive numbers on the balance sheet and again as positive numbers on the cash flow statement. Both these liabilities have increased over the last year. Because ABC's sales have gone up, there should be proportionate increases in some expenses because ABC should have had to buy more materials to create more products to sell. Still, this increase must be closely watched.

The long-term liabilities on the balance sheet are shown as the sum of the cash flow from financing activities on the cash flow statement. On the cash flow statement, you can see a little more detail about the financing activities. Debt borrowings and debt repayments are broken out so you can see how much cash came in or went out as a result of these activities.

ABC MediCompany had a total of $500,000 in borrowings for this last year. They repaid $50,000 of their borrowings during this last year. The final number—$450,000—of cash flow from financing activities is the same as the $450,000 on the balance sheet for long-term liabilities.

There is one other item to note between the liabilities and owner's equity on the balance sheet and the cash flow statement. That is how owner's equity is shown on the cash flow statement. In this case, ABC MediCompany retained all net profit. It did not pay out any distributions to shareholders. For this reason, owner's equity and net profit are the same on ABC's cash flow statement.

What About the Cash?

The last item to compare on the balance sheet and the cash flow statement is the cash itself. On the balance sheet, cash on hand is usually listed as the first asset. On the cash flow statement, cash is the last line. It is calculated from what are called the sources and uses of cash. Sources of cash are incoming or positive numbers on the cash flow statement. Uses of cash are outgoing or negative numbers on the cash flow statement. Figure 6-8 demonstrates the connection between cash on the balance sheet and cash on the cash flow statement.

The final cash number on the cash flow statement should equal the amount of cash shown on the balance sheet.

So, is what you see on the cash flow statement good or bad? The goal for an organization is to make sure that it always has enough cash to meet its obligations and to make necessary investments in the organization without having too much cash on hand. Too much cash is not good in that it invites managers to become lax in their controls and purchases as well as introducing the possibility of illegal activities such as embezzlement from the extra cash flow.

Figure 6-8. Comparing cash.

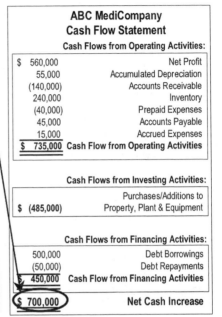

NORMAL LAYOUT

ABC MediCompany
Balance Sheet Changes
From Last Year to This Year

Assets:	*Change*
Cash	$ 700,000
Accounts Receivable	140,000
Inventory	(240,000)
Prepaid Expenses	40,000
Property, Plant & Equipment (PPE)	485,000
Accumulated Depreciation	(55,000)
Liabilities and Owner's Equity:	
Accounts Payable	$ 45,000
Accrued Expenses	15,000
Long-Term Liabilities	450,000
Owner's Equity	560,000

REVERSE LAYOUT

ABC MediCompany
Cash Flow Statement

Cash Flows from Operating Activities:

$ 560,000	Net Profit
55,000	Accumulated Depreciation
(140,000)	Accounts Receivable
240,000	Inventory
(40,000)	Prepaid Expenses
45,000	Accounts Payable
15,000	Accrued Expenses
$ 735,000	**Cash Flow from Operating Activities**

Cash Flows from Investing Activities:

$ (485,000)	Purchases/Additions to Property, Plant & Equipment

Cash Flows from Financing Activities:

500,000	Debt Borrowings
(50,000)	Debt Repayments
$ 450,000	**Cash Flow from Financing Activities**
$ 700,000	**Net Cash Increase**

Figure 6-9 lays out ABC MediCompany's cash flow statement using the Senior management financial yardstick.

As you can see from figure 6-9, ABC has a surplus of cash at this moment, about $700,000 worth. In this case, the surplus was planned in part due to a one-time increase in long-term debt. This increase was made to allow ABC to make some necessary improvements in PPE and adjustments to its marketing strategy. It is important to be cautious about one-time increases in cash from sources such as extraordinary income from the sale of assets, from new stock issues, or from long-term debt. Over the years an organization needs to be generating enough cash from continuing activities to remain healthy. Too many one-time instances of extraordinary measures without generating enough cash from continuing activities will sink the organization. For this reason, it is important to pay particular attention to the cash flow from operating activities. This section of the cash flow statement can be an indicator of trouble or success. Cash flow from operating activities can tell you if an organization is doing well or poorly in supporting itself from continuing activities. In ABC's case, cash flow from operating activities was $735,000. This is a positive indicator for ABC.

Figure 6-9. Cash flow statement graph.

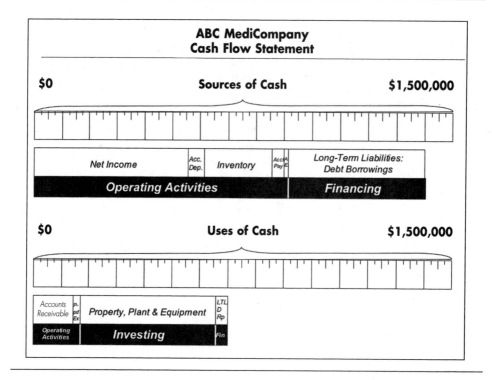

Could the cash flow statement for ABC MediCompany have looked quite different? Absolutely. As noted earlier, ABC's management is very pleased with the improvements in inventory management. These improvements were spurred in large part, however, because in prior years' inventory, older equipment, and aggressive competitors had been threatening ABC's cash and profit margins. If ABC's management had not taken action, it could easily have had much less cash from net profits and inventory to add to the debt it will use to make necessary investments planned over the next three years.

Remember, Senior management's timeframe is often three to five years to carry out its vision for the organization. ABC is making its moves in alignment with its vision to be in the position to generate positive cash flow from its ongoing activities well into the future. Whether they are the right moves will only be known over time.

To communicate value based on the cash flow statement, you will use many of the same measures that you used to communicate value from the perspective of profit or position. This is because the figures on the cash flow statement are pulled from the income statement and the balance sheet. Therefore, the same WLP solutions that drove the changes in those statements will drive changes in cash flow. The difference in your value chains will be to substitute cash as the starting point for your Senior managers. A sample value chain for ABC is shown in figure 6-10.

Figure 6-10. Sample cash financial value chain.

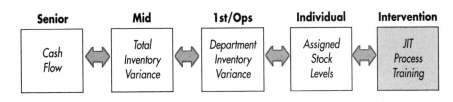

Change management is hard to do well. If training or a performance improvement intervention was done well as part of ABC's successful JIT inventory improvement project, the case can be made that WLP has provided a portion of the value from the JIT project.

Create Your Own Value Chain

Now that you have had a brief introduction to cash flow statements, this is a good time to document the cash flow measures that are most important in your organization and to create a cash flow value chain for your target organization. In exercise 6-1, fill in what you can and make notes of what you need to learn about your organization or your target organization.

 LET'S REVIEW: ─────────────────────

- ◆ This chapter provides details for the cash component of step 3 of the financial value process: identify financial imperatives.
- ◆ Cash is different from profit because profit can be tied up in non-cash items such as inventory or AR. An organization might be making a great profit, but if all the profit is in non-cash assets, then the organization will stop running. Senior executives must always be looking forward to ensure that there will be enough cash on hand to pay employees and creditors and to keep the organization in operation.
- ◆ A cash flow statement is where the organization tracks its increases and decreases in cash over a specified period. Cash flow statements have three sections. The first shows changes in cash from normal

---

Exercise 6-1. Your cash flow measures and financial value chain.

Directions: Complete the following steps for this exercise to conclude your work on step 3 of the financial value process: identify financial imperatives. If you prefer not to write in this book, go to the companion Website (astd.org/astd /publications) to download a PowerPoint file for this exercise.

1. Fill in the names of as many measures as you can for the four audience levels that you identified in exercise 2-1 in which you defined your audience. Don't worry if you have them exactly right. Treat this as a brainstorming exercise or a rough draft that you can use as an aid for later research into more complete lists of measures.
2. Use some of your measures to complete a financial value chain. Take this chain to some of your co-workers or customers for their insights on this or other value chains.
3. Make sure to take note of research you need to complete or questions that you would like to ask your boss or a mentor. Add these to the questions you had for research into profit and position measures. The next chapter will give you hints on how to find more business intelligence about your organization or your target organization.

Step 3: Identify Financial Imperatives

Cash Flow Measures:

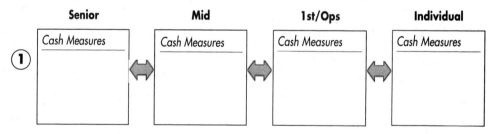

Cash Flow Value Chain:

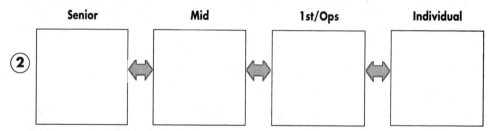

Cash Flow Research Notes:

③ _____
_____
_____

operating activities. The second shows changes in cash from investing activities, and the third shows changes from financing activities.

◆ All items on the cash flow statement are linked to items on the income statement and the balance sheet. The net profit (or loss) on the income statement becomes the first line of the cash flow statement. The changes from last period to this period for the assets, liabilities, and owner's equity of a balance sheet are transferred to the cash flow statement as changes in operating activities, investing activities, or financing activities.

◆ Changes in assets move in the opposite direction as cash. If the asset increases, cash decreases.

◆ Changes in liabilities or owner's equity move in the same direction as cash. If a liability or owner's equity increases, cash increases.

◆ Too much cash on hand can be as much of a problem as too little. Senior management must make sure there is a wise use of cash at all times.

◆ You may already have connected the value of your solutions to the income statement or the balance sheet. Knowledge of your impact on cash gives you even more variety and opportunity to point out the value of those same solutions to your organization.

In the last three chapters, you have been asked to complete profit, position, and cash flow value chains for your target organization. But, what if you don't know where to find the measures necessary to complete these chains? The next chapter will give you ideas about where to look.

———————————————————————➤

Business Intelligence: Researching What an Organization Will Value

 IN THIS CHAPTER: ————————————————

- ◆ How to carry out step 2 of the financial value process: research financial information
- ◆ Some general notes about business intelligence research
- ◆ Sample checklists for researching Senior, Mid, 1st/Ops, and Individual measures
- ◆ A case study of how a consultant used business intelligence research to prepare for an important meeting at ABC MediCompany.

You've been introduced to the language of finance and how that language connects to the language of performance. The last five chapters were critical in helping to complete step 1 of the financial value process (define audience) and step 3 (identify financial imperatives).

Now that you know what you are looking for, it is time to go back and complete step 2 (research financial information). You need to establish a regular flow of relevant financial information without becoming lost in the mountains of data you could find or, conversely, frustrated by your lack of access to the data that you want.

Research Roadblocks

The process of gathering information differs depending on whether you are internal or external to your target organization. External to an organization, you may have to deal with the fact that you may not have access to all the financial information you'd like. For corporations, you may be interested in only one segment of their business. Companies usually disclose little or nothing about individual subsidiaries or divisions with the only exception being that corporations are required to disclose results by "industry segment." If the portion of the corporation that you are interested in is large enough, you may be able to find more details about it.

Alternatively, you may be interested in a privately held organization. Privately held organizations are not required to publish their financial information. If you are interested in a corporation based in another country, and that corporation trades stock on the U.S. stock exchanges, that corporation must disclose information in the United States according to the rules of the U.S. Securities and Exchange Commission (SEC). If the corporation is not traded on U.S. stock exchanges, you will find that other countries have different laws about what must be disclosed. The information you want may be provided in unfamiliar formats or not publicly disclosed at all. If you are interested in a government organization, still other rules apply for what must be published in each province, state, city, or country.

To allow for a wide range of examples for business intelligence research, this chapter focuses primarily on research information on publicly traded corporations. For each audience level—Senior, Mid, 1st/Ops, and Individual—the externally available information is reviewed first, followed by internally available information.

Internal Versus External Views

If you are internal to an organization, you'll want to perform the types of research suggested for both the external and internal WLP professional. If you are external to an organization, you'll want to perform the appropriate external research and then prepare questions that you would ask of an internal person to help you find out more details and to clarify where you can add financial value.

Note that the research suggestions given here are not exhaustive. They are meant just to give you ideas of the types of information you can look for. Every organization is unique. Use your imagination and creativity to find sources for other information you may need. You'll find several useful references listed and described in the Additional Resources section of this book.

Research Takes Time

Performing business intelligence research will take time. The process resembles a good exercise program in many ways. Consistent application is necessary to get good, long-lasting results. It initially takes time to locate the sources of information you think you need, but over time you will become more efficient at the process. You'll also find that once you begin paying attention to how changes in the business affect finances that you will notice more information as it quickly moves through the press or passes in conversation. Eventually, other people will bring information to you simply because they know you are interested. It's important to make sure you allow yourself enough time to be successful and see results.

Business Intelligence: Senior Level

Table 7-1 summarizes suggested external Senior-level business intelligence that you can gather, along with places for you to look for this information.

Because understanding profit, position, cash, and the balance among them is fundamental to creating financial value chains, the first items of business intelligence that you'll need to obtain are the company's annual report, quarterly financial statements, and any reports of material changes or events required by the SEC. These statements are known as 10Ks, 10Qs, and 8Ks.

Where to Look

For annual reports, check your company or your target company's Website. Most companies have an investor relations page that will allow you to download their annual report free. If the report is not available online, you will usually find contact information for the company's investor relations department where you can request a copy of the report to be sent to you. Some companies will also post copies of their SEC filings on their Websites. If you cannot find this information, try the SEC at www.sec.gov. If you are a consultant and looking for financial information, you might even invest in a share of stock so that you will regularly receive financial news from them. You can find some information on the 500 top private companies at www.forbes.com. Keep in mind that private companies are not required to publish financial information; therefore, the information you will find at this site will be more general in nature. For more in-depth information, check Hoover's at www.hoovers.com. Some of Hoover's reports are not free, but paying for data may be a very economical way for you to get valuable information fast.

Other Information

While you are on the company's Website, don't forget to look for other information such as press releases, mission statements, and new product releases.

Press releases may alert you to major new deals or ventures that will imply changes in revenues, long-term investments, or market share. Mission

Table 7-1. External Senior-level business intelligence checklist.

	Source	Where to Look
Organization Information	Annual report Press releases Mission statements New product releases	The organization's Website, or www.forbes.com/2002/1/o7 /privateland.html if a large private company, or Hoover's business information services at www.hoovers.com
Investor/External Financial Information	Annual SEC report (10K) Quarterly SEC reports (10Q reports) SEC material changes or events report (8K reports)	www.sec.gov
Industry and Competitor Information	Industry statistics Competitor information Market share distribution Trends, especially best-in-class New developments in markets, legal issues, R&D, or customer sentiment	Industry publications, industry Websites, stockbroker, investors' Websites, business information sites, competitors' Websites

statements can give you an idea of what the company will emphasize in the way they do business, such as "highest quality in the industry." Such statements can indicate their approach to costs or services. Wal-Mart is a huge U.S. company. As an example, Wal-Mart is known for its devotion to low prices. To maintain such low prices, Wal-Mart must employ great diligence in cost control and purchasing negotiations. Other things to look for may be new products, which can imply major cost investments or a temporary dip in revenue from other product lines that could affect cash flow.

Useful Facts About the Industry

In addition to information that you can get directly about the company itself, you also need to obtain information about the industry that the company is in. Your Senior management closely watches industry statistics, competitor information, market-share distribution, trends, and new developments that could favorably or adversely affect your target organization.

 Senior managers make financial adjustments to meet the demands of their industry. As a WLP professional, you'll be ahead of the game if you anticipate these moves.

Where to Find the Facts

Even though we live in a world that Googles for almost any bit of information, the public library is still a good place to find business intelligence. You can find industry magazines listed in *Bacon's Magazine Directory: Magazines and Newsletters*. The SRDS Business Publication Advertising Source provides advice to its database subscribers on industry publications in particular industries.

Many articles in business publications report on trends, organizations, and business practices that are considered best in class. What is considered best in class today will be expected of all businesses in that industry within three years in order to maintain a competitive position. Senior managers surely will be focused on ensuring that best-in-class changes occur within their organization within a three- to five-year period.

Other Sources

Security analysts at investing firms create a wealth of reports on a wide variety of industries. You might be able to get access to some of these reports through a stockbroker. Of course, Websites are always available. Four excellent information sources are Dun & Bradstreet at www.dnb.com, the Brandow Company at www.bizminer.com, Hoover's Online (www.hoovers.com), and Zacks at www.zacks.com.

Internal Fact Finding

Some details about what executives are measured on may be widely communicated. Others may be very confidential. Table 7-2 summarizes suggested internal Senior-level business intelligence that you can gather, along with places where you can look for this information.

Internally to an organization, you may be able to obtain copies of what are known as management versions of the income statement, balance sheet, and cash flow statement. Management versions of financial statements

Table 7-2. Internal Senior-level business intelligence checklist.

	Source	Where to Look
Financial Information	Management financial statements	Finance or accounting department, executive office
	Budgets and variance reports	
	Balanced scorecards	
	Business plans	
	Venture capitalist reports, major or private investor reports	
	Turnaround plans	
Individual Measures	Compensation plans	HR department, executive office
	Balanced scorecards	
Key Strategies	Technology strategy	Information technology, HR, sales and marketing, various departments
	Executive white papers	
	Market expansion plans	
	Succession plans	

provide more detail than published versions. More detail will allow you to determine more measures, issues, and trends. High-level budget reports that give information on variances and trends will also be critical for you to obtain. These documents will be treated with great confidentiality and sensitivity, so you may need to explain why you would like to examine them.

Compensation plans and balanced scorecards are excellent sources of information about the measures that mean the most to an executive's wallet. The finance and accounting department is a likely source for documents on compensation plans, or you may obtain them from the executive office of your organization. If your organization uses a balanced scorecard, by all means, obtain a copy for the Senior level. The executive office or your HR department will likely have this information.

Information about key strategies will lead you to obvious impacts on costs, revenues, assets, liabilities, or cash. Executive **white papers** often discuss the future of one or more key areas of the business.

> *Technology strategies or market expansion plans are just two examples of key strategies that you may need to understand so that you can position your WLP inter- ventions to support them. **Succession plans** can also give you hints about what behaviors and capabilities will be needed in the future. Your information technology department, marketing, HR, and other departments may have this information.*

Having Difficulty?

If you are having difficulties obtaining copies of high-level internal documents, don't give up. Enlist the help of your managers. Devote some time to explaining why you would like access to this information and ask if they can request the information for you. You may want to read ahead in this book to the chapters on positioning your value. Chapter 11 offers a useful format for explaining how you will use existing data and where you are targeting improvements for the organization.

Another way that you can build the trust that gets you access to inside information is by following Jim's example. Jim (not his real name) is a professional trainer who was laid off along with his entire department from a company where he had worked for several years. He was hired as a contractor by a firm that delivers specialized software and training classes for labs around the country. Jim knew that it would take time for the managers at his new company to learn to trust him. From the moment he began working under contract, Jim was very enthusiastic in suggesting ways to improve the training and at the same time pointed out how the suggestions would improve the company's bottom line. After a few months, Jim had become the confidant of several line managers. He was told that he was looked on as a member of their own staffs. In record time, he earned favored status for training assignments, inside information, and an extension from a one-year to a three-year contract. The extension in his contract significantly improved Jim's personal financial situation.

> *It may take time for the managers in your organization to get accustomed to your focus on the company's finances. The higher the level of the manager, the more time it make take to work your way up the chain of confidence. Nevertheless, if you are trustworthy and keep what you learn in confidence, and if you are consistent, enthusias- tic, and diligent in looking for opportunities to improve the bottom line, you will eventu- ally be rewarded with the additional trust and information you seek.*

Business Intelligence: Mid Level

Table 7-3 summarizes some external Mid-level business intelligence that you can gather and suggests some places for you to look for this information.

	Source	Where to Look
Large-Scale Process or PPE Investments	Press releases about large deals awarded to vendors Vendor success case stories	Use search engine to find target organization's name on vendors' or other Websites, organization's annual report, investor research
Legal or Societal Issues	New regulations Legal actions by or against organization Environmental issues or plant shutdowns Investigations, special-interest group protests, lobbying efforts	Industry Websites, industry publications, www.sec.gov, news articles, political watchdog sites
Trends	Industry conference proceedings Benchmarking studies	Conference or industry publications

Table 7-3. External Mid-level business intelligence checklist.

External to the Organization

Business intelligence on information technology investments, for example, can be found by searching the Web for press releases about major deals awarded to a vendor. Searching for vendor success case stories can also tell you about an organization's investments and goals. New regulations or legal requirements that may affect how a business is managed can be found in many trade publications or even the general press. Litigation can significantly affect the organization's cash flow and its ability to continue sales or other operations. If a business has experienced a shutdown due to environmental or other issues, it will be easy to find articles about it. The same will be true for special investigations or public protests.

Read the articles you find with a critical eye. Recognize that the writers may have been biased in their presentation of the facts either for or against the business. Lobbying efforts will also tell you what is important to a business or industry. Political watchdog or industry Websites may discuss specific lobbying activities.

By searching through the proceedings from industry conferences, you can sometimes find excellent case study presentations of how a particular company or one of its competitors solved a problem in an innovative way. By reading such case studies with an eye to their effect on financial imperatives, you can make educated inferences about what was valuable to the Mid-level management within that organization.

Many companies participate anonymously in industry **benchmarking** studies. Although you may not be able to identify a particular company within a benchmarking study, you will be able to find critical information about the trends that Mid-level managers are expected to keep up with. Benchmarking studies and industry proceedings usually are not free, but you may be able to borrow a copy from a public library. Don't forget to ask about interlibrary loan programs. University libraries often have larger collections of specialty information.

Internal Business Intelligence Searches

Table 7-4 summarizes suggested internal Mid-level business intelligence that you can gather, along with places for you to look for this information. You'll find some overlap between this list and the business intelligence lists for the Senior and 1st/Ops levels, especially when it comes to internal information. Just as the Senior-level measures cascade into lower-level measures, so business intelligence resources tend to repeat themselves but with more and more levels of detail.

Inside your organization, you'll find helpful any memo giving financial status as it applies to divisional or group business plans and budgets. Budget and budget variance reports are also important but may be easier to obtain if you are asking for information on a specific division rather than the entire company. Compensation plans, more detailed versions of balanced scorecards, succession plans, and leadership development plans may be available from your human resources or from high-level line management.

R&D projections, product road maps, and new product introduction plans can explain anticipated revenue streams. Product quality reports can highlight areas for cost savings or improved revenues. The R&D, manufacturing, service, and marketing departments are likely to have this information.

Realignment, merger, or acquisition plans can be very helpful in determining financial and performance needs. Employee satisfaction surveys and customer satisfaction surveys highlight excellence levels that need to be maintained or issues that are costing the organization in turnover, lost sales, or complaints. Building long-term relationships with counterparts in other departments will go a long way toward helping you get the information you need easily.

Table 7-4. Internal Mid-level business intelligence checklist.

	Source	Where to Look
Financial Information	Memos or presentations with financial status	Finance or accounting department, routing and distribution via email or interoffice mail, meetings, intranets, networking
	Divisional or large, group-level business plans	
	Budgets and budget variance reports	
Individual Measures	Compensation plans	HR department, high-level line management
	Balanced scorecards (more detailed breakdown from higher-level scorecards)	
	Succession plans	
	Leadership development plans	
Product Strategies	R&D projections	R&D, manufacturing, service, and marketing departments
	Product road maps	
	New product introduction plans	
	Product quality reports	
Other Key Strategies	Restructuring plans	High-level line management, HR department, marketing department
	Merger and acquisition plans	
	Employee satisfaction surveys	
	Customer satisfaction surveys	

Business Intelligence: 1st/Ops Level and Individual Level

Table 7-5 summarizes suggested external 1st/Ops and Individual-level business intelligence that you can gather, along with places for you to look for this information.

If you are external to an organization, one way to find out about likely requirements, costs, or procedures is to examine industry standards or certification requirements. Another is to look at books or Websites with tips for how

Table 7-5. External 1st/Ops-level and Individual-level business intelligence checklist.

	Source	**Where to Look**
Standards and Procedures	Industry standards (e.g., ISO 9000)	Standards and certification organizations, bookstores, Websites
	Certification requirements	
	How-to books	
Job Descriptions and Responsibilities	General job descriptions	*Occupational Outlook Handbook* (U.S. Department of Labor, 2003), job search engines (e.g., www.monster.com), job postings on your target organization's Website
	Specific job responsibilities and measures	

to manage a particular type of operation. Standards, certifications, or how-to recommendations may spell out what types of measures a 1st/Ops or Individual contributor may have as part of their job responsibilities.

It can be difficult to find external information on measures, job responsibilities, and other issues at this level. One source for information that is often overlooked is job search engines such as www.monster.com. By searching on a company name, you may be able to glean where the company is hiring and what types of measures and responsibilities are expected of the applicants. Alternatively, you can look at your target organization's Website to find out if it has posted job openings online.

If you cannot find job postings for your target organization but you have a general idea of the type of job that your WLP intervention is likely to affect, you can always look up a generic description of that job in the *Occupational Outlook Handbook,* published by the U.S. Department of Labor (2003). It offers a wealth of information about particular jobs including the expected education levels, job responsibilities, and expected growth or decline in each type of job in the next few years. The *Handbook* sometimes describes job measures, but even if it does not you can often infer them from the job descriptions.

Internal Sources

Table 7-6 summarizes suggested internal 1st/Ops and Individual-level business intelligence that you can gather, along with places for you to look for this information.

Table 7-6. Internal 1st Ops- and Individual-level business intelligence checklist.

	Source	Where to Look
Financial Information	Memos or presentations with financial status	Finance or accounting department, routing and distribution via email or interoffice mail, meetings, intranets, networking
	Department-level business plans	
	Department-level budgets and budget variance reports	
	Monthly or quarterly status reports	
Individual Measures	Compensation plans	HR department, line management
	Personal balanced scorecards (more detailed breakdown from higher-level scorecards)	
	Job descriptions	
	Individual development plans	
Product/Process	Service-level agreements	R&D, manufacturing, services, or marketing department
	Process maps	
	Procedure manuals and guidelines	
	Quality reports	
Other Key Strategies	Information technology project plans	High-level line management, HR department, marketing department
	Hiring and staffing plans	
	Sales forecasts and results	
	Major account plans	

Internally to an organization, you'll be looking once again for memos, budgets, business plans, compensation plans, and balanced scorecards, but for a narrower scope or period of time. You should work to get on the distribution lists for monthly or quarterly departmental status reports. Job descriptions and individual development plans can give you a place to start with measures if you have not yet been successful at obtaining higher-level data.

Service-level agreements, either that your organization must live up to or that your organization requires of its suppliers, can tell you a great deal about costs and risks to the organization if performance is not maintained in critical areas. Process maps, procedures, and quality reports can sometimes tell you the same thing. Various departments will have these reports or manuals.

Sales forecasts and results, major account plans, hiring and staffing plans, and information technology project plans are other types of information that you can look for. The level of detail at the 1st/Ops or Individual level can be overwhelming in contrast to the measures you are looking for. In some cases, suggesting lunch with someone in the department you are interested in may tell you exactly what the measures are or point you to the most relevant documents to obtain.

What if You Can't Get Enough?

What if you just cannot get enough information to draw your financial value chains? There are the two other key actions you must be prepared to take to be able to determine the appropriate priorities and measures for your target organization.

First, you must learn to ask. Your 1st/Ops, Mid, and Senior managers know what their measures and metrics are. Even if they do not consciously think in terms of financial value chains, when you demonstrate the concept, they are able to help you fill one or more portions. This is important for you to do even if you believe you know the chains that your intervention impacts. You may have overlooked something. More important, you'll begin to build creditability and respect by demonstrating your focus and commitment to financial success.

The Road to Success

Workplace learning and performance professionals can improve their lot by taking a few simple actions including the simple exercise of asking the right questions based on key information.

Darlene is a knowledge management (KM) consultant. Darlene was invited to meet with the head of KM for ABC MediCompany.

Because KM has such broad potential application, Darlene wanted to be prepared to discuss a number of options for how her expertise could help ABC's financial performance. Darlene approached her business intelligence research task with the goal of learning as much as she could from a Senior management perspective and of creating an excellent set of questions that would focus her conversation with the ABC KM manager.

Darlene started her research by obtaining copies of ABC's financial reports. She examined the same financial statements that were presented in chapter 4 to learn more about the company's profit, position, and cash. Darlene read ABC's Website and purchased a report on ABC's industry from bizminer.com. Darlene checked investor research and competitor Websites to find out more information on how ABC compared within its industry.

Knowledge management is often applied to document critical knowledge that senior managers or key employees have gained over many years. Because ABC MediCompany had been around for several years, Darlene found the names of several principals in the company and used search engines to see if she could find any interesting facts about some of the top employees listed in ABC's annual report. Darlene also read industry Websites and visited a large city library to read some articles in industry magazines. Darlene assembled table 7-7 to summarize where she did her research, the key points she learned, and the most important questions she wanted to ask.

Darlene's questions allowed her to focus during her meeting for maximum benefit to herself and her potential client. During the conversation, Darlene showed her potential client how to draw a financial value chain. Together, they were able to brainstorm possible financial value chains based on ABC's priorities and Darlene's questions. Her potential client was impressed with the conversation because these were exactly the types of conversations he needed to have with his executives.

By talking with Darlene, the head of ABC's KM could see how to position his contributions and could see how to implement interventions with Darlene's expertise. As it turned out, ABC's excellent ROA was partially due to R&D and manufacturing innovations from ABC's key product designers. ABC wanted to protect this competitive advantage. Top management believed it needed to capture more knowledge from these designers to keep ahead of its industry. Darlene was invited back for additional conversations to pursue exactly how her services could help ABC's bottom line.

Other Paths to Success

The first road to success was described as being able ask good questions. A second road can help you, too. You can join trade or other associations for your target industry and organization. Being connected to HR or WLP associations is important and necessary. It is equally important to be familiar with industry buzzwords, emerging trends, and industry leaders. Trade newsletters and publications will often alert you to value chains that you may not have thought about before. Conversations with others in an industry will often help you see connections that have eluded you in the past.

Table 7-7. Summary of ABC business intelligence research.

I	II Research Source	III Key Points and Discoveries	IV Questions
STEP 1: Audience 1	Annual report ABC Website	CEO is Ashton Scott. Names of other executives identified.	*Narrowing the Audience:* a. Is there a particular Senior- or Mid-level executive who is especially supportive of your role or who is expecting to work closely with you?
STEP 3: General 2			*General Financial Expectations:* a. Why was the position of director of knowledge management created? b. What are your key goals for helping the company? c. Do you have clear priorities, dates, or timeframes for what you must achieve, or is it up to you to propose solutions?
3	Annual report ABC Website	Key executives are nearing retirement.	*Broad Financial Impact:* a. What would be the effect on ABC's profits, assets, liabilities, or cash flow if ABC were to lose the knowledge of some of its top executives?

(continued on page 96)

Table 7-7. Summary of ABC business intelligence research (continued).

	I	II	III	IV
		Research Source	Key Points and Discoveries	Questions
4	STEP 3: Profit	Industry magazine article	ABC's competitors are moving to an inside/outside sales team approach where the inside salesperson focuses on capturing and sharing data and knowledge about customers over the phone with salespeople located around the company.	*Revenue:* a. How much impact do you believe your competitor's new sales strategy has had or will have on your revenues in the next one to two years? b. Is ABC planning to make changes in its sales strategy? If so, how important will good KM practices be to ABC's success?
5		Industry Website, notes in annual report about potential changes to business	New regulations will come into effect next year regarding the distribution and maintenance of ABC's products.	*Cost of Goods Sold:* a. How will the new laws affect ABC's cost of goods sold? b. Is it a priority for the KM team to help ABC meet its regulatory obligations? If so, are there dates, costs, or other measures that must be met?
6		Industry magazine article	ABC has one of the most creative and innovative designers in its field on its staff. Industry insiders cite these people as giving ABC an edge and revolutionizing ABC's industry in past years.	*Operating Earnings:* a. What would be the impact on ABC's R&D efforts or competitive position if ABC lost the knowledge of its top designers? b. Could you describe that impact in terms of changes in quality measures, manufacturing costs, changes in sales, or changes in R&D costs over time?

I	II	III	IV
	Research Source	**Key Points and Discoveries**	**Questions**
7 **STEP 3: Position**	Balance sheet	Inventory has reduced a great deal over the last year.	*Assets: Inventory* a. ABC has made great improvements in its inventory levels. Is ABC planning to make more improvements? If so, is KM important to this process? b. How would success be measured at each level in ABC's organization?
8	Income statement and balance sheet	Excellent return-on-assets (ROA) compared to industry average.	*Assets: Balance or Ratio* a. ABC has an excellent return-on-assets compared to the industry average. Is there a secret to how ABC manages this? Does KM play a key role?
9 **STEP 3: Cash**	Cash flow statement	ABC has significant amounts of surplus cash for the moment.	*Surplus Cash Flow:* a. ABC has taken on significant amounts of new debt to generate cash. Does top management have some significant new strategies in mind? b. Will any of this money be spent on KM and how would KM be expected to help? Are there any dates or specific measures for your results?

Create Your Research Notes

Now it is time for you to identify your research sources, the important points you are learning from your research, and the next questions you would like to ask in exercise 7-1. Take a look at the suggested business intelligence gathering tables and the case study process earlier in this chapter to help you figure out where to go in your own organization or for your target organization.

The Benefits of Good Business Intelligence

Knowing your ratios, margins, and breakdowns are the building blocks for your financial value chains. They change from quarter to quarter and year to year. Watching trends will alert you to key issues that your Senior managers will be facing and explain what is causing the sleeplessness in your organization.

If you can see the issues well before the others around you, you will have much more time to research your options, create your interventions, and build your proposals. You'll be in the position to answer what previously may have appeared to be sudden questions about your value. By understanding the position of your Mid

---

Exercise 7-1. Business intelligence checklist.

Directions: Complete the following steps for exercise 7-1. Accomplishing this exercise finishes your work on step 2 of the financial value process: research financial information. If you prefer not to write in this book, go to the companion Website (astd.org/astd/publications) to download a PowerPoint file for this exercise.

1. Select a business intelligence source such as a Website and list the key points and discoveries in the most appropriate row of column III as you read your source. The most appropriate row depends on whether your discovery relates to knowledge about your audience (STEP 1), about general financial information (STEP 3: General), or about profit (STEP 3: Profit), position (STEP 3: Position), or cash (STEP 3: Cash).
2. Make sure to note the source of your point or discovery in column II. You may need to go back and check your reference later, and it might be hard to remember where you learned your information.
3. Write any additional questions that you would like to have answered in column IV. This will help you work more efficiently in future meetings, conduct research more rapidly, or write emails or memos looking for additional information.
4. Repeat steps 1 through 3 of this exercise as necessary. It's helpful to plan on keeping an ongoing worksheet of business intelligence because information is always changing. In chapter 11, you'll see why planning to update your research and communicating your value on a quarterly basis makes a big difference as to how your value is perceived by your audience.

I	**II** Research Source	**III** Key Points and Discoveries	**IV** Questions	
1				
STEP 1: **Audience**	2			
	3			
	4			
STEP 3: **General**	5			
	6			
	7			
STEP 3: **Profit**	8			
	9			
	10			
STEP 3: **Position**	11			
	12			
	13			
STEP 3: **Cash**	14			
	15			

and Senior managers, you will be able to connect their concerns as stewards to what you can do to improve the bottom line as a WLP professional. The links in your chains will become more obvious and familiar over time.

You may be thinking that now that you understand how value chains need to be built and where the information comes from, that you are ready to go off, do good deeds, and communicate your value.

Not so fast! There are other perspectives on value and financial numbers that you need to understand. Even if they produce financial results, not all interventions will be applauded with enthusiasm. Even for those interventions that receive initial enthusiasm, the attention you continue to receive depends on how well you can match your communication strategy to business activity cycles and how you address common perception challenges.

 LET'S REVIEW: _____

- This chapter gives pointers and tips for how to perform step 2 of the financial value process: research financial information.
- The types and amounts of business intelligence research that will be available to you will be different depending on whether you work internally or externally to an organization. No matter whether you are internal or external to an organization, there will be business intelligence that you can gather for every level: Senior, Mid, 1st/Ops, and Individual.
- External business intelligence research usually involves getting copies of financial reports and reading Websites, industry publications, and newspapers. Internal business intelligence research involves the same activities, plus reading internal memos, reports, processes, procedures, job descriptions, plans, white papers, and more.
- In either case—internal or external—business intelligence research requires patience and persistence to build trust and to get the information you want.
- You must not be afraid to ask for the information you need and you must be willing to explain why you would want it. Using your business intelligence research to build a list of questions to gain additional information can lead to very powerful conversations with key influencers and decision makers.

Now that you have explored the basics of financial numbers, let's move into the next part of the book to take a look at how perceptions and business cycles can affect the value others see in your performance.

Part Two

Positioning, Delivering, and Measuring Value

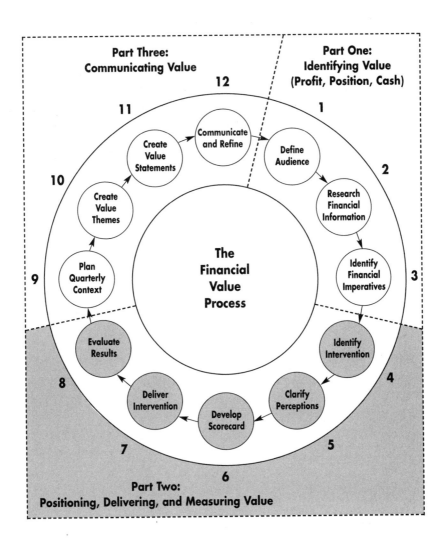

Part Three:
Communicating Value

Part One:
Identifying Value
(Profit, Position, Cash)

The Financial Value Process

- Communicate and Refine
- Define Audience
- Research Financial Information
- Identify Financial Imperatives
- Identify Intervention
- Clarify Perceptions
- Develop Scorecard
- Deliver Intervention
- Evaluate Results
- Plan Quarterly Context
- Create Value Themes
- Create Value Statements

Part Two:
Positioning, Delivering, and Measuring Value

Communicating your value continues with knowing the solution you want to provide; understanding how your solution may be perceived by your audience; and arranging to continuously define, measure, and track your value in financial terms. The second part of this book will cover the next five steps in the financial value process:

◆ Step 4: Identify Intervention
◆ Step 5: Clarify Perceptions
◆ Step 6: Develop Scorecard
◆ Step 7: Deliver Intervention
◆ Step 8: Evaluate Results.

In chapters 8, 9, and 10, which comprise Part Two of *Quick! Show Me Your Value,* you will

◆ be introduced to a model that can explain why so much of what you do is taken for granted and how your financial value becomes "invisible"
◆ discover how to create a scorecard that allows you to track financial value from your WLP solutions and keep the perception of your value high, as that value inevitably drifts over time to being taken for granted
◆ learn what different types of evaluation data must be presented to some audiences but not to others, if your value is to be accepted by every audience you communicate with.

8

---→

What Have You Done for Me Lately?

 IN THIS CHAPTER: ————————————

- ◆ What step 4 of the financial value process (identify intervention) really means
- ◆ Why step 5 of the financial value process (clarify perceptions) is so important to your ability to communicate value
- ◆ An explanation and examples of givens, conscious negotiables, and unknown expectations
- ◆ How your value slides even if your interventions are successful
- ◆ A case study demonstrating changes in value perception.

In previous chapters, you've seen how to use financial numbers to create value chains tailored for the specific audience you are communicating with. It's time to wow them! Right?

Well, not so fast. Before you jump into the communication fray, let's take a quick look at steps 4 and 5 of the financial value process. Once you know which intervention you wish to communicate about, it's important to examine that intervention within a model of perception that, even if you are correct with your numbers, will affect what your audience is able to see, hear, and accept as valuable. You'll see how the effects of time and familiarity create challenges in communicating the value of your **interventions.**

Are You Matching a Need to an Intervention or an Intervention to a Need?

There are two basic situations readers of this book will find themselves in. The first is the situation of identifying and understanding a business need so that the most appropriate learning or performance intervention can be applied to solve the need. In this sense, the financial information in this book augments and supports the groundbreaking work of many WLP professionals in shifting the focus of the profession from training to learning and performance. Excellent books such as the *Handbook of Human Performance Technology: Improving Individual and Organizational Performance Worldwide* (Stolovitch and Keeps, 1999) and *Performance Consulting: Moving Beyond Training* (Robinson and Robinson, 1995) offer detailed methods and guides for looking at cause and effect, setting expectations, and deciding upon appropriate interventions. When in this situation, the WLP professional must use his or her knowledge of financial value to convince others that the new intervention is cost effective and should be purchased, funded, or supported in some way to solve the business need.

The second situation is to have an intervention already in place that must be shown to be valuable or at least valuable enough to continue in its current state. This situation is as applicable for the individual trainer who passionately believes in the value of a health and safety course as it is for the workforce development manager who suddenly needs to justify why his entire department shouldn't be outsourced to another company that says it can do the same job at a lower cost. For this situation, the information in this book helps the reader communicate the value of what is already being done in terms that are current, relevant, and striking for the audience.

No matter which situation the reader encounters (some will encounter both), step 4 (Identify Intervention) is not about using WLP techniques to determine the best intervention to solve the business need. It is about *focusing your communication*. In step 4, you must select a particular intervention or a limited number of interventions, programs, or interventions that you want to use to communicate value for your organization. There are three reasons for selecting an intervention for your value communication:

1. Learning to track and communicate value takes time. You will be more successful if you limit your focus so that you can do an excellent job with your communication.
2. Your audience has little time to hear about your value. You want to focus the audience's attention on what will have the most impact.

3. Even if you need to communicate the value of something broad, such as the worth of your entire department, you need to use specific examples to prove your worth. To do that, you'll need to focus on specific interventions or programs so that you can quickly communicate value in a short period of time.

For some readers the choice will be obvious. Whether the intervention is one that you are selling as an external vendor, one that you believe passionately about and want to support more, or one that you have been informed that you must justify or lose, the choice of how you will focus your value communication is easy.

Others may have a more difficult time. Often that difficulty doesn't arise because you can't prove decent financial numbers but because of your audience's perceptions and filters about those numbers.

Clarifying Perceptions

Examine figure 8-1. Understanding the concepts behind this picture is a critical link in unlocking the mysteries of value perception. This model of value perception is modified from an original concept introduced in the late 1970s at the height of the **Total Quality Management** movement. That concept was called the **Kano Model of Product Quality** (Kano, 1984).

Figure 8-1. Unknown, conscious, and unconscious expectations.

Unknown Expectation (Surprise)
High satisfaction, little or no dissatisfaction

**Conscious Expectation
(Negotiable)**
Satisfaction if met, dissatisfaction if not met

**Unconscious Expectation
(Given)**
No satisfaction if met, only dissatisfaction if not met

Unconscious Expectations: Givens

At the bottom of the model shown in figure 8-1, notice the area labeled unconscious expectation (given). An unconscious expectation is something that a person cannot tell you that he or she expects. This is something so taken for granted that, no matter how much effort it takes to create, perform, administer, or accomplish, your audience may never acknowledge what has taken place on its behalf. You may think relatively few of your programs would be considered a given, but this phenomenon is extremely common. Left to a natural course of events, it is nearly inevitable for every WLP program, service, or intervention.

Here is an example you may recognize from your own experience: Let's say that you are traveling for an important business meeting. After a very late departure, a missed connection, and further delays, you finally make it to your hotel. You breathe a sigh of relief because your room has not been given away. Once in your room, you quickly get ready for bed. You pull back the bedcover only to discover . . . no sheets!

Now did you ever, during your long ordeal, suddenly think to yourself, "I should have told the travel agent that I wanted sheets on my bed when the agent made my room reservations!"? Of course not. You assumed a hotel room would have a bed, a bedspread, and clean sheets under that bedspread. For you, it was a given that the sheets would be there. Of course, now that the lack of sheets is discovered, you are a very dissatisfied customer.

This story illustrates two important points about unconscious givens: First, if the sheets had been there, you would never have noticed. If someone asked you the next day if you had sheets on your bed the night before, you'd probably wonder what kind of person would ask you such a strange question. If you decided it was appropriate to answer, then you'd have to reflect for a moment before you could reply yes. Second—and this is important—the reason you could feel confident in your answer was not because you remembered there *were* sheets on your bed. The reason you could answer was because you know you would have remembered it if the sheets *were not* there!

This leads to the second point about givens. You can't satisfy people by delivering an unconscious given. Why? They simply can't see it. You can only dissatisfy your audience if suddenly what they took for granted is not there. More important from a financial point of view is that the value of givens has already been factored into the income statement, balance sheet, and cash flow statement. Even if you point out that the given has taken place, your audience will shrug, take it for granted, and be unable to recall the conversation 10 minutes later.

If you are working internally to an organization, do you often feel as if managers in other departments wonder what you really do? Do you ever ask yourself, "How could they not know what we do?" If you have to ask yourself that question, you are probably in the dangerous and vulnerable position of spending a huge proportion of your time or your department's time on unconscious givens.

In this position, you are a target for having your budget cut because others take you for granted and can't see what you do. You may have a hard time getting attention, and you are in a difficult spot to establish continuous financial value even if you are doing the best job in the industry. Your value has become invisible.

Conscious Expectations: Negotiables

Next up from givens on figure 8-1 is conscious expectations, or negotiables. A conscious expectation means that a client or manager can describe what is desired, and you can describe what you will do to satisfy that need. You can estimate how much it will cost, and you have a general feeling for how much benefit you expect to obtain for that cost. The majority of new WLP projects, consulting contracts, and other interventions start at this expectation level.

Unlike a given, you *can* satisfy someone when you deliver what was expected. Like a given, you can also dissatisfy someone if you don't. The most important point about a negotiable is that it is very hard to surprise your client in terms of the delighted surprise that comes with an unexpected intervention or benefit.

Wait a minute! If you do an excellent job, can't you delight someone? Won't your audience be happy with you? Well, yes, they will be happy, but it is still hard to excite them in the way that true creativity and innovation does. In a conscious situation, your client or internal customer already knows what to expect because you have both negotiated and agreed upon it. It is possible to communicate the value of fulfilling your agreement but difficult to get your client to believe you have delivered overwhelming, unexpected value.

Unknown Expectations: Surprise

At the top of figure 8-1 is shown the unknown expectation. This is the kind of unconscious expectation that could be described as an untapped need. Your intervention has surprised and excited your audience because of the excellent possibilities they suddenly realize exist. You've solved a problem they didn't know could be solved, at least not in the way that you've done it before. This unknown expectation benefits the organization because the new intervention invariably is more effective or efficient at accomplishing a necessary task. That **effectiveness** and **efficiency** typically translate into larger cost savings or greater revenue than could have been consciously negotiated.

By solving a problem or delivering something in a way that others didn't know could be done, you are in a wonderful situation. It is hard to dissatisfy an audience when you've produced a financial windfall. You have created a sense of customer satisfaction that instills credibility, confidence, and an easy venue to communicate value.

So, what's the catch? Despite your best efforts, trying to satisfy your audience's expectations is like running up the down escalator. Notice the direction of the arrows in figure 8-1. The moment you have surprised someone with a new intervention, method, or program, it becomes a conscious expectation that you will do it again. Without careful management of your audience's perceptions, what is consciously expected quickly drops into an ever-growing pile of givens that you are expected to provide without anyone noticing what you do anymore. This is the "What have you done for me lately?" phenomenon. No matter how big the surprise, what delighted people last year can be completely taken for granted the next. How quickly they forget!

The trap that many WLP professionals fall into is expecting the respect that they generated when introducing a successful program or intervention to last forever or at least much longer than it does. They are then completely unprepared when they realize that the perception of their services has dropped into a given. They are even more shocked when they realize that if they ask their audience to estimate the financial value of a given that the estimate is either far too low, a breakeven at zero financial value, or even a negative estimate of being perceived as a costly program with no financial value.

When communicating value, it is critical to know how your services, programs, and interventions are perceived right now. It is also important to know how quickly improvements are worked into the assumptions of the financial statements so that you can plan ahead to keep the perception of your value high.

Your executives are looking for every competitive advantage they can find. They value more than just your ability to do the basics of your job. When the executives in the Twin Cities study were asked what knowledge, skills, and abilities they expected of human asset professionals, they didn't even mention WLP and HR skills because they were givens! Just as important—or perhaps even more important than your ability to perform WLP functions—is how consistently you introduce additional financial gain and how well you keep what you have introduced consciously valued within the organization. You can take measures to keep the perceptions of your value high, but only if you recognize the pace of your own "down escalator" and take active steps to keep your communication ahead of that value slide.

Meet Marcella

To help you understand the concepts here and throughout the rest of the book, you will be asked to consider a fictitious WLP professional working at ABC MediCompany. Her story will help you see the signs and the effects of the movement from surprise to given. Although Marcella is fictitious, her story is based on a composite of similar situations that real WLP professionals have faced across a number of companies and government agencies.

Marcella is a new training manager hired to work at ABC MediCompany. The product sold by her firm enjoys a special niche in its target customer space. ABC's product is sold by highly trained sales representatives and is almost always purchased with a one- to three-year support contract. The contract renewal department is responsible for calling each customer every year to make sure the information on the contract is up to date. This department is also responsible for asking customers if they would like to upgrade or renew their support contract.

Because support contracts are a very profitable portion of the business, pressure is intense for the contract consultants to renew or upgrade as many contracts as possible. The work is done over the phone, with a contract consultant only requesting the help of a sales representative to call on the customer in person if the contract is over a certain size and in danger of not being renewed. New contract consultants quickly find out that their job is complex, confusing, and often exhausting as they are expected to make many calls every day with a very low error rate on contract changes and updates.

When Marcella was hired, new contract consultants spent three weeks in class to learn all the terminology and systems required to manage contracts. Managers were not happy about the three weeks set aside for the class. They wanted their new hires on the phones and being productive much more quickly. After graduating from the class, the graduates' high error rates affected customer satisfaction and employee morale. Experienced contract consultants spent time helping new employees by answering their questions and demonstrating how to handle more difficult system issues. This put extra strain on the experienced employees to keep up with their own workloads. Turnover was a big problem, which made it difficult to improve the quality and quantity of renewals.

After six months at her new job, Marcella changed the format for new hire training from a three-week class to a two-week class with a one-week formal mentorship updating real contracts over the phone with an instructor's help.

Error rates dropped. Renewal rates went up. Employee morale improved because experienced contract consultants were able to spend more time on their own workload. Turnover rates dropped slightly with both new hires and experienced contract consultants. Although no one gathered solid numbers to quantify the impact, management was delighted and awarded Marcella a bonus. Marcella was thrilled. She continued to look for ways to enhance the program. After nine more months on the job, Marcella improved the on-the-job coaching by the instructors and added another week of formal mentorship to the program. Marcella's instructors told her they were sure the new hires had improved in all areas again, but no one actually quantified the level of improvement. Marcella's managers patted her on the back and told her with a smile that these types of results were just what they'd come to expect from her.

Nine months later, Marcella was asked to help the company by cutting expenses within her department. Sales of the ABC MediCompany's product had hit some new competition and top management knew it had to make some changes to manufacturing, inventory management, and marketing. Top management started to make those investments, but to do so they still had to cut money and budgets from some departments to give to others. Money was extremely tight for the customer service department.

Marcella made a few small adjustments in the new hire program that, quite frankly, she had been thinking about anyway. This allowed her to glean some small savings. Marcella was aware that some managers thought that her program was too expensive and that she had not done enough to trim her budget, but given how much more effective new hires were now than when Marcella first started, Marcella was convinced that the program was exactly what was needed to ensure the contract renewals continued to run smoothly.

Nine months later, or nearly three years since Marcella was hired, Kathleen, Marcella's new manager surprised Marcella by cutting her budget for new hire training down to one week with no mentorship on the job. Marcella could not convince Kathleen that this was a poor move. As a matter of fact, Marcella could not dissuade Kathleen from her belief that the program was costly and offered little financial benefit to ABC. Many people were sympathetic, but no line managers were willing to come forward to help. Marcella worried that errors and turnover would go up, that renewals would slide, and that she would be blamed for poor and expensive training when, in fact, she was sure her program made a great contribution to the company over the prior three years.

Was Marcella right? Should she have been able to avoid this whole situation? Unfortunately, Marcella made a common mistake when introducing each new level of value in her program. She approached her WLP services with a one-time mentality instead of from a mindset of continuous value management.

With a one-time mentality, WLP professionals tend to believe that once they have shown they can deliver phenomenal value (a surprise) then they have met the challenge of proving their worth and that the managers around the WLP professional will recognize what a valuable contributor the WLP professional is. The tendency at that point is for WLP professionals to feel that they can relax and focus on the mechanics of their job, assuming that the surrounding managers will accept, support, and nurture the WLP professional almost indefinitely.

> *By focusing on repeatedly delivering programs and interventions, WLP professionals with a one-time mentality fail to recognize value slide. Their interventions are no longer surprises or even negotiables; they are becoming unconscious givens. The WLP professionals do not realize that they must demonstrate ever-higher levels of value from their interventions. Figure 8-2 shows how WLP professionals who operate with a one-time mentality have a large and growing proportion of their deliverables in the given and or low negotiable states.*

Figure 8-2. Unmanaged and continuously managed value perceptions.

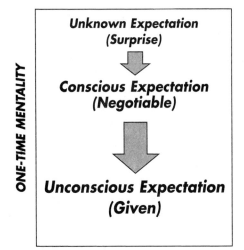

Why the Disconnect?

The general managers around the WLP professional are constantly under pressure to improve processes, costs, and revenues. After all, inflation alone can turn their net profits into net losses very, very quickly. Because WLP expenses are usually much easier to cut back on than, say, long-term equipment or real estate leases, WLP professionals need to take the perception of their value very

seriously. WLP professionals must work to maintain a much higher proportion of their value in the conscious/negotiable and surprise states to offset the
tendency to cut or change critical programs, as shown on the right-hand side
of figure 8-2.

 *Without a continuous value management approach WLP professionals will find that
their audiences have less and less time, money, and patience for what their audiences
perceive as less and less valuable. This is especially true when that audience has
come to depend upon a certain pace of new financial value from the WLP function.*

Constantly Thinking About the Numbers

You, as a workplace learning and performance professional, must use a continuous value management mindset. You have to work to keep the balance of
the perceptions within your organization weighted to the conscious or surprise levels. This transition requires a shift away from a one-time mentality
of using an ROI study as a quick fix for the perception of your value or of
finding some other way to once again prove your worth, so that you can go
back to just focusing on the mechanics of your job. With a continuous value
management approach, you must constantly think about the numbers. After
all, the numbers are the principal focus of all levels above the Individual
performer.

To ensure that the perception of your value remains high throughout the
organization, you should

♦ Create a **financial imperatives scorecard.** You'll learn all about this
  tool in the next chapter, but essentially such a scorecard tracks the
  costs and benefits of a chosen intervention and connects the intervention to the organization's financial imperatives.
♦ Invest in appropriate evaluation and feedback for your programs. You
  can make all of the financial value claims that you want, but you
  must eventually back up your claims with data from different types of
  evaluations. If you don't have such evidence of your value, you risk
  losing your creditability. The definition of credible data changes with
  each level of your audience. You'll learn more about how to match
  evaluation data to audience levels in chapter 10.
♦ Create a quarterly communication plan. Value must be communicated
  regularly to counteract value slide. Even so, value is not heard if it is
  not connected to the urgent and important activities that occur
  during each quarter of the year. A quarterly communication plan is

tailored to the context of a business's activities. This is the focus of chapter 11.

 If Marcella had taken a continuous value management approach, she would have reset the baseline for her contributions each time they changed, and she would have had documented evidence of performance improvement over the last three years to review with Kathleen. That way, she could have avoided an unpleasant discussion based on invisible value and different opinions.

In addition, Marcella would have performed different types of evaluation over time so that she could have verifiable financial data and numbers that matched the type of information that each level of her audience needed to hear.

Finally, if Marcella had a communication plan, it would have helped her to manage her value and to negotiate for what she needed to perform even better rather than reacting to what seemed to be an unreasonable demand from her management team.

Choose Your Focus and Note Perceptions

Before moving on, this is a good time for you to choose the intervention you would like to focus on for the rest of this book, and note how you believe it is perceived. Try your hand at exercise 8-1.

LET'S REVIEW:

- ◆ By completing step 4 of the financial value process you will have identified an intervention, meaning that you have chosen a focus for your value communication.
- ◆ If your intervention is viewed as an unconscious expectation, or a given, its true value can no longer be seen by your audience. All performance interventions become givens over time, especially if value communication is left unmanaged. This is known as the value slide.
- ◆ If your intervention is viewed as a conscious negotiable, you and your client or manager can discuss what is to be designed or delivered and set a reasonable approximation on its value. Many new projects or consulting contracts start at this level.
- ◆ If your intervention is an unknown expectation, your audience will be delighted with your contribution, and its financial value will be seen as very high.

Exercise 8-1. Identifying an intervention and clarifying perceptions.

 Directions: Completing this exercise wraps up your work on steps 4 and 5 of the financial value process: identify intervention and clarify perceptions. If you prefer not to write in this book, go to the companion Website (www.astd.org/astd /publications) to download a PowerPoint file for this exercise.

1. Because perceptions shift over time, the first part of this exercise is to note today's date.
2. Write the name or a brief description of the intervention you would like focus your value communication on.
3. It is possible for your intervention to be taken for granted at one level and to be a potential surprise at another. For each level, put a check in the perception box that best describes how you believe your audience at this level perceives the value of your intervention.
4. Note a reason in the rightmost column as to why you arrived at a particular value perception for each level.
5. After you've completed this exercise, this might be a good time to have an informal discussion with your Senior, Mid, or 1st/Ops managers about how they perceive your value.

Steps 4 and 5: Solution and Perception

① **Today's Date:** _____

② **Your Solution:** _____

③

LEVEL	PERCEPTION			REASON
Senior	☐ Surprise	☐ Negotiable	☐ Given	
Mid	☐ Surprise	☐ Negotiable	☐ Given	
1st/Ops	☐ Surprise	☐ Negotiable	☐ Given	
Individual	☐ Surprise	☐ Negotiable	☐ Given	

◆ All unknown expectations slide into givens if unmanaged. The pendulum of how your audience perceives the value of the intervention swings abruptly from very high to very low in a relatively short period of time.
◆ Clarifying how your interventions are perceived is critical to understanding how to approach your audience when communicating value.

The next three chapters discuss the basics of continuous value management: what it takes to set baseline costs and benefits, define appropriate evaluation and feedback, and develop a quarterly communication plan.

The Financial Imperatives Scorecard

 IN THIS CHAPTER:——————————————

- ◆ Step 6 of the financial value process: develop scorecard
- ◆ How to define your scorecard so that you are always comparing apples to apples
- ◆ How to use your financial value chains to fill in the benefits part of your scorecard
- ◆ How to fill in the costs in the second part of your scorecard
- ◆ How to finish your scorecard by summarizing your value
- ◆ Why you should update your scorecard every time you change or improve your intervention
- ◆ Some rules for tracking and presenting data from your scorecard
- ◆ Tips for special cases
- ◆ A case study of a financial scorecard for Marcella, the fictitious WLP character introduced in chapter 8.

In the previous chapter, you were briefly introduced to the concept of the financial imperatives scorecard. As you followed the exploits of Marcella, you were able to see that she might have avoided budget cuts had she been able to continuously communicate value and discuss how much she had improved versus where she started.

That's where the financial imperatives scorecard comes in. Using a financial imperatives scorecard is a continuous, disciplined effort. It is important to create and maintain your scorecard to demonstrate how much benefit you are delivering versus how much it is costing to obtain that benefit.

Your financial imperatives scorecard is personal. You don't have to show it to anyone if you don't want to. You can use sophisticated spreadsheets or a napkin that you scribble notes on every so often, just so long as you commit to the discipline of using a scorecard and follow a few rules. If you are an external consultant, you probably keep some type of case or scorecard for yourself, but can take the concept further by discussing how you can help your clients create scorecards for themselves.

Building and Using a Financial Imperatives Scorecard

The basic layout of the financial imperatives scorecard is shown in figure 9-1. There are a few rules you should rely on when creating and using the information from a scorecard. As each scorecard item is discussed in the sections that follow, you'll have an opportunity to examine a completed scorecard that Marcella might have used to describe the value she created with her changes to the new hire training program described in chapter 8. This approach will help you see how the scorecard is built piece by piece.

Creating the Scorecard: Intervention and Basis

The first part of the scorecard to examine is the two lines at the top labeled Intervention and Basis. Completing the intervention line is easy. Simply name the intervention that you will be tracking with your scorecard.

Basis is a bit more difficult, but not much. The first decision that you must make for your scorecard is to define how you will count your numbers. Basis refers to how you will count so that you are comparing like to like, or apples to apples, so to speak. There are three parts to your basis: monetary units, intervention units, and time units. The term *monetary units* simply means the currency you are counting your value in. For many of you, this will be an easy choice because you will be tracking interventions that only occur within one country. For those who are working across national boundaries, it is critical to note if the numbers reflect U.S. dollars, Canadian dollars, yen, euros, pounds, or some other unit.

Intervention units define how you will count benefits and costs in terms of either the participants in the intervention or some other countable item that is to be changed for the business. Examples of intervention units may be per participant, per workgroup, or per assembled product.

Time units are used with benefits and refer to how often your benefits will be counted. Examples may be hourly, daily, weekly, monthly, quarterly, or yearly. To compare like to like, it is important to know that you are counting benefits over the same periods of time.

Figure 9-1. Layout of the financial imperatives scorecard.

You may go to the companion Website (www.astd.org/astd/publications) to download a PowerPoint file for this scorecard.

INTERVENTION:

BASIS: (Monetary units), (Intervention units), (Time units)

	MEASURE / CATEGORY	VALUE ADD #1			VALUE ADD #2		VALUE ADD #3	
	I	II	III	IV	V	VI	VII	VIII
		Baseline #1 Date: Timing Note:	**Baseline #2** Date: Timing Note:	**Change** (× number in intervention and units of time)	**Baseline #3** Date: Timing Note:	**Change** (× number in intervention and units of time)	**Baseline #4** Date: Timing Note:	**Change** (× number in intervention and units of time)
1	**Benefits (Senior Measure)**	$	$	$	$	$	$	$
2	Individual Measure (1st/Ops Measure) (Mid Measure)							
3	Individual Measure (1st/Ops Measure) (Mid Measure)							
4	**Total Gross Benefit**			$		$		$
5	*Divided by # of Intervention Unit*							
6	**Benefit Per Intervention Unit**		$	$	$	$	$	$

BENEFITS

(continued on page 120)

Figure 9-1. Layout of the financial imperatives scorecard (continued).

		Cost (Per Intervention Unit)	Total Cost (× number in intervention)	Cost (Per Intervention Unit)	Total Cost (× number in intervention)	Cost (Per Intervention Unit)	Total Cost (× number in intervention)
COSTS	7	**Intervention Costs (Senior Measure)**						
	8	Cost Category:	$	$	$	$		
	9	Cost Category:						
	10	Cost Category:						
	11	Cost Category:						
	12	**Total Costs**		$		$		$
	13	Divided by # of Intervention Units						
	14	**Cost Per Intervention Unit**	$	$	$	$	$	$
VALUE SUMMARY	15	**Total Net Benefit (Senior Measure)**		$		$		$
	16	**Benefit-to-Cost Ratio**		%		%		
	17	**ROI**		%		%		%

During Marcella's 3-year tenure as a training manager at ABC MediCompany, she has made several changes to new hire training for the contracts renewal department. The changes are perceived as having varying degrees of value by managers at ABC MediCompany. The actual value of Marcella's changes is summarized in the completed financial imperatives scorecard shown in figure 9-2. In Marcella's case, her intervention is the contract renewal new hire training. The basis of her scorecard is to count in U.S. dollars, per new hire, per month.

Creating the Scorecard: Calculating Benefits

The next thing to observe are the benefits listed on the blank scorecard in figure 9-1, lines 1–3, in the Measures/Category column. This description of your benefits is where you tie your work in identifying financial value chains in chapters 4, 5, and 6 to your financial imperatives scorecard. In line 1, you'll see a notation for Senior Measure under the word Benefits. In lines 2–3, you'll see notations for Individual, 1st/Ops, and Mid measures. In your own scorecards, you can always add more measures (more value chains) by adding more lines.

To tie your scorecard to your value chains, you need to note which Senior-level measures you intend to impact with your intervention. As you recall from chapters 4, 5, and 6, Senior-level measures include contribution profit margin, operating earnings, current assets, current liabilities, and cash flow. The rest of the measures in lines 2 and 3 of the benefits section are also taken directly from your value chains. The first measure on each line is the Individual measure that you are affecting with your intervention. Underneath each measure, it is very helpful to list the 1st/Ops and then the Mid measures so that you can literally see the value chain(s) that you are tracking by reading down the Measures/Categories column of your scorecard.

In Marcella's case, the changes that she made to the new hire training increased renewals, decreased turnover, decreased lost work hours due to experienced employees being required to repeatedly explain procedures to new employees, decreased errors, and improved the cost of the training program itself.

By reading ABC MediCompany's income statement (chapter 5), Marcella was able to identify a critical Senior manager measure for ABC MediCompany: the contribution profit margin. The contribution profit margin is the first profit margin line on an income statement. It is created by subtracting from revenue the cost to manufacture or provide products, as well as other expenses incurred by an organization to sell its products. It is often very closely watched by Senior managers because if the contribution profit margin is too

Figure 9-2. Marcella's completed financial imperatives scorecard.

INTERVENTION: Contract Renewal New Hire Training

BASIS: Monetary units = U.S. Dollars, Intervention units = Per New Hire, Time units = Per Month

	MEASURE / CATEGORY	VALUE ADD #1			VALUE ADD #2		VALUE ADD #3	
	I	II	III	IV	V	VI	VII	VIII
		Baseline #1 May 2001 (Before 1st change)	**Baseline #2** Feb 2002 (9 Months Later)	**Change** (x 9 New Hires x 9 Months)	**Baseline #3** Nov 2002 (9 Months Later)	**Change** (x 11 New Hire x 9 Months)	**Baseline #4** Aug 2003 (9 Months Later)	**Change** (x 10 New Hires x 1 time change when in training)
1	**Benefits (Senior Measure = Contribution Profit Margin)**	$10,000	$10,800 (Additional $800 per new hire per month)	$64,800	$11,275 (Additional $475 per new hire per month)	$47,025	$11,275 ($0 additional change)	$0
2	Individual Measure = Monthly Renewal Rate (1st/Ops = Team Renewal Rates) (Mid = Six Month Renewal Revenue)							
3	Individual Measure = Lost Work Hours (1st/Ops = Processing Cost Per Contract) (Mid = Cost of Goods/ Services Sold)	350	225 (Savings of $125 per new hire per month)	10,125	180 (Savings of $55 per new hire per month)	5,445 ($0 savings)	180	0

BENEFITS

INTERVENTION: Contract Renewal New Hire Training

BASIS: Monetary units = U.S. Dollars, Intervention units = Per New Hire, Time units = Per Month

	MEASURE / CATEGORY	VALUE ADD #1			VALUE ADD #2		VALUE ADD #3	
	I	II	III	IV	V	VI	VII	VIII
4	Individual Measure = Not Applicable (1st/Ops = Training Program Savings) (Mid = Cost of Goods/Services Sold)	0	0	0	0	0	510 ($510 per new hire, one time)	510
5	Individual Measure = Average Error Cost (1st/Ops = Team Error Cost) (Mid = Other Sales Driven Expenses)	500	445 (Savings of $55 per new hire, per month)	4,455	422 (Savings of $23 per new hire, per month)	2,277	422 ($0 savings)	0
6	**Total Gross Benefit**			$79,380		$54,747		$5,100
7	*Divided by # of New Hires*			9		11		10
8	**Benefit Per New Hire**		$980	$8,820	$553	$4,977	$510	$510

BENEFITS

(continued on page 124)

Figure 9-2. Marcella's completed financial imperatives scorecard (continued).

INTERVENTION: Contract Renewal New Hire Training

BASIS: Monetary units = U.S. Dollars, Intervention units = Per New Hire, Time units = Per Month

	MEASURE / CATEGORY I	II	VALUE ADD #1		VALUE ADD #2		VALUE ADD #3	
			III Cost (Per New Hire)	IV Total Cost (× 9 New Hires)	V Cost (Per New Hire)	VI Total Cost (× 11 New Hires)	VII Cost (Per New Hire)	VIII Total Cost (× 10 New Hires)
COSTS								
9	Intervention Costs (*Cost of Goods/ Services Sold*)							
10	Analysis		$100	$900	$15	$165	$10	$100
11	Design		150	1,350	30	330	0	0
12	Development		250	2,250	60	660	5	50
13	Implementation		300	2,700	65	715	34	340
14	Evaluation		60	540	30	330	0	0
15	**Total Costs**			**$7,740**		**$2,200**		**$490**
16	Divided by # of New Hires			9		11		10
17	**Cost Per New Hire**		**$860**	**$860**	**$200**	**$200**	**$49**	**$49**
VALUE SUMMARY								
18	**Total Net Benefit (Contribution Profit Margin)**			$71,640		$52,547		$4,610
19	**Benefit-to-Cost Ratio**			10 to 1		24 to 1		10 to 1
20	ROI			925%		2,388%		940%

small, Senior management will have to take drastic measures to ensure that there is a final net profit for the business.

The focus in *Quick! Show Me Your Value* is on tangible benefits that can be converted to monetary terms. Intangible benefits are defined as benefits that cannot be, or are not cost effective to be, converted to a monetary value relative to the solution that created them. Though intangible benefits will not be addressed further in this book, do not underestimate the ability of intangibles to support the financial value statements you will make. WLP professionals who have presented the results of detailed ROI studies report that such intangible benefits as increased morale, improved customer satisfaction, greater likelihood for high-potential employees to remain with an organization, or decreased stress are very favorably received in the boardroom.

 Marcella believed that turnover rates would be too hard to quantify, so she simply noted them to herself as a possible intangible benefit. Marcella put the rest of the changes from her new hire intervention into contribution profit margin financial value chains, as shown in figure 9-3.

Figure 9-3. Marcella's financial value chains.

①

Senior	Mid	1st/Ops	Individual
② Contribution Profit Margin	**Six Month Renewal Revenue**	Monthly Team Renewal Rates	Monthly Renewal Rate
③ Contribution Profit Margin	**Cost of Goods/Services Sold**	Processing Cost Per Contract	Lost Work Hours
④ Contribution Profit Margin	**Cost of Goods/Services Sold**	Training Program Savings	
⑤ Contribution Profit Margin	**Other Sales Driven Expenses**	Team Error Cost	Average Error Cost

If you compare figure 9-3 to figure 9-2, you can see that the number 1 above the Senior measures in the picture of value chains corresponds to line 1 of figure 9-2, the completed example of Marcella's financial imperative scorecard. All of her value chains point to the Senior measure of the contribution profit margin. If you look at the numbers 2–5 next to each value chain in figure 9-3, you can see that these value chains correspond to lines 2–5 of Marcella's scorecard shown in figure 9-2. By reading each line in the scorecard, you can see at a glance all of the value chains being tracked for a particular intervention and how all of the chains are related to each other.

Rule #1: Track Benefits. Workplace learning and performance professionals who have some experience in measuring or estimating benefits know that trying to figure out a realistic amount of benefit takes time and sometimes a great deal of effort to track down the right numbers. If figuring out benefits were easy, many more WLP professionals would already be doing it regularly.

Rule #1 of financial imperative scorecards is to never present costs without drawing a connection to the benefits that those costs have brought to the organization. Here's why working out the benefits to the organization is absolutely critical to your success. Many WLP professionals know that they are expected to be more financially savvy, so they talk about the only numbers they have easy access to: the numbers that describe the costs of their WLP programs. Your costs or the costs of your department are already known to influential members of your audience. If they already know your costs and cannot figure out what benefit they are receiving from them, they will draw their own conclusions.

Just as in the children's game of Rumor, your audience's conclusion may be nothing like what you expect them to conclude. That can be disastrous. Highlighting your costs without pointing out offsetting benefits only makes your situation worse. Presenting costs without expected or actual benefits simply reinforces a subconscious belief that the costs must be out of line or unnecessary. If the perceptions of your value have fallen into a given state, your audience's conclusions about your value will be especially harsh.

Your audience will not tell you the value of what you have done. That's your job. You can only draw your audience's attention to financial benefits if you have worked them out for yourself first. The discipline of creating a financial imperatives scorecard allows you to present a more balanced picture between benefits and costs. It is critical that you do the work of naming your benefits and then quantifying them.

Rule #2: Quantify the Value Add. Now it's time to move across the scorecard and fill in the numbers that tell how much financial value your interventions have created for the organization. In the blank scorecard in figure 9-1 you can see that there are enough columns to reflect three different sets of changes in an intervention. You can add or remove as many columns as are needed to reflect your own situation.

These changes are referred to as **value adds.** Value adds are calculated by first estimating or assigning a numerical value to each of the performance measures of the Individual contributor. The first baseline in column II is noted as the original baseline. This means that the value of each of the performance measures for the Individual was measured as it existed before the intervention was introduced. Each of the other baselines was estimated or measured again after each change in the intervention. The dates that each baseline is estimated or measured and notes about the amount of time between measurements are noted in columns II, III, V, and VII of the blank scorecard in figure 9-1.

Now, take a look at Marcella's situation. As described in chapter 8, Marcella made three changes to the new hire training over a multiple-year period. Marcella's first changes were implemented six months after she was hired. Marcella changed a three-week classroom training program into a two-week classroom training program with an additional one-week on-the-job mentorship in performing renewals.

In order for Marcella to know how much value she did (or did not) add, she first needed to measure how much renewal revenue the new hires were bringing in per month and how much cost was being spent on lost work time and errors per month *before* the improvements in the new hire training were introduced. These numbers are reflected under Baseline #1 in column II in figure 9-2. Marcella documented her measurements in May 2001 and noted that these measurements were taken before her first change to the program.

Marcella measured how well the new hires were doing nine months later and documented the changes in column III. In column IV, Marcella multiplied the amounts of additional revenue and cost savings by the amount of her intervention basis (nine new hires) and amount of her time basis (nine months) to get the total impact of her changes on the organization.

Marcella's second change to the new hire program was to update the mentorship and add an additional week of mentorship for each new hire. Marcella used the numbers in column III as her baseline of how new hires performed before the second set of changes took effect. Marcella measured again nine months later and documented the additional revenue and cost savings in column V and her totals in column VI.

Marcella's third change involved cutting a few costs from the new hire training budget without really modifying the format of the intervention in any way.

When she made her third change, she documented the effect of her changes in column VII and the total impact to the organization in column VIII.

Rule #3: Be Disciplined About Your Value Adds. Tracking benefits for long periods, sometimes for years, requires foresight and discipline, but it is important to your ability to continuously communicate value. Rule #2 of financial imperative scorecards is to keep your scorecard up-to-date because as noted in chapter 8, once you have communicated the value from your scorecard, it becomes a given expectation. Salespeople know that once they have communicated their story, they must have something new to say or they wear out their welcome for more conversations with their customer. Without regular updates on your financial contributions, you won't be welcome for long either.

The third rule is a corollary to the second: Capture the data right away, as it is happening. Data and memories fade astonishingly fast. It is almost impossible to recreate data when your intervention has dropped into a given state, you've adopted a defensive position, some of the people originally involved are no longer around, and you can't remember critical details about what happened. It is far easier to document something while or immediately after it has occurred. It is also much more credible. It is easier for your audience to agree with you or to correct your numbers when the situation that produced them is fresh and recognizable. Without such numbers, it is difficult to ask for more support later or to reactively defend your value to the organization.

 Although Marcella did document numbers several months after her changes, she had new hires who were actively demonstrating the desired behaviors and value at the time she captured her data. This rule holds as true for capturing costs as it does for capturing benefits.

Creating the Scorecard: Summarizing the Benefits

A little later in this chapter, you'll read some important points about isolating the impact of your interventions from other changes or initiatives within the organization and about the importance of being very conservative with your numbers.

For now, assume that Marcella was taking very conservative credit for numbers that she could show were created only by her changes to the new hire training. This being the case, you can see that on line 8 of Marcella's scorecard, the gross benefits that Marcella generated for her first changes in the new hire program were $79,380. The gross benefits from the second round of changes were $54,747, and the gross benefits from the third changes were $5,100.

On the blank scorecard in figure 9-1 and on Marcella's scorecard in figure 9-2, you can see that there a line for the total gross benefit to be displayed and a calculation for the cost per intervention unit. This is displayed on lines 5 and 6 of the blank scorecard and lines 7 and 8 of Marcella's example. Marcella's intervention unit is per new hire. Later, in chapter 13, you'll see how to use this kind of number in communicating value to certain audiences. For now, assume that Marcella not only knew what the total gross benefit of her changes were (something that will be of interest to Mid and Senior managers), but she also knew what this meant for each new hire (something that will be of interest to 1st/Ops and Individuals). For her first change, each new hire brought in or saved an additional $8,820. For the second change, per new hire benefit was $4,977. For the third change, per new hire benefit was $510.

Creating the Scorecard: Categorizing Costs

The next section for your scorecard is the costs section. On the blank scorecard, line 7 contains the heading Intervention Costs and a notation for the Senior measure. This Senior measure may be different from the one for your benefits. This Senior measure is the area of the income statement where the costs of your interventions will be allocated. The costs of your intervention are most likely to show up under the contribution profit margin or in operating expenses, depending on how your organization or target organization tracks WLP costs. It is a good idea for you to find out what part of the income statement the costs of your interventions are charged to.

The next four lines in figure 9-1, lines 8–11, reflect cost categories for you to track the costs of your interventions. There is no one right way to categorize the breakdown of costs in your scorecard. You simply need to be consistent in your categories and in what types of detailed items you group together in your categories.

You can see in figure 9-2 that Marcella chose to categorize her costs according to the ADDIE model. As a model for developing interventions, ADDIE has been around for decades. ADDIE is an acronym that stands for analysis, design, development, implementation, and evaluation (Kruse, 2002). Marcella's cost categories are shown in lines 10–14 in column I of figure 9-2.

Moving across the columns in the scorecard, it is important to track costs each time you change your intervention. Costs are tracked per unit of intervention and added together to a total for each category. In figure 9-1, columns III, V, and VII are set aside to track costs per intervention unit. Columns IV, VI, and VIII are used to total the costs for each cost category. In Marcella's case, she has tracked the costs per new hire to analyze, design, develop, implement, and evaluate each of her changes in columns III, V and VII. She totaled her cost categories in columns IV, VI, and VIII.

In lines 12–14 of the blank scorecard and lines 15–17 of Marcella's example, the costs for each change are totaled and, then, for use later, divided by the intervention unit. In Marcella's case, the total cost for each of her three changes was $7,740, $2,200, and $490, respectively. The cost per new hire was $860, $200, and $49, respectively.

Creating the Scorecard: Showing Your Value

Now that you have calculated your benefits and your costs, you can summarize your value—that's what executives really want to see. Finally, you are able to compare the relative value of your contributions against all the other competing ways that executives could have spent the organization's money to gain the most good for all.

Your executives want you to act like a general manager or a salesperson. General managers know that there are always too many demands for the too little money that the organization has available to it. It is rare for a general manager not to deal with this issue daily. As stewards of their organizations, general managers must answer questions such as, "Do we truly need this?" or "What would happen if we didn't spend this money?" or "What other ways can this organization get to the same answer for less cost?" or "If this is the right solution, are we getting the most we can for the least amount of money?"

Successful salespeople know that they must be able to answer these questions and create a compelling case for why their solution is the best use of the organization's money. They must be able to discuss why they bring the best total benefits for the lowest costs. Salespeople are never without the case for their solution. As a steward for your people, your job is to never be without yours so that you can demonstrate your value at a moment's notice.

Rule #4: Be Ethical. When creating your scorecard, rule #3 is to track the obvious and be consistent in counting costs. A WLP professional can make any intervention look better if he or she ignores some known costs or doesn't include some of the costs of delivering the intervention.

Such behavior has led to major corporate scandals. Don't fall into this trap. There is always a bit of skepticism in every audience when someone is communicating his or her own value. Your ability to communicate your value rests on how consistent and credible your audience believes your numbers to be. If your audience discovers that you do not have a good explanation for why you haven't included some costs, your credibility will suffer—perhaps irreparably. Credibility is one of your most precious assets in communicating value. Once gone, it will be very, very difficult to get back. Rule #4 is to track the obvious and be consistent in how you track what your solutions cost your organization—every time.

Creating the Scorecard: Summarizing Value

The final section of the financial imperatives scorecard is the value summary. Lines 15–17 in figure 9-1 (the blank scorecard) and lines 18–20 in figure 9-2 (Marcella's scorecard) are set aside to summarize value.

The first value summary line lists total net benefit, which is calculated by subtracting total costs (line 12 in figure 9-1) from total gross benefit (line 4 in figure 9-1). This calculation is done for each value add.

> In Marcella's scorecard, she subtracted line 15 from line 6 to get a total net benefit of $71,640 for her first change, $52,547 for her second change, and $4,610 for her third change. Marcella's total net benefits are shown on line 18 in figure 9-2.

The second value summary line is the **benefit-to-cost ratio.** This ratio is a quick, shorthand way of telling your audience how many dollars it got back for every one dollar it invested in your intervention. The benefit-to-cost ratio is calculated by dividing total gross benefits by total costs.

In Marcella's case, the benefit-to-cost ratios for her three changes were:

Total Gross Benefits ÷ Total Costs = Benefit-to-Cost Ratio
Change #1: $79,380 ÷ $7,740 = 10.25
Change #2: $54,747 ÷ $2,200 = 24.88
Change #3: $5,100 ÷ $490 = 10.40

These ratios means that Marcella's first change gave back $10 in benefit for every $1 in cost. Her second change was even better, giving back almost $25 in benefit for every $1 in cost. When described as a ratio, Marcella's third change looked as good as the first. The third change returned $10 in benefits for every $1 in costs. In figure 9-1, benefit-to-cost ratios are shown on line 16. In Marcella's scorecard, you can see her benefit-to-cost ratios on line 19.

The third value summary line is return-on-investment, or ROI, which appears on line 17 of figure 9-1. The ROI is calculated by subtracting the total costs from the total gross benefits. This number is then divided by the total costs. The result of the division is multiplied by 100 to get a percentage.

Marcella's ROI numbers are shown on line 20 in figure 9-2. To summarize, the ROI for her three changes were:

[(Total Gross Benefits – Total Costs) ÷ Total Costs] × 100 = ROI
Change #1: [($79,380 – $7,740) ÷ $7,740] × 100 = 925%
Change #2: [($54,747 – $2,200) ÷ $2,200] × 100 = 2,388%
Change #3: [($5,100 – $490) ÷ $490] × 100 = 940%

Marcella's first change had a 925 percent ROI. The second had a 2,388 percent ROI. Marcella's third ROI looked even a little better than the first at 940 percent.

As you can see from the scorecard, Marcella had a significant impact on the bottom line with her first change (line 18 of figure 9-2). Nearly $72,000 over a nine-month period was a significant difference to her company's contribution profit margin. It could be argued that Marcella's improvements were even better with her second change, because it took her proportionately less cost to achieve almost another $53,000 in benefits. These findings are reflected in the comparisons between her first and second benefit-to-cost ratios and ROI percentages.

So, where did Marcella take a wrong turn? Over the period covered by Marcella's first two changes, her managers came to expect this type of payback from the changes that Marcella rolled out. Unfortunately, with her third change (line 18, column VIII of figure 9-2), Marcella does not make the same level of contribution to the organization's financial imperatives. Her third improvement is less than 10 percent of the size of her last one nine months ago, and it is certainly not impressive at a time when everyone in the organization is being asked to do more with less.

Yet her benefit-to-cost ratio and ROI percentage are nearly the same or better as for the first change she made only six months after she joined the organization. Only a few months after Marcella's third change, her budget was cut. Why? Marcella's ability to make big contributions to the bottom line had become taken for granted. For Marcella, "big contributions" meant the final size of the impact on the financial statements, not just the size of the benefit-to-cost ratio or the size of the ROI. Marcella ran into the downside of givens (chapter 8). Marcella really had made excellent contributions to the bottom line. In the minds of the managers around her, it was time for her to do it again. Yet for her third change, Marcella did not stay consistent within her established pattern of contribution. By not staying consistent, she bucked her trend.

Marcella may, in fact, have had excellent judgment in not cutting costs further for the new hire program, but to manage perceptions she needed to aggressively make her case for why this was so. Instead, Marcella let others draw their own conclusions. Kathleen did not have the history in the organization to fully understand what benefits Marcella had previously contributed. At the same time, Kathleen was under intense pressure to create a bigger size of impact on the financial statements.

Marcella had not been tracking numbers the way it's been demonstrated in this chapter. She had assumed that the value of her interventions was well understood by line and staff managers and was subconsciously estimated to be as high as what Marcella herself believed the value to be. Marcella let others draw their own conclusions. The results of Kathleen's conclusions showed up later in the forced cuts to Marcella's budget.

Effectiveness Versus Efficiency. Marcella's story is very predictable for many WLP professionals. Excellent, but repeated, interventions often level out in terms of the size of the contribution that additional improvements can make on the bottom line. This is the law of diminishing returns—the economic concept that it takes more and more effort and cost to gain smaller and smaller additional results. For this and other reasons, an intervention often stabilizes in a certain format. At the same time, the perception of the intervention's value is usually dropping into a given state. Because it is likely that a WLP professional's management team will change every two to four years, many WLP professionals who work within an organization (or who have continuously sold the same product or service to an organization) run the risk of Marcella's story playing out at some time in their own careers.

> *The discipline of measuring and updating scorecard numbers goes a long way toward changing the end of the story because that discipline helps improve communication and perceptions. The scorecard brings another potential benefit for the WLP professional: It helps the WLP professional manage the trend of the numbers as the numbers shift from reflecting effectiveness to reflecting efficiency.*

Effectiveness in WLP interventions means creating new or additional impact on an organization's financial measures or financial statements such that the impact makes a significant or sizable difference to the success of the organization. Marcella's first two changes were changes of effectiveness. Large, consistent changes in effectiveness go a long way toward earning you a seat at the table with your executives. Efficiency is defined as delivering the same level of benefit as has been had previously, but at a lower intervention cost. Marcella's third change was a change in efficiency. It is possible, but often much more difficult for changes in efficiency to have the same type of impact on the bottom line that changes in organizational effectiveness can have.

Because the same formulas are used to calculate ROI or benefit-to-cost ratios whether you are talking about effectiveness or efficiency, effectiveness and efficiency can be thought of simply as convenient ways of noting what and how much has changed each time you communicate your value.

 The more effectiveness you can communicate, the more likely it is that you can keep your value perceptions between surprise and the high end of the negotiables (chapter 8).

Be Cautious When Communicating ROI. When using benefit-to-cost ratios and ROI, there are a couple of points to be careful about when summarizing your value. On one hand, the difference in productivity between high performers and low performers can be astronomical, as has been documented in research studies (Hunter, Schmidt, and Judiesch, 1990). This means that the size of WLP ROI and benefit-to-cost ratios can, quite legitimately, be huge. But, even if your numbers are consistent, conservative, and correct, their size can simply seem impossible to managers who are used to the types of returns available from investments in property, machinery, or short-term market securities. Using such a large ROI number without carefully explaining how conservative you were in counting costs and in isolating the cause of the improvement can lead your audience to scoff and stop listening.

 Savvy managers know that you can get a large ROI from a very small set of numbers, as Marcella did with her third change. It is important to be able to quantify your actual contribution, rather than just using ROI percentages to communicate value. This practice can help you maintain your creditability.

Timing. The time to gather all the information that you need to demonstrate your value is *not* when you are in a crisis. To be sure, using the format of a financial imperatives scorecard will help you even then, but the best time to make sure you have your case put together is before you need it. You'll be thinking much more clearly then.

The very act of gathering data and making estimates can be turned to your favor. Updating data often leads to new ideas and more perceived value by the client. As you learned from Marcella's dilemma, had she maintained financial imperatives discussions, she might either have garnered more support from other managers when her budget was cut or she would have discovered that she needed to have made more effort, connections, or changes. Marcella could then have adjusted her efforts far earlier and avoided an unpleasant and awkward situation. In any case, she wouldn't have been caught unprepared.

Rule #5: Be Conservative. It is very educational, but usually very time consuming to research all of the potential costs or benefits resulting from WLP interventions. Many WLP professionals do not have as much time as they would like to perform detailed financial analysis.

If you are external to an organization, you may not have access to the information you want. Because time is always limited and you will never have all the information you could possibly want, tracking solution costs and organization benefits necessarily involves estimation. Estimates absolutely beat no data at all because when you have no idea where you stand it is very difficult to counteract a downward value slide. For this reason, adhere to rule #5: Be conservative in your estimates to preserve your creditability.

One way that WLP professionals tend to overstate their benefit estimates is by not acknowledging the potential contribution of others to those same benefits. Don't claim all cost savings, increased sales, or better morale in an organization because you ran training or some other performance intervention programs. WLP professionals rarely work in a vacuum within an organization. There may easily have been other initiatives within the organization that could also have created some of the same benefits at the same time. Being able to credibly separate your contributions from the contributions of others is known as isolating the effects of your intervention. Jack Phillips has made many contributions to the WLP profession, including many recommendations on how to be conservative and credible in presenting information about the ROI for WLP interventions. Some of his most valuable work has been to research, develop, and promote isolation techniques. A reference to one of his books describing isolation techniques can be found in the Additional Resources section.

In Marcella's case, some of the reduced errors were because of the change in class format and on-the-job mentorship, but some of them could also have come from an information technology system redesign to make the renewal process more straightforward. When it was noted earlier in this chapter that Marcella was careful to isolate the benefits for her training program, this meant that she subtracted out of the total contract renewal benefits from the impacts of the change in the information technology system and the impacts of other possible changes. She left herself only what she could reasonably verify as benefits resulting from the training program itself.

Challenging Situations: A Few Pointers

There are a couple of situations that can make creating a financial imperatives scorecard more of a challenge. What happens if you have many participants in the same class who believe it will bring each of them different benefits? This happens with courses that are offered to a general population with many different types of jobs. The people who sign up for the course are different every time it is offered. Examples could be a presentation skills course or a stress management course. Such a class could have factory workers, administrative assistants, supervisors, and programmers all taking the course together.

The impact of the course could show up in fixed expenses, inventory, revenue, COGS, or any number of other places on the financial statements. The solution in this situation is to ask. You can query the participants themselves to tell you what benefits they expect and what they think the benefits may be worth when you ask them for feedback about the class. Or, if you have many classes but it is possible to group participants from different classes, ask their managers for an estimate of how this WLP intervention helps their people.

Jack Phillips has created an excellent method for asking others to estimate their own benefits, as part of his work on isolation.

What if you are proposing something that has never been done before in your organization? How do you get your first baseline? Suppose you are a new training manager and you believe that your department would benefit from investment in on-demand e-learning modules but there are no off-the-shelf solutions for your needs and you don't know many counterparts who have ventured into e-learning. You still need to create a scorecard that includes solution costs and estimates of the benefits to your organization. You simply need to research industry literature, interview multiple vendors, make some industry connections, and get creative in who you talk with to validate your estimates. You also needed to be more comfortable with wider margins of risk and error in your initial estimates and need to explain your assumptions as you are convincing others to invest the upfront money to bring the projected benefits to the organization.

Create Your Own Financial Imperatives Scorecard

It's easy to read about financial imperatives scorecards, but you'll learn even more by beginning the process. Take the time now to create a cost and benefit analysis for your chosen intervention and target organization. Exercise 9-1 contains a template you can use to document your own benefits, costs, and financial value connections.

Exercise 9-1. Creating a financial imperatives scorecard

 Directions: Complete the following steps for this exercise to finish up the work on step 6 of the financial value process: develop scorecard. If you prefer not to write in this book, go to the companion Website (www.astd.org/astd /publications) to download a PowerPoint file for this exercise.

Top of Scorecard

1. Name the intervention that you are tracking at the top of your scorecard.
2. Determine your basis in terms of monetary units (currency), intervention units (per participant, per unit, etc.), and time units (hourly, daily, weekly, monthly, quarterly, yearly).

Benefits

1. Use your financial value chains to name the benefits in column I, under Measures/Category. This will be in lines 1–3. Add more lines as needed for your intervention.
2. Estimate or measure your performance baseline for your benefits *before* your intervention was or will be introduced. Note these figures in column II (lines 2 and 3) and the date and timing for these figures in line 1.
3. Estimate or measure your performance baseline *after* your intervention was introduced. Note these figures in column III (lines 2 and 3) and the date and timing for these figures in line 1.
4. Calculate the difference between your two benefit baselines and write your calculations on lines 2–3 in column IV.
5. Total your gross benefits on line 4.
6. Write in your number of intervention units on line 5, column IV.
7. Divide your total gross benefits on line 4 by the number of intervention units on line 5 and write the result on line 6 (Benefit per Intervention Unit).

Costs

1. Note the Senior measure where your intervention costs will be assigned in column I, line 7.
2. Determine how you would like to track your costs and write the names of your cost categories in column I under Measures/Category. This is in lines 8–11. Add more lines as needed for your intervention.
3. Write in the cost per category per intervention unit in lines 8–11 in column III.
4. Multiply the cost per category per intervention unit by the number of intervention units and write the result in lines 8–11 in column IV.
5. Add the total costs for each category together (lines 8–11, column IV) and write the result in line 12, column IV.
6. Write in your number of intervention units on line 13, column IV.
7. Divide your total costs on line 12 by the number of intervention units on line 13 and write the result on line 14 (Cost per Intervention Unit).

Totals

1. Note the Senior measure for your net benefits in line 15, column I.
2. Subtract your total costs on line 12, column IV from your total gross benefit on line 4, column IV. Write the result on line 15, column IV, for total net benefits.
3. Calculate your benefit-to-cost ratio according to the formula:

$$\text{Total Gross Benefits} \div \text{Total Costs} = \text{Benefit-to-Cost Ratio}$$

   Write your result in line 16, column IV.
4. Calculate your ROI according to the formula:

$$[(\text{Total Gross Benefits} - \text{Total Costs}) \div \text{Total Costs}] \times 100 = \text{ROI}$$

   Write your result in line 17, column IV.

INTERVENTION:					
BASIS: (Monetary units), (Intervention units), (Time units)					
		MEASURE / CATEGORY	**VALUE ADD #1**		
		I	**II**	**III**	**IV**
BENEFITS	1	**Benefits** *(Senior Measure)*	**Baseline #1** Date: Timing Note:	**Baseline #2** Date: Timing Note:	**Change** (× number in intervention and units of time)
	2	Individual Measure (1st/Ops Measure) (Mid Measure)	$	$	$
	3	Individual Measure (1st/Ops Measure) (Mid Measure)			
	4	**Total Gross Benefit**			$
	5	*Divided by # of Intervention Unit*			
	6	**Benefit Per Intervention Unit**		$	$

				Cost (Per Intervention Unit)	Total Cost (× number in intervention)
COSTS	7	**Intervention Costs (Senior Measure)**			
	8	Cost Category:			
	9	Cost Category:			
	10	Cost Category:			
	11	Cost Category:			
	12	**Total Costs**			$
	13	Divided by # of Intervention Units			
	14	**Cost Per Intervention Unit**		$	$
VALUE SUMMARY	15	**Total Net Benefit (Senior Measure)**			$
	16	**Benefit-to-Cost Ratio**			
	17	**ROI**			%

LET'S REVIEW:

- This chapter covered step 6 of the financial value process.
- Financial imperative scorecards provide a concise, single place to consistently track the amount of value you are creating from your interventions. The discipline of creating and updating your scorecards is critical to your long-term ability to keep the perceptions of your value high.
- Rule #1 of the scorecard is to never present costs without drawing a connection to the benefits that those costs have brought to the organization.
- Rule #2 is to keep your scorecard up-to-date.
- Rule #3 is to capture the data right away, as it is happening.
- Rule #4 is to be ethical by tracking the obvious and being consistent in counting costs.
- Rule #5 is to be conservative.
- Your scorecards must have a consistent basis or definition for how you count your numbers so that they can always be compared to each other.

◆ Your benefits are taken directly from your financial value chains.

◆ Tracking benefits reliably can be time consuming, but it is critical to never present cost data without offsetting benefit data.

◆ Scorecards must track costs as well as benefits. Costs need to use the same definition for counting numbers so that they can be subtracted from or divided into benefit numbers.

◆ Value in your scorecard can be summarized in terms of total net benefit, as benefit-to-cost ratios, or as an ROI percentage. Be cautious when using benefit-to-cost ratios and ROI percentages when communicating value. Big ratios and ROIs can be generated from very small numbers. If your audience believes this is what has happened, you'll lose your credibility.

◆ Value is created in terms of effectiveness and efficiency. The more effectiveness you can communicate, the higher you can keep the perception of your value into the conscious states for your audience.

◆ There are creative and proven ways to research realistic benefit and cost numbers if you have never offered a particular type of intervention before or if your participants come from widely varying parts of your organization.

In the next chapter, you'll examine the next steps in continuous value management. The financial value process hinges on the assumption that the intervention has eventually taken place. Once your intervention has occurred, you must be able to validate the numbers you claim on your scorecard. Validation requires some form of evaluation. Different types of audiences require information from different types of evaluation methods. You must ensure that you are gathering the right types of evaluation data to match the needs of each level of your audience.

10

Value and the
Levels of Evaluation

 IN THIS CHAPTER: ─────────────────

- ◆ Steps 7 and 8 in the financial value process: deliver the intervention and evaluate results
- ◆ Why delivering an intervention changes what your audience expects to hear when you communicate value
- ◆ How to match types of evaluation data to the data each level of your audience needs to hear
- ◆ Why Senior management needs optimization data
- ◆ What penetration, sustainability, and speed mean to effectiveness
- ◆ Some tips for getting the evaluation data you need.

It's time to make another important transition in the financial value process. Up to now, it has been possible to define audiences, perform business intelligence research, create value chains for the most important financial imperatives in an organization, focus your communication on a particular intervention, clarify perceptions, and even start a scorecard—all without ever delivering anything. At some point, however, the intervention must take place, and the value you have been planning must be delivered. This is step 7: deliver intervention.

How an intervention is delivered is unique to every situation. Hundreds of books discuss WLP delivery methods, techniques, and alternatives. How well an intervention is delivered is a matter of experience, skill, planning, teamwork, support, work environment, and other factors. Nevertheless, no matter how it takes place or how well things go (or don't go), delivering the intervention creates an important psychological turning point in the minds of your audience. Up to now, you have been able to discuss the value of your intervention in terms of what it *will* do. To maintain your credibility and your ability to communicate value, you must now prove that you delivered what you promised.

Crossing the Threshold

Once the critical delivery threshold has been crossed, it's time to deal with the next step in the financial value process: evaluate results. That's the focus of step 8 in the financial value process. One of the most underestimated areas in gaining a seat at the table is how much of a difference regularly measuring your value makes in your stature and your credibility. If regular measurement is underestimated, then one of the most misunderstood areas in communicating the value of WLP interventions is that once a commitment is made to measure, different levels of your audience require different types of data from different forms of evaluation. One size does not fit all.

When communicating your value, making the mistake of not gathering the data at all or mismatching the type of data to the level of your audience can lead to failure. If you don't provide the data that your audience is subconsciously expecting at their level and in the audience's terms, you're leaving the audience to draw its own conclusions. Just as in the game of Rumor described in chapter 2, those conclusions may not be anything like what you think they ought to be.

 To communicate your value, you need to remain in control of how you will prove your value. After having achieved so much in identifying and delivering value, the last thing you want to do is to fall short in your communications by not understanding the need for and appropriate use of evaluation data.

So, just what type of evaluation data does each level of your audience need? It might not be what you would expect.

A Little Background on Evaluation

One of the most widely used evaluation models was originally described by Donald Kirkpatrick (1994) in the 1950s and updated in the mid-1990s. It was extended to include return-on-investment (Phillips, 1997). Kirkpatrick defined four levels of evaluation as

- Level 1—reaction
- Level 2—learning
- Level 3—behavior
- Level 4—results.

Phillips's fifth level is known as level 5—ROI. Kirkpatrick's method was originally developed for training programs. Together, Kirkpatrick's and Phillips's methods can be applied to a broader range of WLP interventions. See table 10-1 for a brief explanation.

Levels of Evaluation

The levels of evaluation described in table 10-1 are not the only possible types of evaluation. Not everyone in the worldwide WLP community agrees that all of these levels are, in fact, forms of evaluation. Nor does everyone agree that presenting these types of evaluation in a hierarchy of levels is appropriate.

These differing points of view are often very useful as WLP professionals search for the most effective ways to study the impact of their interventions. Unfortunately, these very conversations can distract attention from an important realization when communicating value. In the Twin Cities study cited in chapter 1, when Senior executives listed the competencies they wanted from human asset professionals, knowledge of WLP or, in this case, determining what is or isn't correct about different models of evaluation was not even mentioned. Knowledge of the basic elements of the WLP profession itself was so taken for granted that it didn't even make the list of critical skills executives were looking for in WLP professionals.

Because knowing the craft is a given and because audiences often look at WLP professionals as if they just didn't get the code, it's time to step back to reflect. Rather than trying to determine if a particular model of evaluation is or isn't really evaluation, let's look at what types of data your different audiences need so that you will be able to successfully communicate your value.

What Your Audience Wants to Know

In figure 10-1, the four financial audience levels are once more depicted, this time reinforcing the timeframe that each audience level is typically concerned with. Underneath the financial value chain are displayed the five levels of evaluation.

Table 10-1. Levels of evaluation (Kirkpatrick, 1994; Phillips, 1997).

Level	Definition
1. Reaction	Determines if the participants in a program liked the program. Level 1 evaluation forms are commonly referred to as smile sheets. This level of evaluation is collected immediately following an intervention and is the most commonly used form of evaluation. The belief is that if participants reacted well to the training or other intervention, they are more likely to implement it. If they did not like it, they are less likely to apply it back on the job.
2. Learning	Determines if the participants learned the information, skills, or behaviors presented in the intervention correctly. Participants may have liked their training or other intervention, but if they learned incorrectly, then their application of what they learned will not have the desired impact on the job.
3. Behavior	Determines if the participants implemented some or all of the desired behaviors back on the job. The participants may have liked the intervention and learned well, but if they don't do what they were supposed to do, there is no benefit to the organization.
4. Results	Determines if there was a benefit to the organization in the participant's application of new knowledge, skills, or behaviors. It is possible for participants to apply what they learned but to have no change or even a negative change in financial impact to the organization. One way that results can be thought of is as tracking gross benefits to the organization. Gross benefits means that the costs of the intervention have not yet been accounted for. It is important to determine if the changes from the learning or performance intervention were worth more than the cost to implement the intervention.
5. ROI	Phillips introduced a fifth level of evaluation. That level is ROI evaluation. A simple way of looking at ROI evaluation is to determine the net benefits to the organization or, in other words, to account for the costs of implementing the intervention versus the isolated gross benefits gained. A gross benefit less its costs is said to be a net benefit. (See chapter 9 for method of calculation.)

Levels 1 and 2

In figure 10-1, levels 1 and 2 are aligned under the Individual level of your audience. This is because evaluation levels 1 and 2 are concerned with data that Individual contributors need to know in order to discern if the training or other intervention will help them meet their measures. Individuals ask themselves questions such as, "Is it going to be worth my time to be in this class" (reaction) and "Will I learn enough by being there?" (learning). Evaluation levels 1 and 2 help answer those questions.

Figure 10-1. Aligning value and levels of evaluation.

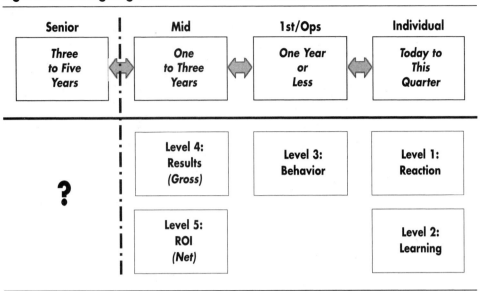

Level 3

It is not until level 3, that you begin to move up the financial value chain to get data that your first management level is going to be interested in. Yes, some managers at every financial level will want to know if the learners liked the intervention and if they learned well. But, for the most part, for everyone above the Individual layer knowing that the intervention was well constructed and kept people awake, engaged, and learning correctly is a given. They think to themselves that, of course, this is the case or else it is time to find a different WLP professional to manage the WLP tasks.

 You cannot satisfy the Senior, Mid, and 1st/Ops levels of your audience by showing them level 1 or level 2 data. You can only dissatisfy them if they ask to see it and it is not there!

The 1st/Ops level is interested in level 3 behavioral data because this data corresponds to what they have the most day-to-day control over and are held accountable for. Yes, many 1st/Ops managers are interested in results or ROI data, but being able to change organizational level 4 and level 5 numbers is often out of their control. For example, any single 1st/Ops manager may have had a great result within his or her own group, but he or she cannot control the results of his or her peers. Level 3 data is the most useful and directly applicable data for the 1st/Ops layer in the financial value chain.

Levels 4 and 5

Are some Mid-level managers going to be concerned about level 3 data? Of course, but for the most part, the job of the Mid-level manager is too removed from the day-to-day activities of the Individual contributors to be able to directly influence behavior. For the Mid-level manager, level 3 data is a given.

Mid-level managers think to themselves that, of course, their WLP programs are going to be applied and people will behave differently on the job. Otherwise, why would they waste money on the interventions? Workplace learning and performance practitioners know that in reality ensuring new behaviors can be difficult, that reinforcement is key, and that the support of Mid-level managers is often critical to ensure the transfer of new behavior to the job. Mid-level managers expect that the WLP professional is going to arrange for support, communication, and other reinforcement as required. But, the Mid-level manager is not going to chase the WLP professional down to make sure these "given" activities are going to occur. You cannot truly satisfy a Mid-level manager by pointing out that people actually applied the new behaviors on the job. You can only dissatisfy them if the learners do not!

Mid-level managers are often responsible for level 4 (results) and level 5 (ROI). Mid-level managers have measures such as total revenue, COGS, days inventory outstanding, or other measures as discussed in previous chapters. It often takes time for results and ROI to be able to appear so that they can be calculated. This lag time places ROI in the timeframes between the long end of the 1st/Ops level and well into the Mid level of your audience.

If you are communicating ROI percentages to an audience for the first time, it will need to hear more details about the other levels of evaluation to convince them that you have built a solid case and are presenting a valid ROI. In addition, telling the whole story of a great accomplishment can be just as valuable to the participants as it is to the people who manage them. Nevertheless, if you've earned your credibility and people are hearing an update to a continuing story, presenting other levels can lead to the too-much-information syndrome. Symptoms of this syndrome include glazed eyes, sleepiness, and fidgeting in your audience. If you sense that your audience is being overwhelmed with too much information, get to the point with the level of information your audience is most interested in.

What Does Senior Management Need?

If levels 4 and 5 data are of interest at the Mid layer of your audience, will this same information satisfy your Senior managers? At this stage of business maturity for the WLP profession, the answer is yes and no. Many Senior managers are very interested in ROI numbers, but ultimately Senior managers are looking for something more. They are looking for a true business partner who can help them set visions and drive the success of the entire organization.

On the one hand, many Senior managers have never had the opportunity to understand how ROI numbers can be reliably gathered and calculated within their organizations. Such an understanding would give Senior managers critical insights into what the norms are for their organization and what the potential payoffs might be from additional WLP investments versus other possible investments. Senior managers intuitively know that learning and performance improvement pays off. They simply have never been able to validate by how much or for how long. They have had to rely on guesses and gut feelings, which could be wildly off the mark. They cannot risk the future of the organization on such unreliable guesses and opinions. For many Senior managers, gaining a better understanding of how they can measure and control the ROI from WLP interventions is an untapped need, or as discussed in chapter 8, it is an unknown expectation. Satisfying an unknown expectation creates a condition of delight.

On the other hand, once their need to know how to measure and control WLP ROI is satisfied, then it rapidly becomes a given that the WLP professional will provide interventions that make a difference to the bottom line.

> *Before you demonstrated that you were providing great value all along, Senior managers were unsure if they were getting any value at all or enough value to sustain the investment. This led them to keep increasing the pressure for you to demonstrate your value until they got the type of information they were looking for. Once they are assured that the value is there, however, then proving a positive ROI is no longer enough. Senior managers will then ask themselves what else was the WLP professional hired for?*

In the long run, you can't satisfy a Senior-level executive by proving results or ROI. You can only dissatisfy them if you don't. So if a Senior manager is looking for a true business partner, what does a Senior level manager need to hear when you are communicating your value? Take a look at figure 10-2.

Aligning Value at the Senior Level

Senior managers are responsible for setting the vision and pace for the organization. They are ultimately responsible for the organization's profit, position, and cash, as well as the balance that must be maintained among them. As a quick review, recall that profit is shown on the income statement and consists of the remainder of incoming revenue after the costs of doing business have been subtracted from that revenue. Position is shown on the balance sheet and describes what assets or liabilities the organization is using to gain its profit.

Figure 10-2. Value and Senior management expectations.

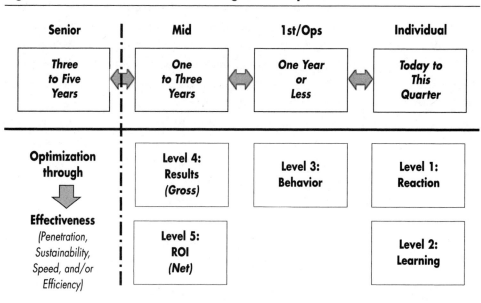

Cash is like the lubricating oil in a car engine. A certain percentage of the organization's assets must always be kept in the form of cash so that the business can keep paying its bills and running smoothly. If the cash ever dries up— even for a moment—the business grinds to a halt and stops running. Running out of oil in a car can destroy its engine. Running out of cash in an organization can destroy the organization. Cash is shown on the cash flow statement.

Balance is the act of keeping the best mix of profit, position, and cash in place at all times. Balance is measured through ratios. Ratios use figures from different financial statements to calculate balance.

Senior Management and Optimization

Senior managers know that oftentimes a phenomenally low rate of learning from WLP interventions transfers from the initial intervention to the workforce. Senior managers have much experience with different types of interventions. Most have learned the hard way to expect only a 10 to 20 percent transfer rate, with the payback being gained from a relatively small number of people.

But, Senior managers also know that even a very small transfer rate can generate incredibly high ROI numbers. As one Senior manager points out, "The top 10 percent of my people are going to get it anyway. I'm going to get a really good return from the whole program if just those people perform better." A good one-time ROI number did not impress this Senior manager. For him, a good one-time ROI number was a given. He knew he was going to get that anyway.

Senior managers are responsible for broad-scale change. They know that their WLP interventions must constantly be optimized through ever-increasing effectiveness and efficiency. In chapter 9, effectiveness was defined as creating new or additional impact on an organization's financial measures or financial statements such that the impact makes a significant or sizable difference to the success of the organization.

Three Components of Effectiveness

Effectiveness hinges on three critical components: penetration, sustainability, and speed. Penetration is the total number of WLP attendees or intervention participants who successfully applied the intervention on the job. Penetration describes the characteristics of the adopting participants, such as their number of years of experience, location, or salary level. Senior managers know that they can see a high ROI produced by a small number of people. Senior managers are looking for results from a broad population; therefore, comparing an ROI to the percentage of participants who apply the WLP intervention back on the job raises your credibility.

Sustainability is the length of time participants who apply the WLP intervention continue to do so. Many WLP professionals know that their interventions may be initially applied on the job, but behavior will often drop rapidly without proper reinforcement. When application and behavior drop, the benefits to the organization are not sustained. It's possible to measure a one-time ROI before application and behavior drops. This can make the intervention look really good on paper. Senior managers know this. Senior managers are looking for long-term, sustained benefits, thereby demonstrating more than a one-time ROI or, in other words, showing the permanency or sustainability of the WLP intervention.

Speed refers to how quickly the benefits of the WLP intervention can be obtained for the entire target population. If the full population has not yet applied the intervention, Senior managers want to know how quickly you can increase effectiveness when addressing additional segments of the target population. In other words, can you do whatever you did to get excellent results even faster in your next go-around?

Efficiency means delivering the same level of benefit as has been had previously but at a lower cost. No matter how much effectiveness you've achieved, Senior managers want to know how you can provide the same benefits for less cost in the future.

So What Did the Senior Manager Want to Know?

In the case of the Senior manager who pointed out that "his top 10 percent were going to get it anyway," what he wanted to know was if the WLP intervention could ensure that:

- the impacts of the intervention went far beyond the top 10 of his people (penetration)
- the effects of that intervention created long-term change (sustainability)
- those numbers were created and collected as fast as possible (speed).

That kind of broad-scale change can take years to implement and sustain, which is exactly the timeframe that a Senior-level manager is responsible for in his or her financial statements. That kind of information requires more than a one-time ROI study; it requires a continuous value management approach. This Senior manager needed proof that a continuous pattern of broader and deeper ROI was consistently being achieved. He didn't want to waste time on discussions that didn't give him the answers he was looking for.

The problem with many WLP professionals' approach to ROI is that they view it as a one-time proof of their ability to deliver financial results. As was discussed in chapter 8, if they can prove that they've achieved a great ROI at least once, then the inference is that they know what they are doing and should be supported and nurtured in doing whatever it is that they do indefinitely. This approach means that the WLP professional is not analyzing, or, to use the term in a slightly different context than in many WLP discussions, this means that the WLP professional is not evaluating his or her performance from a Senior executive's point of view. This can cause many a promising career to run into major bumps.

But, Who Has the Time?

There are two rules of thumb in performing higher-level evaluation. One is that the higher the level of data that you want, the more time consuming and frustrating it will be to get it. The other is a corollary to the first: The higher you go, the more expense you incur to get the information you need. You certainly cannot perform formal evaluation to levels 3, 4, or 5 on every program you offer, or you will never have the time or money to do anything else! On the other hand, who has the time to have their budget cut, capability questioned, lay off members of their staff, or find a new job?

If you are external to your target organization, your ability to get evaluation data is even more constrained. Many clients are not willing to pay for an expensive evaluation process on top of the original WLP services they asked for in the first place. To them, it's a given that the intervention is going to work well or else you shouldn't be selling it to them.

What's the Answer?

The answer is in adjusting your approach to get what you can within the limits of your environment and always to be selling the benefits of additional data in helping the organization get even better results. If your organization, or target organization, is willing to pay for a formal evaluation program, by all means take full advantage of the opportunity to get some excellent data for yourself, your intervention, and your department. But, even if they are not willing to foot the bill, here are some pointers that may help you find the answers:

1. Focus your efforts for formal evaluation on programs that are most important to your organization. These interventions are often highly visible, expensive, or risky.
2. Start with a rough guess. To approximate some types of data, you may need to rely more heavily on projections, sampling, indicators (such as if a certain rate of errors goes up or down), and inferences from those indicators. In other words, be willing to make a rough guess of financial value, penetration, sustainability, or speed based on any data you can get. Getting anecdotal information can alert you to any particularly positive use or lack of use of your performance intervention. You must recognize and make clear, however, that your inferences carry a much wider margin of error than data from a formal evaluation program. From hallway conversations to quick and dirty surveys, short phone calls to on-the-floor observation, less formally structured feedback can cover a lot of ground. Just make sure you document what you start with and then take your rough estimates to potential members of your audience so they can help you refine your numbers. Once your audience realizes that your numbers can help them show what a great job they are doing too, you might be surprised at the support and cooperation you get. Never underestimate how much easier you make it for your audience to help you if you put what you are trying to calculate in a rough form so your audience can quickly grasp where you're trying to go. More than anything else, the key to getting more formal data often starts with a rough guess.
3. Start small and build up. Perhaps you have an ideal set of evaluation data that you would like to track on an ongoing basis. But, tracking that much data seems overwhelming to your managers because you haven't proven you really need it all yet. Start with a subset of the data to answer some questions and leave the door open for other subsets. An example might be

to find out how much improvement has been made in sales for each region of a company, but to leave the question of why the eastern half of the country did so much better than the western half until your audience is demanding that you go find the answer for them. It never hurts to leave your audience wanting a little more. After all, once your audience is demanding the data, how can it fail to provide you the budget or the support you need to go get the answers?

4. Arrange for a continuous flow of feedback. Build up your personal network of participants and managers. Make sure that people know that you want feedback. If you have the names of your attendees, don't be afraid to spend five minutes to pick up the phone and call. If you are internal to an organization and have the support of the line management, you can simply state that you are collecting informal feedback and will keep their comments completely anonymous. If you are external to an organization, ask your client if they would mind you making a few phone calls after the training or performance intervention just to get validation and future feedback. If you promise to keep the people anonymous but share the general conclusions, you'll find participants and clients who are open to your proposal.

5. Position your data gathering as an experiment. You may have heard that people hate to change but love to experiment. If you are just starting a formal evaluation program, make sure you let people know that they will be safe if they talk with you and that your first efforts are just an experiment until you find out what really works for everyone.

6. Ask how your clients will prove the intervention's value to their managers. This is especially helpful for external vendors. Oftentimes, a 1st/Ops or Mid client has the discretion to pay for an intervention but doesn't look ahead to how they will handle value communication months down the road. If you ask them to think ahead about what they would like to be able to say and what proof they will need to say it, it may be possible to negotiate your contract so that you can add some data-gathering services. An e-learning vendor in the Denver area has used this technique with great success.

A Story to Illustrate the Point

A training manager working with trainees spread all over the United States and Canada found that the most effective way to provide new training was to host monthly audio conferences supported by Web-based presentation materials. Because the training participants did most of their work over the phone, this medium allowed realistic role plays and useful job aids. The training manager immediately established the routine that after each audio conference she would pick a semi-random list of four or five people from the audience to call. The training manager would leave a voicemail that asked what the participants liked about the training and thought should be kept for the future, what they thought should be changed or that they still needed information about, and what they needed training on in the future. The remarks were kept anonymous.

Most of the time, the training manager received a three-minute voicemail reply. Sometimes the training manager would talk personally with an attendee. Yet even if the voicemail or phone call lasted only three minutes, she could get a wealth of information that gave her hints on reaction, learning, behavior, and results. Because the training manager documented the costs of each audio conference, she could calculate ROI and because she did this consistently every month for a couple of years, she knew how to improve penetration, sustainability, and speed. From the training manager's perspective, the effort wasn't that big: a couple of hours of calls and note taking each month. Perhaps this practice does not meet all the rules for formal evaluation methods, but over time, it became obvious that the payoffs were huge. Sometimes those three-minute voicemails were surprisingly enlightening.

Your Turn

Now it's your turn to decide how you'll get your data. Exercise 10-1 will help you get started. In this exercise, you'll briefly describe how you plan to get the type of data needed for each audience and how often you plan to gather it.

Exercise 10-1. Your evaluation plan.

 Directions: Complete the following steps for this exercise to help ensure you have the right data for each audience and to finish up step 8 of the financial value process: evaluate results. If you prefer not to write in this book, go to the companion Website (www.astd.org/astd/publications) to download a PowerPoint file for this exercise.

1. Because plans often change over time, the first action is to note today's date.
2. Write the name or a brief description of the intervention you will be evaluating.
3. For the Individual level of your audience, write in a short name or description for how you plan to gather level 1 (reaction) data, level 2 (learning) data, and how frequently you plan to do so for each. Data gathering activities may be handing out an evaluation form at the end of a class, informally contacting a subset of the participants, or sending out an email survey. For frequency, you may plan to do this at the end of each class, once a month, or at some other time interval.
4. For the 1st/Ops level of your audience, write in a short name or description for how you plan to gather level 3 (behavior) data and how frequently you plan to do so. Examples of data-gathering techniques may include periodic observation, supervisor interviews, or surveys. The frequency of your data gathering depends on your situation. Examples could be hourly, weekly, monthly, or quarterly.

Exercise 10-1. Your evaluation plan (continued).

---

5. For the Mid level of your audience, write in a short name or description for how you plan to gather level 4 (results) data or level 5 (ROI) data and how frequently you plan to do so. Gathering results and ROI data may be done by conducting interviews, attending status presentations, or reading some of the documents you identified in your business intelligence research discussed in chapter 7. The frequency of your data gathering will depend on the frequency that the behavior is displayed and the frequency that financial or other measurement data is available.
6. For the Senior level of your audience, write in a short name or description for how you plan to gather optimization data. Optimization data is defined as effectiveness (penetration, sustainability, and speed) and efficiency. Penetration, sustainability, and speed are often tied to behavior data, so your frequency may be the same as for your level 3 data gathering. In other cases, effectiveness and efficiency are better analyzed along with level 4 (results) and level 5 (ROI), so the frequency may be tied to how often you will be looking at this information. Each situation is unique, so the best advice is to use your own judgment. Your judgment will improve with experience.

Step 8: Evaluation Worksheet

(2)   (1) **Today's Date:** _____

Your Intervention: _____

AUDIENCE	DATA GATHERING PLAN	FREQUENCY
(3) Individual	Level 1: _____ Level 2: _____	_____ _____
(4) 1st/Ops	Level 3: _____	_____
(5) Mid	Level 4: _____ Level 5: _____	_____ _____
(6) Senior	Optimization: _____ _____	_____

LET'S REVIEW: ────────────────────────────

- Delivering your intervention changes your audience's expectations of the value you communicate. Prior to delivery, you could communicate in terms of future expectations. After delivery of your intervention, you need to prove that you have delivered what you promised.

- Levels of evaluation data were presented as level 1 (reaction), level 2 (learning), level 3 (behavior), level 4 (results), and level 5 (ROI).

- Each level of your audience needs to hear different types of evaluation data. Individuals need to hear reaction and learning data to find value. The 1st/Ops level needs to hear behavior data. The Mid level needs to hear results and ROI data. The data needed for one type of audience is a given for the next level up of your audience.

- For Senior management, the initial proof of ROI and learning how to reliably measure and control ROI from WLP interventions creates delight. Once this ability is proven, however, results and ROI become givens. Senior management needs optimization data in terms of ever-increasing effectiveness and efficiency.

- Effectiveness was further defined in terms of penetration (how much of the total number of participants in an intervention actually provided financial return), sustainability (whether those participants were able to continue to provide financial return indefinitely or for a long enough period of time), and speed (how fast the organization was able to obtain financial benefit).

- It is important to always be selling the idea that the organization needs good evaluation data.

- If you are having trouble getting enough evaluation data, some ways to make your task easier are to focus your efforts, start with a rough guess, start small and build up, arrange for a continuous flow of feedback, position your data gathering as an experiment, or ask how your client will prove the intervention's value to managers.

Now that you understand how you should approach and align the worth of what you do to the organizational level you are trying to reach, the next section of the book will show you how to put all of your research and data gathering into successful communication. In the next chapter, you'll learn how to put together a quarterly communication plan on a rolling three-month basis. Not only does periodic communication continuously remind those financial types of your worth today, but it creates a cycle that increasingly improves your ability to communicate in the future.

Part Three

Communicating Value

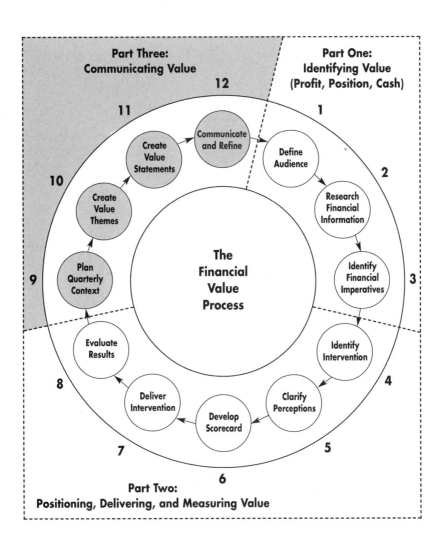

Part Three:
Communicating Value

Part One:
Identifying Value
(Profit, Position, Cash)

12

11

1

Communicate
and Refine

Create
Value
Statements

Define
Audience

10

2

Create
Value
Themes

Research
Financial
Information

The
Financial
Value
Process

9

Plan
Quarterly
Context

Identify
Financial
Imperatives

3

Evaluate
Results

Identify
Intervention

8

Clarify
Perceptions

4

Deliver
Intervention

Develop
Scorecard

7

5

6

Part Two:
Positioning, Delivering, and Measuring Value

Communicating your value is easier when you know how to place your value in the context of the urgent and important activities of your audience, create themes and statements that help you clearly and concisely communicate your value, and know how to continuously refine your communication plans to keep up with the changes in your organization and your career. The third part of this book will cover the final four steps in the financial value process:

- ◆ Step 9: Plan Quarterly Context
- ◆ Step 10: Create Value Themes
- ◆ Step 11: Create Value Statements
- ◆ Step 12: Communicate and Refine.

In chapters 11, 12, 13, 14, and 15, which comprise Part Three of *Quick! Show Me Your Value,* you will

- ◆ be shown how to connect your value to the predictable but important activities that preoccupy your audience throughout the year
- ◆ learn how to create flexible value themes that help you communicate value in a variety of situations
- ◆ be shown how to create high-impact value statements that get your point across in 30 seconds or less
- ◆ refine your value communication plans so that you'll have the important information you need always at your fingertips
- ◆ receive some encouragement to begin communicating your value.

Building Your Context Plan

 IN THIS CHAPTER:

◆ Step 9 of the financial value process: plan quarterly context
◆ Why you have to make sure your value is relevant to the "urgent and important" of today
◆ The three lifecycles that enable you to plan your relevance in advance
◆ When to time your communication to take advantage of fiscal vision, budget setting, implementation, and validation phases
◆ A method for planning whom you will talk with and when you'll show them your value and relevance.

Regular, quarterly communication is critical to managing perceptions of your value and keeping the support you need to deliver that value. Yet, even if you have successfully analyzed the financial priorities for your organization or target organization, dealt with perceptions, kept a scorecard, validated results, and made sure that others know how well you can deliver solutions, you may still find it difficult to get the attention of your Senior, Mid, or even 1st/Ops managers on a regular basis. Why?

Although the job description of upper-level managers includes setting visions and looking to the future, the reality for Senior, Mid, and other managers is that they must spend huge proportions of their time managing the "urgent and important" of today to make sure those visions of the future become reality. As stewards of their organizations, life for many Senior managers means long hours, little sleep, a rapid-fire pace, and a never-ending stream of tasks that these managers could never complete even if they worked 24 hours a day, seven days a week. One of the first things that successful leadership development programs teach new 1st/Ops and Mid managers is how to prioritize their time and ignore the majority of things that do not have immediate relevance to the urgent and important of today.

> From your audience's point of view, excellent **value communication** means that you know how to create relevance between what you are communicating and what is important to them today. If you can connect your value to the current business context, it will be much easier for your audience to see why it is important to pay attention to you now. How do you do that every quarter? You can do it by understanding the three basic lifecycles of an organization: the fiscal lifecycle, the new product lifecycle, and the seasonal lifecycle.

Fiscal Lifecycle

The first and most important lifecycle to examine is the fiscal cycle. Fiscal patterns are pretty much the same whether an organization is large or small, a for-profit or nonprofit, a publicly traded conglomerate or a privately held business, a government department or an educational institution. All organizations must pay taxes, prove their nonprofit status, or collect taxes, usually quarterly or annually.

All organizations have a **fiscal year**. In some organizations the fiscal year has the same dates as the **calendar year.** A new calendar year always starts on January 1, has 12 months, and always ends on December 31. A fiscal year also has 12 months, but it may begin on the first date of any month. It ends on the last day of the month that falls 12 months later. Many organizations align their fiscal years to begin and end on the same dates as the calendar year. Many others do not. Microsoft, for example, begins its fiscal year on July 1. The U.S. federal government begins its fiscal year on October 1.

> The legal requirement to pay taxes drives the managers in your organization into quarterly and annual behavior patterns. If managers are driven into predictable behavior patterns, what they pay attention to as being relevant to the urgent and important of today also follows a predictable pattern that you can use to get your value across.

The key to understanding fiscal context and the fiscal value lifecycle is knowing when an organization's fiscal year ends. In addition, you also need to know the beginning dates of each quarter within that year. A quarter is defined as three consecutive months within a fiscal year. For planning reasons, quarters are typically referred to as the first quarter, second quarter, third quarter, and fourth quarter (figure 11-1). If the fiscal year begins on July 1, then the first quarter consists of July, August, and September. The fourth quarter is April, May, and June.

Figure 11-1. Example of a fiscal year.

1st Quarter	2nd Quarter	3rd Quarter	4th Quarter
July August September	October November December	January February March	April May June

---

Finding a Fiscal Year

Finding the date when an organization's fiscal year begins is easy. If you are part of an organization, you are probably aware of your organization's fiscal year because you may have certain budgetary requirements (if you are a WLP manager) or it might just be in the jargon of the organization. If you don't know the fiscal year of an organization, you can go to the Website of most publicly traded organizations and find in their annual report when their fiscal year begins and ends. If you are dealing with a small or private organization, this is one of the first business intelligence questions you should ask in your networking or informational interviews.

Quarter by Quarter

Fiscal context may also be thought of in terms of the annual budget and planning cycle of an organization. Examine figure 11-2 to take a closer look at fiscal context.

Context begins in the fourth quarter with budgeting. The fourth quarter is an extremely important time of the year because that is when money is set aside for the most critical priorities in the next 12 months. If money is getting set aside, then this must be the time that you would want to propose your projects and communicate your value, right?

Figure 11-2. The fiscal lifecycle.

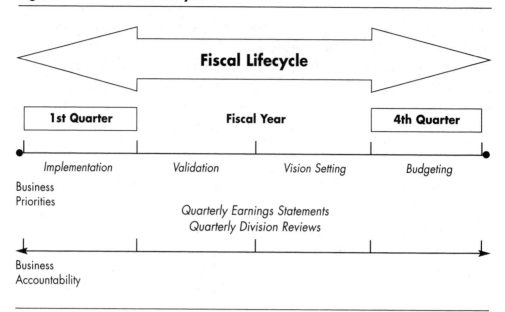

> ! You definitely want to be communicating your value during every quarter of the
> year, but the fourth quarter is not when you should propose new projects! Fourth
> quarter is a tactical time when all of the possible projects are already known. If you
> haven't made the consideration list before the fourth quarter starts, the odds are less likely
> that you'll get funding.

If you want funding for your projects, you need to have proposed them during the third quarter. The third quarter is the vision-setting and proposal-review period. This is when department heads form alliances with other department heads or work on strategies to protect or increase their allocations of money for next year. The third quarter is when managers spend significant time communicating up the chain about the value of what they have done and why they should be the ones to keep and grow their portion of the budget.

But, if you need to communicate your value and accomplishments by the third quarter, you need to have been gathering and summarizing data about your performance and validating your results before then. But, wait! You didn't have the money to implement new interventions until the beginning of the first quarter so there may not be a great deal of data about results until the second quarter. That's why figure 11-2 labels the first quarter as the implementation quarter and the second quarter as validation.

When Does the Real Work Get Done?

When examining the year this way, it may seem as though only half of the year is spent getting any real work done and the other half of the year is spent planning for the next year. Looking at the year this way does not mean that ongoing business operations stop for new initiatives, validation, visions, or budgets. It is a given that the ongoing work of the organization will continue to be managed every day.

The fiscal context in figure 11-2 is referring not only to the ongoing core of the business, but also to the extra initiatives and changes that are always required to keep the core of the business profitable, operational, and competitive. Remember that if ABC MediCompany did nothing each year to protect its 5.6 percent net profit margin, inflation alone would remove approximately 2 percent of the net profit. New initiatives, along with the core of the business, will always be there.

> *To communicate value, you need to connect your value to the given core of the business, and you must make sure your contributions to the new initiatives that keep the business profitable, well positioned, and competitive are obvious every quarter. Contributions are most easily recognized when it is obvious how those contributions support the current urgent and important Senior, Mid, or 1st/Ops tasks within the implementation, validation, vision-setting, or budgeting activities.*

Why Communicate Quarterly?

Notice in figure 11-2 that there is a line labeled Business Accountability under each of the quarters in a fiscal year. For publicly traded businesses, which must not only pay taxes but which must file SEC statements and announce earnings, tracking accountability every quarter is a legal requirement. To be able to make informed statements about their earnings, Senior managers require their Mid-level managers to report on the status of their operations each quarter. To get up-to-date information, Mid-level managers require status reports from 1st/Ops. To get their data, 1st/Ops ask for information from their Individual contributors. To be viewed as a true business partner, you need to be established as a team player who consistently contributes to this quarterly information-gathering cycle and who helps others to contribute to it as well.

When communicating value, it is inordinately time consuming to have to communicate to everyone at all times about your own value. In addition, there is always a bit of wariness when others listen to someone talk about him- or herself, especially if they seem to hear him or her do it all the time. The ideal way to communicate your value is to get others to do it for you.

It's one thing to say that you've helped improve inventory turns by 5 percent, thereby saving hundreds of thousands of dollars in the first three months of implementation. It's even better when your inventory control manager publicly gives credit to the WLP department for improvements in inventory turns. Your communication strategy needs to be timed such that you have information about how you have supported the urgent and important (such as the implementation of a new initiative) in the hands of each of your audiences as they are gathering the information for their status updates. When it comes to relevance, give them news they can use at the right time. When done in an inclusive way, this news not only makes you look good, but also it helps the Senior, Mid, 1st/Ops, and Individuals you are communicating with look good too. *That's news they'll want to share, every quarter!*

If you are managing a department, having your people cited by a number of managers in different departments leaves a powerful impression. If you are an external vendor, you know the power of word-of-mouth advertising. The key to your communication plan is making sure succinct summaries of your value are in the hands of the right audience at the right time each quarter. It's the equivalent of a regular WLP press release. You won't always be cited by everyone, but just as consistent discipline pays off when creating and updating baselines, consistent discipline in communicating within context pays off.

As you demonstrate your value within the fiscal context, it becomes easier to arrange meetings with your managers to ask them what they would value for the future so that they can meet their fiscal obligations in the next one, two, or three quarters. At these meetings, you can discuss your proposals, ask for specific types of help, and agree upon the dates when you will provide status updates. These dates should be close to the time when they will need to be making their quarterly status reports. Gradually, you should be able to get your managers to expect communication from you that they can use to talk about successes in their own departments. You should also be able to get them on a schedule to discuss the future and arrange for periodic updates from your agreements.

Variations on Fiscal Context

Some companies may find themselves in a more rapid budgetary cycle. Many high-technology companies, for example, find that their markets move so quickly that a yearlong planning cycle is far too long to react to swift market changes. Such companies often go through a budget adjustment process at the half (end of the second quarter). Others use a quarterly budget reallocation process.

What do these terms mean? It means that value communication is constant and that high-quality data showing progress toward goals is an imperative or you will quickly be "outta there!" When fiscal planning cycles are cut in half from annual to twice or four times a year, your communication context must adjust accordingly.

Of course, not all organizations operate on such a strict timeline. The smaller the organization, the less complex the budget planning process becomes and the easier it is for a single manager to make decisions and commitments. Smaller organizations can sometimes be driven more by other value lifecycles.

The fiscal context lifecycle is the most important one to get into the rhythm of whether you are internal or external to your target organization. The other two lifecycles are synchronized to work within the fiscal context lifecycle.

New Product Introduction Lifecycle

New product introductions can have serious effects on cash flow. A company's customers often know when a new product is going to be introduced in a marketplace. When a new product is coming out, many customers put off their purchase of the product in anticipation of the next release or a newer model. Revenues drop. Many customers also don't want to be the first to buy the new product in case there are software bugs, mechanical issues, or other problems. This hesitation further delays revenue and related cash flow. At the same time that customers are not buying the product at the levels they were previously, the company has to put out large sums of money to promote the new product. This additional marketing and sales expense further depletes cash.

New product introductions can be a very stressful time for a company, but these introductions typically follow a defined pattern within a fiscal year.

 Anything that you can do to identify the new product introduction cycle is important in knowing how to put your value in context. Even better, anything that you can do that shows how you have helped improve revenue or reduce costs during the lull in this cycle shows great value!

If you are internal to a company, finding out when the company is introducing new products or services is usually rather easy. If you don't know, a phone call or two can often tell you unless a new project is being kept extremely confidential to protect the company's competitive advantage. If you are external to the company, looking for patterns in old press releases, industry trade publication product reviews, industry analyst reports, or financial statements may be able to help you predict the next new product introduction.

If you have a contact at your target organization or in the industry, you can always just ask. They may or may not be able to divulge information, but you'll be no worse off than if you hadn't asked at all.

Seasonal Lifecycle

Seasonality is defined as naturally occurring periods of much higher or lower sales during the year. Many retailers make the majority of their sales during the Christmas season and use the cash flow generated from September through December to fund their operations during the remainder of the year. In the services sector, accounting firms experience high volumes of sales during tax preparation season. In the food industry, beef consumption reaches a peak during the summer barbeque season and drops to a low point during the winter, affecting cash flows in this business. In the home improvement business, spring and summer are high seasons with some variation depending on the weather in different areas of the country.

What's considered urgent and important changes as managers cope with seasonal hiring, production, distribution, advertising, and other business fluctuations.

 If you understand the seasonality of your target organization, you can time your communication to be in the right place at the right time. You'll also be able to propose meetings for the future quarters that will be much more meaningful for your business managers.

Planning Communication Within Context

To create your communication plan, the first step is to master the timing of the fiscal, product, and seasonality lifecycles. The next step is to plan ahead for the type of quarterly context, the audience to be communicated with, and the dates by which your value must have been communicated to your audience via meetings, memos, voicemail, or any other method you chose.

For some WLP professionals, their audience will always be the same, no matter which of the three cycles they are planning around. For other readers, the audience will be different for each cycle.

Marcella, who works as a training manager at ABC MediCompany, regularly communicates the value of changes in the contract renewal department new hire training. To do so, Marcella created a map to define the fiscal quarters at ABC MediCompany to show her when she should use different fiscal, product, and seasonal context statements.

She wanted to make certain that she communicated her value to key audience members who were in a position to cite Marcella's contributions as part of the improvements within their departments. In Marcella's case, her audience for fiscal, new products, and seasonal sales were always the same.

Finally, for each member of her audience, Marcella noted the dates by which she wanted her value statements in front of them. Marcella's plan is shown in figure 11-3.

Figure 11-3. Marcella's quarterly context plan (step 9).

	1st Quarter: Jan–March	**2nd Quarter: April–June**	**3rd Quarter: July–Sept**	**4th Quarter: Oct–Dec**
FISCAL	. . . as we launch our initiatives	. . . as we stabilize initiatives and gather results	. . . as we create visions for the future	. . . as we plan our budgets
PRODUCT INTRODUCTION		. . . as we introduce our new products		
SEASONALITY	. . . as we work through our seasonal low		. . . as we manage our seasonal high	

Audience and Communication Dates

1st/Ops:	Hans	Jan 15th	May 15th	Aug 5th	Oct 15th
Mid:	Jose	Jan 25th	May 25th	Aug 15th	Oct 25th
Senior:	Nancy	Feb 10th	June 10th	Sept 5th	Nov 10th

Marcella's map allows her to schedule meetings, presentations, and memos in advance. Using good project management techniques, Marcella works backward from the dates that she wants to communicate on to when she must have her evaluation data and updated baselines. Using this kind of plan, Marcella always seems to be in the right place at the right time. Her friends tell her she just seems to be so lucky to get into some of the conversations she does. As the old saying goes, "Luck favors the prepared."

Making Your Plan

Now it's time to plan your luck. Complete exercise 11-1 by filling in today's date, the name of your intervention, your fiscal quarters, the names of people who are your key audiences for each lifecycle, and the dates you want to have your value in front of them.

 LET'S REVIEW: ─────────────────────────

- ◆ To manage the urgent and important of today, Senior, Mid, and 1st/Ops managers learn to ignore anything that is not immediately relevant to their priorities. Step 9 of the financial value plan helps you ensure that your value communication is timely and relevant.

- ◆ In addition to managing the core of the business, your audience must also constantly be working on new initiatives to keep the business profitable and competitive. Because of tax and reporting laws, your audience will be driven into a quarterly behavior pattern to accomplish these initiatives.

- ◆ There are three primary organizational lifecycles that operate within the quarterly nature of a business. These lifecycles enable you to plan your relevance in advance. The three lifecycles are the fiscal lifecycle, the new product introduction lifecycle, and the seasonal lifecycle.

- ◆ The fiscal cycle consists of the first quarter or implementation quarter, the second quarter or validation quarter, the third quarter or vision-setting quarter, and the fourth quarter or budgeting quarter. Especially in publicly traded companies, your audiences report the status of their activities within each of these quarters up through the management chain.

- ◆ You need to be a part of the quarterly status information flow. It is easier to communicate your value when you get others to do it for you.

- ◆ New product introductions and seasonal sales fluctuations can create great stress and cash flow strains within an organization. They also create predictable activities that become urgent and important within specific quarters of a year.

The last thing that you will need to communicate your value is what you are going to say. Even with all of your preparation, your audiences still have very little time. How can you summarize your value each quarter in 30 seconds or less and in a way that your audiences can communicate their value (and by default yours) as well? Read on.

Exercise 11-1. Your quarterly context plan.

Directions: Complete the following steps to make sure that your value is always visible in the right place at the right time. Completing this exercise will help ensure you have the right data for each audience and wrap up step 9 of the financial value process: plan quarterly context. If you prefer not to write in this book, go to the companion Website (www.astd.org/astd/publications) to download a PowerPoint file for this exercise.

1. Note today's date.
2. Write the name or a brief description of the intervention you will be communicating about.
3. Fill in the names of the months that begin and end each fiscal quarter under the headings first quarter, second quarter, third quarter, and fourth quarter.
4. For your fiscal lifecycle, fill in the audience names and the dates in each quarter by which you need to have communicated your value as it relates to the core business and the new initiatives that have been launched and managed within each fiscal quarter.
5. For your new product introduction lifecycle, fill in the audience names and the dates in each quarter by which you need to have communicated your value as it relates to improving new product introductions.
6. For your seasonal lifecycle, fill in the audience names and the dates in each quarter by which you need to have communicated your value as it relates to improving or managing seasonal fluctuations in revenue, costs, or cash flow.

Step 9: Quarterly Context Plan

(1) **Today's Date:** _____

(2) **Your Intervention:** _____

(3) **1st Quarter:**   **2nd Quarter:**   **3rd Quarter:**   **4th Quarter:**
    _____   _____   _____   _____

(4) **Fiscal:**   **Audience and Communication Dates**

1st/Ops: _____	_____	_____	_____	_____
Mid: _____	_____	_____	_____	_____
Senior: _____	_____	_____	_____	_____

(5) **Product:**   **Audience and Communication Dates**

1st/Ops: _____	_____	_____	_____	_____
Mid: _____	_____	_____	_____	_____
Senior: _____	_____	_____	_____	_____

(6) **Seasonal:**   **Audience and Communication Dates**

1st/Ops: _____	_____	_____	_____	_____
Mid: _____	_____	_____	_____	_____
Senior: _____	_____	_____	_____	_____

Your Communication Base: Value Themes

 IN THIS CHAPTER:

- ◆ Step 10 of the financial value process: create value themes
- ◆ The difference between a value theme and a value statement
- ◆ The spectrum of finance to performance
- ◆ The components of a value theme
- ◆ How to use your financial value chains to create value themes for your intervention
- ◆ When to use value themes
- ◆ Value theme examples.

Finally! Throughout this entire book, you have been working through all of the pieces and parts that you must have to communicate value. You know where to get business intelligence, what's important to your organization, what intervention you want to communicate about, and how your intervention is perceived. You have your scorecard, you can validate your results, you know when to communicate, and how to make it relevant, but what should you say? And how can you say it in 30 seconds or less?

Types of Value Communication: Themes and Statements

You need two communication formats when communicating value. The first format is the financial **value theme.** The second is the financial value statement. Both are based on your hard work to identify, position, deliver, and measure your value. Each format is useful in different situations. Figure 12-1 displays the components of value themes and value statements.

For those of you who are tempted to skip ahead, it will be helpful to read this chapter on value themes first, before proceeding to the next chapter on value statements. Some of the basic concepts for building your value themes also apply to creating value statements. Reading this chapter will make the next easier to follow.

The Difference Between Value Themes and Value Statements

Your value theme is the starting point for your value communication. Your theme is a high-level generalization of the value you bring to the organization. The basic layout for your themes is shown under the number 1 in figure 12-1.

Your value statements are specific descriptions of how much performance improvement you've enabled (number 2 in figure 12-1), how much financial value the performance improvement has created (3), why sharing this information is relevant to the urgent and important of today (4), and what you need from your audience to create even more value in the future (5). Both formats are concise, yet each is a necessary part of your repertoire.

Figure 12-1. Building your value communication.

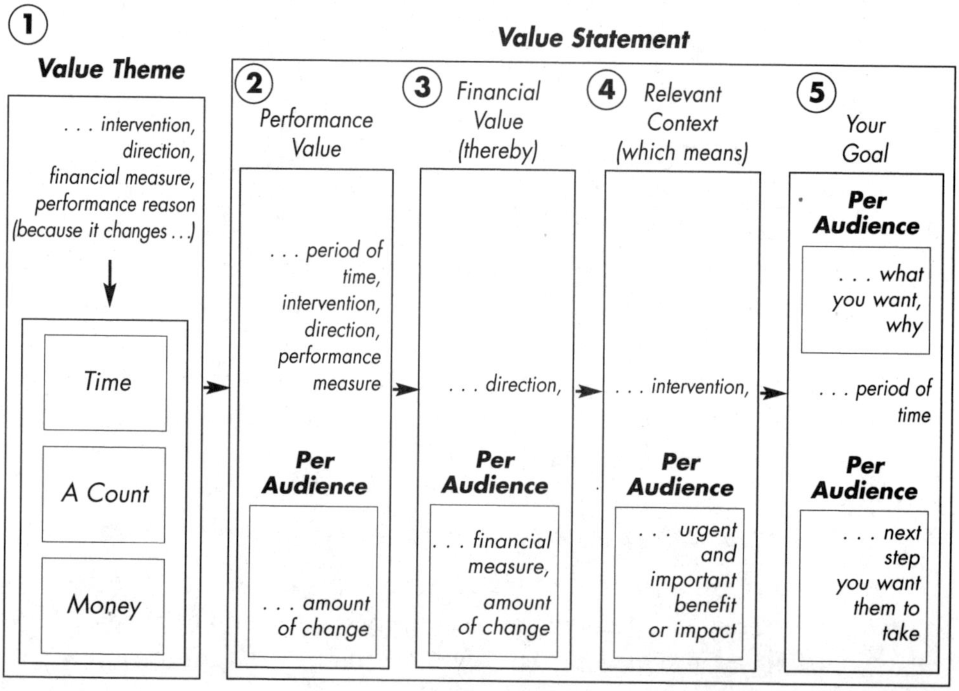

The Basis for Value Themes and Value Statements

Value themes and value statements are based on the financial value chains you have been using throughout this book. First, a quick review: financial value chains describe the four levels of your audience (Senior, Mid, 1st/Ops, and Individual). In a financial value chain, the broad financial measures of the Senior level are broken down into more specific measures for each audience until those measures become the detailed performance measures of the Individual.

In addition to the measures for each level of your audience, financial value chains also help you identify the relative timeframes that each level of your audience is responsible for in delivering value. Senior management is often responsible for creating value over a three- to five-year timeframe. Individual measures often vary from one week to one quarter. Figure 12-2 shows the sample financial value chain that you first read about in chapter 2.

Figure 12-2. A sample financial value chain.

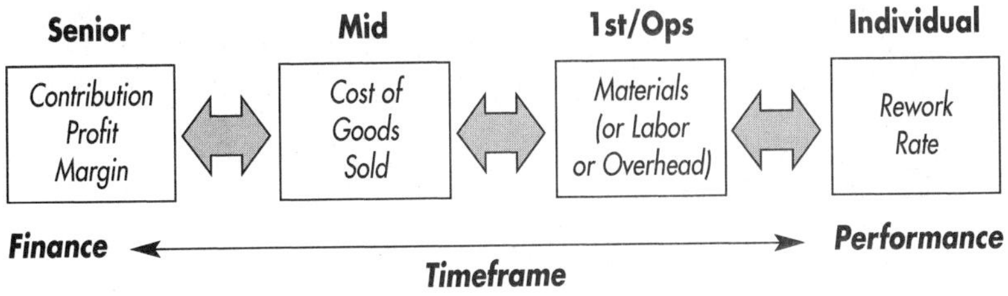

The CPM is what is left over from the initial revenue after all of the costs to produce the goods to be sold and all of the costs to make sales have been subtracted from the revenue. Revenue, COGS, and other sales-driven expenses are all items that go into the CPM and are typical measures that are assigned to Mid-level managers in an organization. In figure 12-2, profit performance needs to be improved and a link is made from CPM to COGS, with COGS being indicated as a key focus for improvement. Materials, labor, and **overhead** are components of COGS and, in this case, materials costs are linked as an important measure for improvement at the 1st/Ops level. Finally, a link is made from materials to rework rates at the Individual level as being an important performance measure in improving financial value.

Financial and Performance Comparisons

Financial value themes (and financial value statements) are based on the principle of drawing a causal relationship between one point on the finance-to-performance spectrum depicted at the bottom of figure 12-2 and another point on the same spectrum. Any two points on the spectrum can be used to draw a causal relationship. The higher or broader measure will be referred to as the financial measure. The smaller or more detailed measure will be referred to as the **performance measure.** The use of broader versus more specific measures gives us the flexibility to use the most appropriate terms depending on whom we are communicating with.

For example, if you are communicating with the CFO about the financial value depicted in figure 12-2, you could use CPM as your financial measure and materials as your performance measure because materials is a smaller, more detailed measure than CPM is. It is not always necessary to go down to the Individual measure to contrast finance with performance. Conversely, if you were communicating with a 1st/Ops manager about financial value in figure 12-2, you could use materials as the financial measure most relevant to the 1st/Ops manager and rework rate as your smaller, more detailed performance measure.

An Example to Help You

This is a good time to pull out the financial value chains that you created in the exercises for chapters 4 (profit), 5 (position), and 6 (cash). Nonetheless, even if you have created your own financial value chains, it may be easier for you to follow the steps for creating financial value themes if you have an example to follow.

Marcella, the training manager at ABC MediCompany, made a number of changes over the last three years in the contract renewal new hire training for ABC. Some of her changes created great value for ABC; others didn't create as much. In chapter 8, you saw the impact of Marcella's assumptions that the value from her interventions would be obvious and indefinitely supported by the managers in her organization. Unfortunately, over the long run, Marcella's assumptions did not hold up as well as she would have liked.

In chapter 9, Marcella chose to manage her value communication differently. She introduced financial value chains for her intervention and created a financial imperatives scorecard to describe the amount of value she had created for each chain. In chapter 11, Marcella mapped her contributions to the urgent and important of her organization.

To see how Marcella created her value themes, examine Marcella's financial value chains, which were first introduced in chapter 9. Marcella's financial value chains are shown in figure 12-3.

Figure 12-3. Marcella's financial value chains.

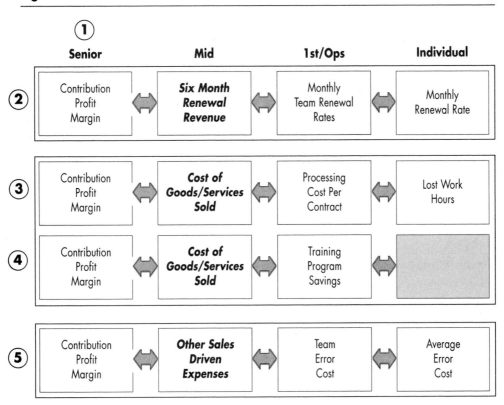

In Marcella's case, all of her value chains use a Senior manager profit measure from the income statement—the CPM—as their starting point. Marcella's first chain addresses how her intervention helped increase the revenue that goes into the CPM. The next two chains affect COGS and the last affects other sales-driven expenses that are subtracted from revenue to reach the CPM.

Having financial value chains that all affect the same Senior measure isn't necessarily the case for every situation. It's possible for multiple Senior measures to be impacted, depending on the intervention. Marcella could also have drawn financial value chains depicting the impact of changes in the contract renewal new hire training on the balance sheet or cash flow statement.

Shortened Value Chains

Before moving on, one another thing to notice in Marcella's chains is that one Individual-level box does not have any measure in it. In the third round of changes that Marcella made to the contract renewal new hire training, the

Individuals were not impacted by the changes Marcella made to the cost structure of her intervention. The first opportunity for Marcella's action to make a
difference to anyone was when the charges for the training were passed on to
the 1st/Ops hiring managers. In chapter 9, effectiveness was defined as creating new or additional impact on an organization's financial measures or
financial statements such that the impact makes a significant or sizable difference to the success of the organization. Efficiency was defined as delivering
the same level of benefit as has been had previously, but for less solution cost.
Effectiveness chains often stretch the entire length of the organization.
Efficiency changes can create slightly shortened financial value chains.

The Value Theme Layout

The general format for a financial value theme is shown in figure 12-4.

Figure 12-4. Format for financial value themes.

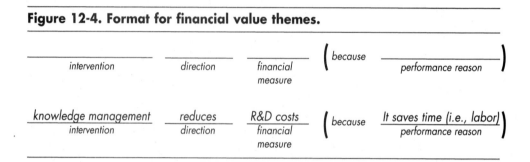

Financial value themes state your intervention, give a direction that you
have moved a financial measure, name the financial measure, and give a performance reason for the movement in the financial measure.

Identifying Your Intervention

The first step in creating your value theme is to state the intervention you are
communicating value for. You can use the principles of value communication
for many reasons and in many situations. Your audience will find it easier to
agree with you, however, when your financial value theme refers to the results
from a specific intervention. Step 4 of the financial value process helped you
identify the intervention that you wanted to focus your value communication
on. A discussion of step 4 was given at the beginning of chapter 8.

Examples of possible interventions include

- new hire sales training
- knowledge management consulting
- problem-solving skills for information technology specialists

- ◆ leadership screening assessments
- ◆ quality improvement training for health care administrators.

Pick a Direction and a Financial Measure

After you've named your intervention, you need to link it to the financial **measure** you expect your intervention to affect, and you need to designate the direction that the financial measure should move. Your financial measures come directly from your financial value chains.

The direction of movement is simply a verb form that describes the type of movement that was created for the financial measure. *Reducing, lowering,* and *decreasing* are all "down" verbs and are best used with a cost measure. *Increasing, raising,* and *strengthening* are all "up" verbs and are best used with a revenue or income-producing measure. *Improving* is a generic term that can be used in relation to either costs or income. Because *improving* is often overused or misused, it is better to choose a verb that more strongly matches costs or income.

"Direction/while" is a special case of showing value. It is possible to write a value theme that shows that you are increasing, decreasing, or maintaining one measure while increasing or decreasing another. For example, you may have been able to increase sales income while maintaining the cost of sales. That's not always easy to do. The first assumption of your Senior managers is that the cost of sales probably went up in proportion to the sales revenue. If you were able to hold costs steady while increasing revenue, this phenomenon is important to point out.

Give the Reason

Finally, if it is not exceedingly obvious in your theme why your intervention affects a particular financial measure, you must state a performance reason why you will or have already moved that measure. Reasons leverage the same direction but name the **base driver** that will change to achieve that direction. Base drivers are a more detailed, specific measure on the same value chain that is used as the performance comparison for the broader financial measure.

Performance measures or base drivers can be summarized as being of three types:

- ◆ labor costs or time
- ◆ resources, a rate, or a count
- ◆ direct receivables or money.

Every performance measure that you are increasing, decreasing, or maintaining saves time, changes a count, or directly brings in more money. Arguably, time can be considered a count, but because labor costs are such a significant portion of income, accrued expenses, and cash flow, it is useful to distinguish time as a category of its own when stating reasons. Eventually, improvements in time and resource counts will be converted to money.

If the audience you are communicating with understands the terminology of your performance measures, it is best to use the name of the performance measure as your performance reason. If the audience that you are communicating with knows nothing about the area of an organization that you have improved, you can substitute a very generic and basic driver, such as saving time, improving the rate of output, or getting more money as your performance reason.

 Marcella can use her financial value chains to create value themes like the ones in figure 12-5.

Figure 12-5. Marcella's financial value themes.

CONTRACT RENEWAL NEW HIRE TRAINING
Value Themes

Each of Marcella's value chains names the contract renewal new hire training as the intervention she is focusing her communication on. Marcella's first value chain names the Mid-level measure of COGS as the theme's financial measure and describes how the intervention decreases (the direction verb) this financial measure because (performance reason) it decreases lost work hours from experienced employees who previously had to spend needed time to help new hires on the job. In generic terms for a performance base driver, this intervention saves time.

Marcella's second value chain names the Mid-level measure of other sales-driven expenses as the theme's financial measure and describes how the intervention reduces (the direction verb) this financial measure because (performance reason) it reduces average renewal contract error rates for new employees. In generic terms for a performance base driver, this intervention improves a count or a rate.

Marcella's third value chain names the Senior-level measure of CPM as the theme's financial measure and describes how the intervention increases (the direction verb) this financial measure because (performance reason) it increases average monthly team renewals by new employees. In generic terms for a performance base driver, this intervention brings in more money.

Why Do You Want a Theme?

If you are just going to create value statements next, why bother with a theme? There are three reasons to create your value themes.

First, figuring out how to translate financial value chains into value statements can seem daunting. Value themes help you both to focus and to clarify. Working out your value theme helps you simplify the process of creating value statements because you'll be comparing the same finance and performance measures in your themes and in your statements. Each piece of your theme is used again in the first half of your value statements. Creating a theme saves you time while still allowing you to customize your value statements even more closely to your audience.

Second, there are times when all you will want to use is your theme. For example, if you happen to be talking with a new acquaintance in your community, you may not know what industry he or she is in or what audience level he or she represents. Using a performance theme allows you to describe your value in general terms. As the conversation progresses, you can provide more specific value statements if that is appropriate.

Third, value themes are very versatile. They can be used as headings during presentations or on marketing brochures. They can introduce sections in reports, be used in conversations, or serve as the lead-in for more detailed value statements.

Why Is This Any Different From What You Already Do?

 Many WLP professionals use something like a value theme every day. There are two ways that a financial value theme differs from how you are currently communicating your value. These critical differences ensure that you make the translation of your value into your audience's frame of reference.

The first difference between a financial value theme and how many WLP professionals communicate their value is that instead of connecting the intervention to a financial measure and a performance reason, the WLP professional simply describes value in terms of performance. This leaves your audience with the task of translating the performance measure into the financial measure that is most meaningful for them.

One of the basic rules in decoding the ROI codeword for your audience is that the translation of value is *your* job. If you leave the translation for your audience to do, they will either not do it or will translate your value into completely unintended meanings. The problem of unintended meanings can be exacerbated depending on whether your intervention is perceived with an unknown, conscious, or given set of expectations, as discussed in chapter 8.

At other times, WLP professionals translate their value directly into a financial measure but do not provide the performance reason. Unless the translation is extremely obvious (such as creating higher dollar sales for each sales representative and thereby bringing in more top-line revenue), your audience is left without an understanding of why you think your intervention changes a financial measure, and they'll have to draw their own conclusions. It is better to state your logic explicitly than assume that the audience will get it right on their own.

Create Your Own Value Themes

Now it's time to try your hand at writing at least one theme for yourself using exercise 12-1.

Exercise 12-1. Your value theme.

 Directions: Completing this exercise completes your work on step 10 of the financial value process: create value themes. If you prefer not to write in this book, go to the companion Website (www.astd.org/astd/publications) to download a PowerPoint file for this exercise.

1. Write the name of your intervention in the first space labeled "intervention."
2. If you have not completed your financial value chains, go back to chapters 4, 5, and 6 to create these for your organization. If you have completed your financial value chains, select a direction and a financial measure for your value theme. Fill in the direction and financial measures in the corresponding spaces in the exercise.
3. Select your performance measure. Fill in the final space in the exercise by repeating the direction verb and stating the performance measure. Alternatively, you can use a generic base driver such as saving time, improving a count, or creating more money.

YOUR VALUE THEME

Define the value theme for your intervention:

_____

intervention

_____   _____

direction   *financial measure*

(*because*   _____)

performance reason
(time, count, or money)

 LET'S REVIEW: ─────────────────────────

- This chapter completes step 10 in the financial value process: create value themes.

- Your theme is a high-level generalization of the value you bring to the organization. A value statement gives more specific data about the performance change, financial change, relevance to the urgent and important of today, and what you need next to bring even more value to the organization.

- Financial value themes (and financial value statements) are based on the principle of drawing a causal relationship between one point on the finance-to-performance spectrum of a financial value chain and another point on the same spectrum. Any two points on the spectrum can be used to draw a causal relationship. The higher or broader selected measure is called the financial measure. The smaller or more detailed measure is called the performance measure.

- Value themes name the intervention, chose a direction that the financial measure will or has already moved, and then give a performance reason for the movement in the financial measure.

- Performance reasons echo the same direction and can be a specific performance measure or, if the audience will not understand the terminology of the performance measure, you can use a generic base driver of time, count, or money as a performance reason.

- Value themes are different from what many WLP professionals currently use because they ensure that the translation from performance to finance is done for your audience and that your audience can see your logic in claiming a type of value.

◆ Value themes can be used in a wide range of places, including marketing brochures, presentations, conversations, or as lead-ins to more specific value statements.

◆ This chapter gave examples of three value themes based on value chains created for ABC MediCompany.

Financial value themes are important, but if themes were enough to gain a seat at the table, you'd already be there. Your peers at the table need more. In the next chapter, you'll create financial value statements that give your audience the specific information they are looking for.

13

---→

Creating Financial Value Statements

 IN THIS CHAPTER:————————————

- How to do step 11: create value statements in the financial value process
- The four segments of a value statement
- How your value theme, financial value scorecards, your evaluation data, and quarterly context plans help you create powerful value statements
- Why you must have a goal in terms of what you want from your audience to complete your value statements
- Value statement examples
- Additional uses for value statements.

N ow it is time to create succinct, 30-second statements that break through the code and speak directly to each member of your audience. You're ready to make sure your value is conscious, contextual, and connected to the critical financial imperatives of your organization.

A special note on reading this chapter: The explanations of value themes and value statements are closely tied together. Some key concepts and terms used in this chapter were introduced in the previous chapter. If you have come directly to this chapter for fast tips and pointers, you may find that skimming the previous chapter will help you grasp the most important points just a little more easily.

Picturing Value Communication

The general structure for **value themes** and value statements was introduced in chapter 12. You saw in figure 12-1 the structure of the value theme as well as the four segments of a financial value statement and the components within each segment. Value themes are a generalized summary of the information you will communicate in your value statements—the topic of this chapter.

Introducing the Four Segments

Value statements are much more specific descriptions of the value you have brought or are proposing to bring to your target organization. They are stated in a concise format that allows you to communicate your value in 30 seconds or less. The first segment in your value statement is your performance value (under the number 2 in figure 12-1). Your performance value serves as an introduction to your work and describes how much value you have added or plan to add in performance terms.

The second segment in the financial value statement is the **financial value.** The components of the financial value part of your value statement are shown under the number 3 in figure 12-1. In the financial value segment, you translate for your audience what the performance improvement means in terms of the financial measures your audience cares most about.

The third segment in the financial value statement is the relevant context. The components of relevant context are shown under the number 4 in figure 12-1. In the relevant context, you draw a connection for your audience from the financial value to how this value supports an urgent and important task that your audience is dealing with today. In this part of the financial value statement, you describe why it is important for your audience to pay attention to you *now*.

The fourth segment in your financial value statement is your goal. The components of your goal are shown under the number 5 in figure 12-1.

If your audience accepts and believes you can create value, it will want to know what help you need to ensure the value is indeed created or what else you would need to create even more. Your audience is signaling an acceptance of you as a valued team member who can accomplish one or more significant objectives for the organization. This is a significant reward for your preparation and hard work to communicate value. This kind of acceptance is a fundamental prerequisite to gaining recognition as deserving of a seat at the table as a steward for your organization.

Let's examine the first three segments of the financial value statement in more depth. The basic components for these segments are shown again in figure 13-1. This time the components are shown in a fill-in-the-blank format, along with a completed example. After you've reviewed these segments, you'll see how to add your goal to your value statements.

Figure 13-1. Three segment layout.

Period of Time	Intervention	Performance Measure	Direction

	thereby	
Amount of Change		Direction

		which means
Financial Measure(s)	Amount of Change	

Intervention	Relevant Benefit or Impact

Example:

Six months	after implementing our stress management program,
Period of Time	**Intervention**

nursing turnover	decreased	by 20%.	This significantly helped
Performance Measure	**Direction**	**Amount of Change**	**(thereby)**

increase	our operating profit margin and free cash	by saving $250,000 in
Direction	**Financial Measure(s)**	**Amount of Change**

out-of-pocket costs.	This means	we have the ability to continue to fund the
	(which means)	**Relevant Benefit or Impact**

salaries for several general administrative staff members within next year's budget.

Breaking the ROI codeword depends on being able to tie your value to what is meaningful from your audience's point of view. When creating a value statement, you'll use the same financial value chains and the same measures you selected previously for your theme, as your performance measure, and your financial measure in your value statement. You may have already noticed that these financial value chains and their measures are also the ones you used to create your financial imperative scorecard in chapter 9.

Your value chains, scorecard, and theme now become key tools for you as you create specific value statements customized for your audience.

Performance Value

A financial value statement starts by stating the performance improvement that is planned or has been made for the organization. This is the performance value segment of the financial value statement. The performance value segment starts by identifying a specific period of time in which the value was or will be obtained.

When communicating value, it makes a big difference if the benefits were obtained in six weeks or six months. Including a period of time is an important part of identifying the rate of change or speed in which value is being brought to the organization. This information is particularly important when demonstrating how you are optimizing value to your Senior executives. In the example in figure 13-1, the period of time is six months. Where would you get a figure such as six months? This is the same period that you selected for a specific value add column on the financial imperatives scorecard created in chapter 9.

Next comes the name of the intervention that has (or will be) implemented, the direction verb, the performance measure, and the amount of change in the performance measure. The intervention is the same one that you chose to focus on in step 4 of the financial value process. In figure 13-1, the sample intervention is a stress management program.

In the last chapter, the performance measure was defined as being a smaller or more specific measure from a profit, position, or cash financial value chain. The chosen performance measure can be any of the measures on the financial value chain with the exception of the Senior level measure. This is because the improvement in the performance measure must be contrasted with an improvement in a larger, broader financial measure. It's hard to contrast the top measure with itself! The direction is simply a verb that describes an up or down movement for the improvement. In this example, the stress management program decreased nursing turnover.

 You'll notice in the example that the direction verb and performance measure were stated in a slightly different order than the template displayed above them. Although the segments and all of the components of each segment should be kept as part of the statement, the order of the components within each segment can be moved so that your value statement sounds natural to you.

Examples of direction verbs are reducing, increasing, lowering, or raising. Depending on the performance measure selected, the amount of improvement can be expressed as a percentage of change in time, a count, or a gross or net dollar amount. The amount of performance change will be drawn directly from the benefits that you have been tracking for your value add on your financial imperatives scorecard. In the example here, the amount of decrease in nursing turnover was 20 percent.

Financial Value

The financial value segment is where a financial value statement becomes significantly different from many WLP claims to value. Many statements frequently stop right after the performance measure and the amount of change. Perhaps they don't even include an amount of change. With such a statement the WLP professional is hoping that the audience will be able to translate what the improvement in a performance measure means.

Unfortunately, the audience won't make this leap to financial value. You must translate performance value into financial terms if you want the audience to understand the value your interventions bring to the organization. That is why the next piece of the financial value statement is always a form of the term *thereby.* You can use the word *thereby* or some variation, such as was used in the example (figure 13-1). No matter how it is done, you must be sure that the next segment of your value statement makes the connection between the language of performance and the language of finance.

After the statement of financial value (*thereby*) comes another direction verb, the financial measure that was impacted, and the amount of change that the performance improvement translated into. Because the basis of the financial value statement is a connection between performance and finance, the financial measure cannot be the same as the performance measure. The financial measure must be a higher-level or broader measure than the performance measure. As long as the financial measure is higher than the selected performance measure, the financial measure can be chosen from any of the four levels of the financial value chain with the exception of the Individual or most detailed performance measure.

In the example in figure 13-1, the direction of the financial measure(s) increased. Many times in a value statement, you'll then simply state a single financial measure that changed as a result of the change in performance.

If you have done the work to create your financial value chains based on multiple financial statements, you can sometimes group two financial measures together to pack a little more punch into your value statement. In the example here, two financial measures were grouped together: the operating profit margin and free cash. The amount of change was $250,000. A quarter of a million dollars is likely to be large enough to catch people's attention and indicate value, but the value statement doesn't stop there.

Relevant Context (Which Means)

Following the financial value or *thereby* segment is one more connection that it is your job to make. That is the connection from the general translation of performance and finance to the urgent and important of today. That connection is expressed by using the phrase or some variation of the phrase *which means*.

> Many times when a WLP professional is trying to communicate value, he or she can be frustrated when their audience says, "I know you're important, but I can't talk to you right now. I have a business to run!" Organizational leaders learn very early to filter out any communication that is not immediately relevant to the urgent and important tasks of today. In chapter 11, you learned about the three lifecycles of a business based on fiscal, new product, and seasonal sales patterns and how these lifecycles drive your audience into a predictable pattern of what is urgent and important for them to accomplish. Now it is time to use your quarterly context plan to connect your value to the most important tasks that your audience is dealing with.

In the layout in figure 13-1, the last two components listed are the intervention and the relevant benefit or impact. Depending on the flow of conversation or what feels natural, you may repeat the name of the intervention or omit it from your value statement at this point. You can see that in the example shown in figure 13-1, the name of the intervention was omitted, and the statement flowed directly into the relevant benefit or impact. the connection to context was made by pointing out that the extra $250,000 in savings made it possible to fund several staff member's salaries for the next year. For all we know, perhaps one of those salaries was the WLP manager's! Or, perhaps this statement was made as the WLP manager was trying to get more of his or her manager's attention focused on retaining key parts of the WLP budget for next year.

The Goal

The final segment in your financial value statement is your goal.

Goals: Why Bother? Having a goal is critical to your success for several reasons.

First, your audience *expects* to hear a goal articulated. To an executive, communication without purpose is noise. In the Information Age, people have no time. If you are going to take the time of a Senior manager, you must be prepared to explain what you want him or her to do next to help you continue to create value. Even if you just want something as simple as some recognition for a job well done because it would motivate you or your staff to keep producing more, you need to tell your audience that. The audience won't know what you need until you say so.

The second reason you must state a goal is because three pieces of information have not yet been included in your financial value statement. This is information regarding **penetration, sustainability**, and **speed**—the optimization information that your Senior managers will be looking for from your value statements. Some information on rate of speed was communicated in your period of time as the first component of your performance value segment. But, because optimization information is really answering questions about the future (for example, how many more need to participate in the intervention, what it takes to sustain the benefits from the intervention for longer periods, how much faster you can gain the benefits in another iteration) then optimization information is really about your future goals. You can draw your Senior executives' attention to how you will bring even more value to the organization through your goals or, in other words, you can draw their attention to how you will optimize their value.

Third, goals build your own confidence and influence. Don't overlook the personal benefits of goal setting. Setting a goal gives you motivation to make sure your value communication pays off. All people need to feel that the effort they put forth is meaningful and worthwhile. Clarifying what you want for your efforts and then asking for it is a good way to build your own confidence and self-esteem.

 If you want a seat at the executive table, you must be able to see yourself as an equal to the others who are there. One of the keys to success is having the motivation and the self-confidence to go after what is important to you as a steward for your people. That gives you a much better footing with your peers.

Pay attention to the basic interactions that build self-confidence. Having the ability to successfully influence others builds the foundation for the belief that one can set and achieve goals. One of the primary ways to influence an audience is to ask the audience to make a commitment, even a small one. Robert Cialdini (1998) describes the top six ways that people influence each other. Commitment and consistency, according to Cialdini, constitute one of the ways to build influence. Once people have committed to an idea, a principle, or some type of support, they do not like to contradict themselves and are likely to commit to it again.

An example of commitment to a principle might be getting someone to agree to the statement that "It is important to show that we support learning for our people." Once someone has committed in a small way, he or she will often be more open to a slightly larger commitment later. A slightly larger commitment might be for an executive to write a memo supporting a particular learning initiative. A slightly larger commitment after that might be to give extra funds to expand the initiative. In other words, the less frequently you set a goal and ask for a commitment, the less influence you have. Connecting what you do to financial benefits that create goodness for the organization make it easier for you to gain commitment in the first place.

One caution: Be careful not to select goals or ask for commitments that cause your audience to give you a resounding "No!" Once people have committed to that position, they will want to stay consistent within it as well.

Goal Layout. Let's continue looking at the layout of a value statement by examining the final segment: your goal. Figure 13-2 consists of a blank layout for your goal and then a completed example.

In your goal, you should first describe what you want and then explain why you want it. What you want and why will change for each member of your audience according to what he or she can provide to help you toward

Figure 13-2. Your goal layout.

_____

_____
What you Want

_____
Why

_____   _____
Period of Time   *Next Step You Want Them to Take*

Example:

_____
I know times are tight, but we need to keep all of the members of our staff
What you Want

if we are to be able to produce these kinds of results again next year.
Why

_____   _____
In the next two days,   *I'd like to meet with you to review a proposal for how we*
Period of Time   **Next Step You Want Them to Take**

can get the CFO to increase next year's budget allocations for workplace learning and performance.

_____

your goal. The last part of your goal is to start a specific period of time and then the next step that you want your audience to take to help you with your goal.

The example in figure 13-2 continues with the value statement that was introduced in figure 13-1. The WLP manager for an organization wants to keep the same size of budget going into the next fiscal year so that he and his staff can continue the excellent work that their department is doing. The WLP manager wants his boss to review a proposal that will go to the CFO to increase the WLP budget allocations for next year.

A Few Recommendations

As you develop comfort, confidence, and skill in communicating your value, financial value statements will become easier and easier for you to use. Here are a few recommendations for you to keep in mind. First, remember to match the appropriate level of evaluation data to your audience as best as possible. For a review of these concepts, please see chapter 10. If your audience needs multiple types of evaluation data, the higher the level of evaluation data you can use, the better.

Amounts that reflect net dollars are better than gross dollars that have not been formally isolated or had costs removed. In general, however, it is a good idea to give the audience an idea of the size of the contribution by using some type of dollar figure. A percentage of adoption for the performance value can also be used, but it's best if this **metric** is compared to a dollar figure for the broader financial measure. Remember that your audience needs to hear the size of your contribution, not just the benefit-to-cost ratio (BCR) or return-on-investment (ROI), as discussed in chapter 9. Many people in your audience know that large ROIs or BCRs can be generated from very small numbers, so it is important to know the actual size of your contribution in monetary figures.

 Always use numbers you can substantiate and will be happy to discuss. If you are successful in catching people's attention—the goal of working through this entire book—you will be asked how you arrived at your conclusions. Be prepared with a solid answer to cement your creditability.

The key to communicating your value is preparation, which includes preparing a draft of your value statements as much as a year in advance. The first, second, third, and fourth quarters happen every year. Studies have shown that people who write down their goals are much more likely to achieve them. By preparing your statements in advance you will not only know exactly what you are aiming for, but you will be able to give yourself much needed practice in helping these statements roll off your tongue. You'll also be in a better position to share your value statements with others, so that they can help communicate your value for you.

Let's return once again to Marcella to see how she has laid out a series of financial value statements for one of the changes she introduced to ABC's contract renewal new hire training. In chapter 12, you saw that Marcella could create three different value themes from her financial value chains.

Great negotiators will tell you that you win more if you pick a focus and stick to it when communicating value. One way for Marcella to prioritize her themes and statements is the order by which they added the most financial gain. This order could change each time Marcella updates her financial imperatives scorecard with new value adds from incremental changes to her interventions. Another way that Marcella could prioritize her themes and value statements is by the type of Mid-level measure they address. If Marcella's Senior management issues a dictate that every sales department will cut other sales-driven expenses, Marcella will be able to show how she has helped the team with these expenses.

Marcella chose to create a series of value statements that highlight the additional revenue gained from her first improvement in her contract renewal new hire training intervention. Let's take a look at how Marcella's financial value statements were the same and how they were different for each level of her audience. Marcella's examples for the first changes she made to the contract renewal new hire program are shown in figure 13-3.

For Marcella, the examples in figure 13-3 are split into the four segments of the financial value statement. Notice that none of Marcella's value statements used input metrics or such metrics as the number of people who attended a particular training program. Business managers do not want to know how many people you had sitting through classes, they want to know what they got out of having them there! Marcella's value statements also did not rely on level 1 (reaction) or level 2 (learning) evaluation data. Marcella could have used this information at the Individual level, but because she was working with salespeople she chose to translate her numbers into percentages or monetary numbers that her audience would want to pay attention to.

The first four lines (lines 2–5) of Marcella's financial value statements are the same for each audience. Notice that these four lines plus her financial measures (line 9) give Marcella her value themes. Marcella can use the format in figure 13-3 for documenting both value themes and value statements in one place.

Figure 13-3. Marcella's sample value statements.

		SENIOR	MID	1ST/OPS	INDIVIDUAL
	I	**II**	**III**	**IV**	**V**
1	**PERFORMANCE VALUE**				
2	Period of Time	In the last 9 months	In the last 9 months	In the last 9 months	In the last 9 months
3	Intervention	Improvements in our contract consultant new hire training	Improvements in our contract consultant new hire training	Improvements in our contract consultant new hire training	Improvements in our contract consultant new hire training
4	Direction	Increased	Increased	Increased	Increased
5	Performance Measure	Our renewal revenue	Our renewal revenue	Our renewal revenue	Our renewal revenue
6	Amount of Change	By $64,800	By an average of $1,800 per team every month	By $800 per new hire each month	By $800 per new hire each month
7	**FINANCIAL VALUE (Thereby)**				
8	Direction	Increasing	Increasing	Increasing	
9	Financial Measure(s)	Our contribution profit margin	Our 6-month renewal revenue	Our average team revenue for our four teams	
10	Amount of Change	By 2.5 percent	By $43,200 and 9-month renewals by $64,800	By $1,800 per team every month	

(continued on page 194)

INTERVENTION: Contract Renewal New Hire Training

DATE: February 2002

Figure 13-3. Marcella's sample value statements (continued).

	I	SENIOR II	MID III	1ST/OPS IV	INDIVIDUAL V
11	**RELEVANT CONTEXT** *(Which Means)*				
12	Intervention	The new hire training improvements	The new hire training improvements	The new hire training improvements	Your new hire training program
13	Relevant Benefit or Impact	Are helping us offset the expected short-term loss in cash flow from our strategic initiative to convert our top 100 customers to new, more profitable contracts.	Are making it easier to achieve our total revenue goals while successfully converting our top 100 customers to the new contract format.	Are making it easier to achieve our total revenue goals while successfully converting our top 100 customers to the new contract format.	Makes it easier for you to be even more successful as you join our team.
14	**YOUR GOAL**				
15	What You Want	With additional funding,	With your reinforcement and communication,	With your reinforcement and communication,	With your dedication,
16	Why	We believe we can gain another $40,000 in improved revenue stream	We believe we can gain another $40,000 in improved revenue stream	We believe we can gain at least another $900 in improved revenue stream per team every month	We believe we can gain another $400 per month for each new consultant.
17	Period of Time	Over the next 9 months	Over the next 9 months	Over the next 9 months	Over the next 9 months
18	Next Step You Want Them to Take	May we arrange a meeting with you to discuss our proposal?	May we present our strategy to you and your team?	We'd like to gather data from your new consultants each month to make sure we are getting the additional revenue and to find out if there are opportunities to gain even more.	Once a month, we'll ask for feedback about how well the program is working for you. This will help us make the improvements that help you meet your quota.

Marcella is using benefits from the top half of her financial imperatives scorecard to help her create her financial value statements plus some other information she has collected about ABC MediCompany. The benefits section of Marcella's financial imperatives scorecard has been reproduced and enhanced in figure 13-4 to help you correlate the two figures.

The financial value statements that Marcella is creating are using

- ◆ financial value chains summarized by combining rows 1 and 2 from column I of the scorecard
- ◆ value add #1 information from columns III and IV, rows 1 and 2 of the scorecard
- ◆ projected numbers from value add #2 in columns V and VI, rows 1 and 2 of the scorecard
- ◆ the size of ABC MediCompany's contribution profit margin documented in chapter 4
- ◆ a little extra information that Marcella knew about the number of teams in the contract renewal department
- ◆ her knowledge of how the fiscal, product, and seasonal lifecycles worked for ABC MediCompany.

You'll see how Marcella made each of her calculations as you review her financial value statements in figure 13-4. To create financial value statements, Marcella could have used the benefits from any of her financial value chains that are reproduced in the benefit rows, or, as time went on, she could have used any benefits from each of her calculated value adds. Alternatively, Marcella could have used a summary of all of the benefits she had created in any value add by using figures at the bottom of her columns from her completed financial imperatives scorecard shown in chapter 9. Marcella could also have used a summary of all of the benefits she had created for any financial value chain by adding the time periods and figures across any of her rows. By tracking her value over time in her financial imperatives scorecard, Marcella has a very versatile tool to use when communicating her value.

Marcella has created four related value statements in figure 13-3, one for each of her Senior, Mid, 1st/Ops, and Individual audiences. Marcella has named her intervention (the contract renewal new hire training) at the top of her financial value statements. The date for these value statements is February 2002—the same date that Marcella documented for her baseline #2 in row 1, column III of her scorecard in figure 13-4.

For the performance value segment of her value statements, Marcella's period of time in row 2 reads, "in the last 9 months." Marcella transferred that period of time from the same column and row in her scorecard where she found

Figure 13-4. Marcella's completed financial imperatives scorecard.

INTERVENTION: Contract Renewal New Hire Training

BASIS: Monetary units = U.S. Dollars, Intervention units = Per New Hire, Time units = Per Month

	MEASURE / CATEGORY		VALUE ADD #1		VALUE ADD #2		VALUE ADD #3	
	I	II	III	IV	V	VI	VII	VIII
		Baseline #1 May 2001 (Before 1st change)	**Baseline #2** Feb 2002 (9 Months Later)	**Change** (x 9 New Hires x 9 Months)	**Baseline #3** Nov 2002 (9 Months Later)	**Change** (x 11 New Hire x 9 Months)	**Baseline #4** Aug 2003 (9 Months Later)	**Change** (x 10 New Hires x 1 time change when in training)
1	**Benefits** *(Senior Measure = Contribution Profit Margin)*	$10,000						
2	Individual Measure = Monthly Renewals *(1st/Ops = Team Renewals) (Mid = Six Month Renewal Revenue)*		$10,800 *(Additional $800 per new hire per month)*	$64,800	$11,275 *(Additional $475 per new hire per month)*	$47,025	$11,275 *($0 additional change)*	$0
3	Individual Measure = Lost Work Hours *(1st/Ops = Processing Cost Per Contract) (Mid = Cost of Goods/*	350	225 *(Savings of $125 per new hire per month)*	10,125	180 *(Savings of $55 per new hire per month)*	5,445	180 *($0 savings)*	0

BENEFITS

INTERVENTION: Contract Renewal New Hire Training

BASIS: Monetary units = U.S. Dollars, Intervention units = Per New Hire, Time units = Per Month

	MEASURE / CATEGORY	VALUE ADD #1			VALUE ADD #2		VALUE ADD #3	
	I	II	III	IV	V	VI	VII	VIII
BENEFITS 4	Individual Measure = Not Applicable (1st/Ops = Training Program Savings) (Mid = Cost of Goods/Services Sold)	0	0	0	0	0	510 ($510 per new hire, one time)	510
5	Individual Measure = Average Error Cost (1st/Ops = Team Error Cost) (Mid = Other Sales Driven Expenses)	500	445 (Savings of $55 per new hire, per month)	4,455	422 (Savings of $23 per new hire, per month)	2,277	422 ($0 savings)	0
6	**Total Gross Benefit**			$79,380		$54,747		$5,100
7	Divided by # of New Hires			9		11		10
8	**Benefit Per New Hire**		$980	$8,820	$553	$4,977	$510	$510

her date of February 2002. In row 3 (figure 13-3), Marcella has again named her intervention and used a direction verb of *increased* in row 4. Because all three of her potential performance measures for each of her audiences use a form of renewal revenue in their name, Marcella used a general form of her Individual measure (revenue) as her performance measure in row 5.

Marcella calculated the amount of change in row 6 to be the appropriate size for each of her audiences. For the Senior level, Marcella simply took the nine months of renewal revenue $64,800 directly from row 2, column IV of her financial imperatives scorecard.

For her Mid audience, Marcella needed to supply the amount of perform- ance at the 1st/Ops level. To convert her number to a 1st/Ops measure of monthly team renewals, Marcella had to know that there were four contract renewal teams. If the total improvement was $64,800 for nine months, shared by four teams, then the average improvement per team every month was $1,800:

$64,800 additional revenue ÷ 9 months ÷ 4 teams = $1,800 per team

To get the performance measure of the Individual to use for 1st/Ops and again for the Individual, Marcella used the notation she had made of $800 per consultant per new hire per month on row 2, column III of her scorecard.

In her financial value segment, Marcella repeated her use of the direction *increasing* in row 8, for each of her three audiences. Remember that the Individual level has only its own performance to refer to, so there is no financial value segment for that audience. Marcella selected her financial measures from the chains noted in her scorecard. Her Senior measure of contribution profit margin (CPM) is from row 1, column I of her scorecard. The Mid and 1st/Ops measures can be read from row 2, column 1 of her scorecard.

To calculate the percentage improvement to the CPM for her Senior audi- ence, Marcella took her amount of revenue change ($64,800), divided it by the size of ABC's latest CPM ($2,500,000) as was shown in chapter 4, and multi- plied the result by 100 to get a percentage.

$64,800 additional revenue ÷ $2,500,000 CPM × 100 = 2.5%

For her Mid-level audience members, Marcella pointed out the financial value to them in terms of their measure of six-month revenue and in terms of the total amount of revenue over the nine-month period. To convert the Mid-level financial measure to get the six-month number, Marcella took the additional $800 per new hire noted in row 2, column III of her scorecard, multiplied it by nine new hires (scorecard row 1, column IV), and then multiplied again by six months:

Marcella simply reused the calculation she performed to get the 1st/Ops performance value previously for the 1st/Ops financial measure on row 10, column IV of her value statements.

Marcella has tied her financial value statements to the relevant context of managing cash flow during the implementation of an initiative to switch customers to a new type of contract (lines 12–13). Marcella's quarterly context plan (see figure 11-3) shows that the first quarter of ABC's fiscal year is January through March.

This means that February—when Marcella is making her value claims—is the middle of the first quarter, the implementation quarter. The new initiative has two downsides in terms of cash flow. Although the new initiative is expected to increase revenues in the long-term, in the short-term it reduces cash flow for ABC MediCompany. In addition, the initiative is being kicked off during ABC's seasonal low in sales, putting even more strain on available cash. By tying the value of her changes to the new hire contract renewal program to the immediate urgent and important task of carrying out this initiative while minimizing the impacts on cash flow, Marcella has captured attention at each level of her audience. You can see in row 13 of figure 13-3 how Marcella customized her relevant benefit or impact for each level.

Marcella's goals can be seen in the last segment of her financial value statements (lines 15–18). On line 15, you can see that from Senior managers, Marcella is looking for additional funding. From Mid and 1st/Ops managers, Marcella wants reinforcement and communication. From the Individual contributors, Marcella seeks commitment and dedication to applying what they have learned from their training.

On line 16 Marcella has used a forecast or estimate of what she would achieve during the next nine months. Marcella originally made this estimate using figures that she tracked in row 2, columns V and VI, for value add #2 on an earlier version of her scorecard, not shown in this book. The numbers you see on the current scorecard are not exactly the same as Marcella's estimates because the scorecard example in figure 13-4 uses the actual numbers that Marcella created over a period of nearly three years. But, you can see that Marcella's original estimates in her value statements were not far off from what actually occurred. Marcella used $40,000 in row 16 for her Senior and Mid value statements, which roughly corresponds to the figure of $47,025 in row 2, column VI of her scorecard (see figure 13-4). Marcella used a similar calculation as she did previously to come up with the average team improvement number for 1st/Ops. For the individual number, she used a notation of $400 from a forecast that is roughly similar to the notation you can see in row 2, column V of Marcella's scorecard.

Marcella used the same period of time—the next nine months—for all of her audiences. Marcella then chose the next step that she would like each audience to take. For the Senior-level manager, Marcella would like a meeting to discuss a proposal for the funding with him. For the Mid-level manager, Marcella would like to present her strategy to the manager and his staff. From the staff, Marcella would like to get support to gather data for her next improvement. From Individuals, Marcella would like their support to give her the data she needs.

Can You Make Value Statements in 30 Seconds or Less?

Each of Marcella's value statements packs a great deal of information into a short format. When delivered at a confident presentation pace, suitable for Senior or other executives, it is possible to make your value statements in under 30 seconds.

Practice before you try using a financial value statement for the first time. Initially, though, you may feel awkward, and you may forget a piece or two. Making these kinds of statements become easier with time. The point is to begin practicing your new skill so that it becomes second nature.

Be prepared to be interrupted with questions about how you arrived at your conclusions. That's great! Questions show that your audience is listening. But, you must be prepared if your audience needs additional information. The types of questions you will get vary depending on whether your intervention is perceived as an unknown expectation (delight), a conscious expectation (a negotiable), or is unconsciously taken for granted (a given).

With the give and take of a normal conversation, you may not make it through to your relevant context or your goal on the first try. You will be prepared, however, to make urgent and important connections and to state your goal as the moment becomes available.

Other Ways to Use Your Financial Value Statements

You've examined financial value statements from the perspective of using them in conversations. Don't overlook how powerful this format can be when included in presentations, memos, letters, executive summaries, and full reports. Putting your financial value statements into a variety of formats reinforces your message and helps your audience recognize your value that much quicker.

Documenting your financial value statements, financial value chains, and scorecards can have other benefits. One of the hardest things to do is to go back and re-create the data to support a great story. It's not always easy to decide how to tell that story. Applying the discipline to track this kind of data can make it easier to apply for grants, awards, or certifications in the future. Social proof is another powerful way to earn credibility. For external consultants and for professionals internal to an organization who are so inclined, applying this type of discipline makes it much easier to support articles, case studies, or professional presentations.

Many readers will have recognized that the format for financial value statements is very similar to the format that many career counselors advise their clients to use when communicating their value in resumes, cover letters, networking conversations, and interviews. Financial value statements can also make it easier for others to write powerful letters of recommendation for you. As you create and update your value statements, don't forget to update one of the most important places that you can use to communicate your value—your résumé.

Finally, if you are external to an organization, your financial value statements can go a long way to helping you with sales. Working on sales is not only important when you are trying to sell a customer for the first time. It is also important to keep selling your value as you meet with more people up and down the organization's financial value chain and as you deliver the service you have contracted for.

If you are having trouble getting in the front door, you might check out Anthony Parinello's book *Selling to VITO: The Very Important Top Officer,* which is listed in the Additional Resources section. Parinello focuses on the top officers of an organization, for sales across all industries. His techniques are not applicable to all audiences that a WLP professional must deal with every day, nor does it describe how to evaluate or make connections from a specific performance intervention to a financial number. Parinello does, however, offer some excellent tips and techniques for using statements somewhat similar to the financial value statements in this book to get meetings with high-level executives.

Creating Your Own Financial Value Statements

You've worked hard throughout this book to create financial value chains, analyze perceptions, document contexts, create a financial imperative scorecard, and write value themes. Take a moment now to leverage all of that work and complete your own financial value statements in exercise 13-1.

Exercise 13-1. Your value statements.

 Directions: Completing this exercise completes your work on step 11 of the financial value process: create value statements. If you prefer not to write in this book, go to the companion Website (www.astd.org/astd/publications) to download a PowerPoint file for this exercise.

1. Write the name of your intervention in the first line labeled "intervention."
2. Date your value statements on the second line.
3. For your performance value segment, fill in the period of time, the intervention, your direction verb, performance measure, and amount of change as is meaningful for each of your audiences. Go back to your financial imperatives scorecard exercise from chapter 9 to get the information you need.
4. For your financial value segment, fill in your direction verb, financial measure, and amount of change. Once again, your financial imperatives scorecard will be very helpful to you, as will other information you have gathered from your business intelligence research on financial statements or on other details about your organization.
5. For your relevant context, make sure you have your quarterly context plan available. Fill in the name of the intervention and then create your relevant benefit or impact based on the fiscal, product, or seasonal lifecycles of your organization and what is urgent and important for your audience to pay attention to today.
6. For your goal segment, write down what you want from each audience and why that is important using estimates, forecasts, or any other data you may have. Fill in the period of time in which you would like your audience to take action, and then write down the next step you want that audience to take.

INTERVENTION:					
DATE:					
		SENIOR	MID	1ST/OPS	INDIVIDUAL
	I	II	III	IV	V
1	PERFORMANCE VALUE				
2	Period of Time				
3	Intervention				
4	Direction				
5	Performance Measure				
6	Amount of Change				
7	FINANCIAL VALUE (Thereby)				
8	Direction				
9	Financial Measure(s)				
10	Amount of Change				

(continued on page 204)

| | | SENIOR | MID | 1ST/OPS | INDIVIDUAL |
	I	II	III	IV	V
11	RELEVANT CONTEXT (Which Means)				
12	Intervention				
13	Relevant Benefit or Impact				
14	YOUR GOAL				
15	What You Want				
16	Why				
17	Period of Time				
18	Next Step You Want Them to Take				

LET'S REVIEW:

- This chapter completes step 11 in the financial value process: create value statements.

- Financial value statements leverage the general value themes that you created in the last chapter. The exercise for creating financial value statements can also be used to document your themes.

- Value statements have four segments: the performance value, the financial value, the relevant context, and your goal.

- The performance value segment begins the translation from the language of performance to the language of finance by describing the period of time in which you have made an improvement for your target organization, what intervention created the change, a performance measure, the direction in which you moved that measure, and the amount of change that you created.

- The financial value segment translates the change in performance into the language of finance. This segment uses the same or a new direction verb depending on what is appropriate for the financial measure that the change in performance will be connected to. The financial segment translates the amount of performance change into an amount of change for the financial measure.

- After the general translation of value from performance into finance is accomplished, the relevant context segment makes sure that your audience cares to hear about your value right now. The relevant context segment ties your value statement to the urgent and important tasks based on the fiscal, product, and seasonal lifecycles of an organization.

- Finally, your goal segment describes what you want now, why you want it, when you want your audience to take action, and what action you want the audience to take to help you create even more value.

- The information in each of your four segments is based on your business intelligence research into your organization and its financial imperatives, on your financial value chains, your financial imperatives scorecard, and your quarterly context plan.

- Having a goal is critically important to your business stature and to gaining a seat at the table. Executives expect you to ask for what you need. They will not know unless you tell them. Goals also create self-confidence and build influence by gaining commitments from others.

◆ A series of value statement examples for Marcella at ABC MediCompany was discussed and reviewed. It was demonstrated where and how Marcella got the data contained in her value statements.

◆ Financial value statements are a concise way to convey a great deal of information very quickly. Be prepared with additional information if your audience has questions for you. The types of questions you'll get depend on how your audience perceives the value of your intervention.

◆ Financial value statements can help you with memos, presentations, reports, and marketing. They can be very helpful as documentation for case studies, articles, or industry awards as well as on your résumé and during a job search. External consultants will find them helpful in sales.

You've worked hard to understand and complete the steps in the financial value process. You're almost through a full turn on your flywheel. It's time to review your plan and make sure that everything is working together smoothly. Your next turn through the flywheel will go much more quickly when it is based on a solid foundation, and the turns after that will spin faster than you imagine. One more chapter to adjust your plans . . . .

Putting It All Together

 IN THIS CHAPTER:

♦ The final stage in the financial value process, step 12: communicate and refine
♦ Pointers to examples, chapters, exercises, and checklists on the CD and on the companion Website (www.astd.org/astd/publications)
♦ A full set of checklists for each step to help you refine your communication plan
♦ Some reasons to make sure this step becomes a habit.

Excellent! You've completed the first 11 steps in the financial value process. You've broken the value code and learned to identify, position, deliver, measure, and communicate value from your audience's perspective. Now it is time to complete step 12 of the financial value process. As you go through the work of identifying, positioning, delivering, measuring, and planning your value communication, your own insights plus changes in the world around you will necessitate periodic adjustments to your plan. Your communication needs to reflect these changes.

A Seat at the Table

The goal of this book is to help you get a seat at the table. That way, you can stop feeling like you are an expendable part of the organization and start attaining a position of respect and being in control of your destiny. To help you along the way, you needed to know a few facts about what is important to the decision makers in your organization (or your target organization), how to present what you do to these decision makers in an understandable and ROI-driven manner, and a value communication plan.

In this chapter, you'll review each step, work through checklists of questions about how you can refine your plan, and complete the book with the familiarity, comfort, and confidence to communicate your value in a way that your audience will appreciate and understand. In other words, when you are finished with this book, the "Showing Your Value" folder on your desk should be complete and ready to put into action!

Is This Last Step Really Necessary?

An important key to successful retention and a deeper understanding of what has been learned is the ability to experiment with the learning and then to step back, reflect, and adjust what has been learned to better fit your needs. You've spent a lot of time looking at the individual pieces, parts, and steps necessary to communicate value.

In the introduction to this book, you read about the concept of pushing a flywheel to generate momentum and power. As you work through each individual piece, the first few turns through the flywheel can feel slow and arduous. Over time, the more turns you complete and more people you can get to push the flywheel with you, the faster you pick up speed and the more momentum you create to carry you forward in the service of your people. Reflection and adjustment creates deeper learning and helps you gain the strength to push your flywheel harder and faster.

Even more important, organizations are dynamic, changing places. Your organization may have significantly changed even as you were working through this book. Perhaps a key member of your audience has changed jobs. His or her successor might have a very different perception about the WLP interventions within the organization. Perhaps a new competitor has launched an exciting new product, creating a serious threat to your own organization's revenues. Or, perhaps the financial imperatives you originally identified have simply become even more critical because other initiatives in the organization are not going as well as planned and that is straining the organization's resources.

In chapter 1, you read about the results of the Twin Cities study of what executives were looking for from human asset professionals. Your executives want you to think more like a general manager or a salesperson and to think strategically rather than tactically. To be successful with top executives, salespeople must be alert for changes that affect their customers. Salespeople must be able to adjust their advice and recommendations immediately to reflect those changes. For general managers to think strategically means that they must also have the ability to scan the horizon and adjust actions within their own departments to help the organization stay on track. All these performers have the ability to adjust action in motion so that they continue to create optimum value every day. The final step in the financial value process is to create a frequent habit of reviewing and adjusting your value communication so that you are always bringing the optimal value to your executives and your organization.

The Financial Value Process

In figure 14-1, you can see the steps in the financial value process. In this chapter, the review of each step will cover the goals and basic principles for that step. If you would like to update your work on any of the exercises in this book, you'll find handy references to the CD and Website to help you find the forms you need. The checklists (also available on the CD and Website) will ask you questions to help you adjust your work on the exercises. The checklists are meant to trigger new ideas for how, where, or when you can communicate with more effectiveness.

Step 1: Define Audience

There are two communication goals addressed in step 1. The first goal is to identify with whom you should be communicating. The second goal is to identify the timeframe that each person in your audience is measured on to create value for the organization. This is the timeframe that they want to hear from you when you are communicating about the value you have brought to them.

To achieve these goals, you need to organize your audiences within the framework of financial value chains. Financial value chains consist of Senior, Mid, 1st/Ops, and Individual levels. Look at the names and positions of the people you want to communicate value to. Look also at their timeframes within the perspective of how the economy affects the urgency for results.

One of the fundamental tenets of the financial value process is that the people in your audience will not translate what your value means to them, or if they try to translate it is likely that they will not reach the same conclusion that you would like them to reach. To be successful in your value communication, you need to make sure you make important translations for them.

Exercise and Examples. Chapter 2 provides some examples of audience and time-frame definitions. The exercise and form for this step are at the end of that chapter in exercise 2-1. If you prefer not to write in this book, or if you'd like
 to print out larger versions or multiple copies of exercises and forms, you can find a complete set of all forms on the CD or on the companion Website (www.astd.org/astd/publications).

Figure 14-1. The flywheel of the financial value process.

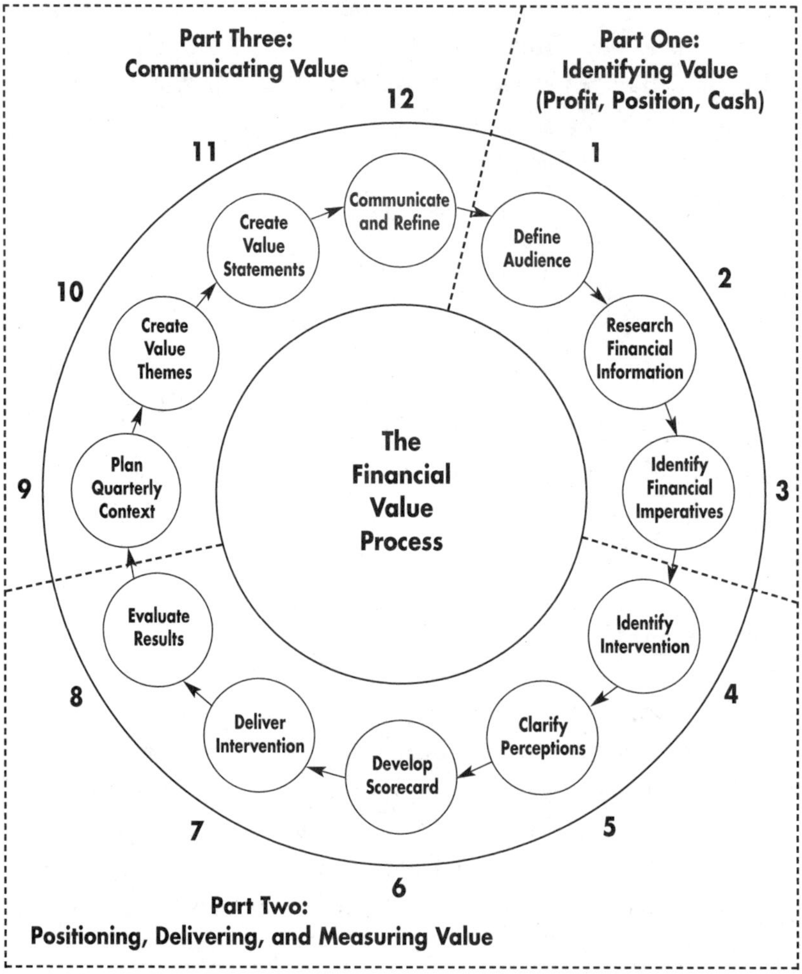

Checklist. Use the step 1 checklist to see if there are any ways that you can improve the definition of your audience. If you need help to complete any of the questions on this checklist, please review the concepts and exercise in chapter 2.

Step 2: Research Financial Information

Step 2 encompasses both a primary goal and a secondary goal. The primary goal is to identify what forms of business intelligence are most helpful to you so that you can gather them. The secondary goal is to keep a steady stream of updated intelligence flowing to you with minimal effort.

Step 1 Checklist. Define audience.

 If you prefer not to write in this book, or if you'd like to print out a larger versions or multiple copies of exercises and forms, you can find a complete set of all forms on the CD or on the companion Website (www.astd.org/astd/publications).

			Yes	No
Your Audience	1.	Have you identified the titles of the people who make up all four levels of your audience? *If not, make sure you know with whom you need to communicate at each level of your organization.*	☐	☐
	2.	Do you know their names? *If not, make the effort to find out. It will make your communication more personal, and you may be able to find out more about how to approach a key person if you know his or her name.*	☐	☐
	3.	Have you checked your list with at least one other knowledgeable person for insights or suggestions? *If not, then check with another consultant or with your manager. Another consultant may see things you have missed, and you should never surprise your manager about your communications to others in your organization.*	☐	☐
	4.	Have any key members for any of your audiences changed since you created your original value chains? *If yes, take the time now to update your chains.*	☐	☐
Multiple Audiences	5.	Do you have multiple audiences (e.g., the same titles but in different divisions or departments or different audiences based on the fiscal, product, or seasonal lifecycles you learned about in chapter 11)? *If yes, begin your financial chains for each of these audiences by completing exercise 2-1.*	☐	☐
Timeframes	6.	Have you verified the timeframes that each level of your audience(s) needs to hear about when you communicate value? *If not, get feedback from others to make sure you understand the perspective of each level of your audience. If you've ever wanted to ask for mentoring from a Senior manager but didn't know how to structure the conversation, you could show him or her the financial value process and ask for input on audiences, timeframes, or other parts of your communication plan.*	☐	☐
Translation	7.	Is anyone in your audience still acting as if you are just not getting it when they ask you about value? Could you still be forcing any level of audience to translate what your value means to them? *If yes, double-check that you have correctly matched your audiences to the best level, timeframes, or measures. See the review on measures under step 3.*	☐	☐

The amount of information available to you varies, depending on whether you are internal or external to an organization. It also varies according to the level of audience you are researching. It is critical to perform research because you must understand what the most important financial priorities are for your target organization to know how to position, deliver, and communicate the most value.

Make sure you give yourself enough time to locate the information you need and to get others into the habit of supplying you with new information regularly. Enlist the help of others and make sure to give them enough time to learn that you are trustworthy and will keep information confidential.

Exercise and Examples. Examples of business intelligence research and a case study of how one consultant managed the task can be found in chapter 7. The exercise and form for this step are at the end of that chapter in exercise 7-1. If you prefer not to write in this book, or if you'd like to print out larger versions or multiple copies of exercises and forms, you can find a complete set of all forms on the CD or on the companion Website (www.astd .org/astd/publications).

Checklist. Use the step 2 checklist to see if there are any ways that you can improve your financial information research. If you need help to complete any of the questions on this checklist, please see the concepts and exercise in chapter 7.

Step 3: Identify Financial Imperatives

The measures and concerns of the Senior management of an organization will drive the measures and focus of everyone else in that organization. Senior managers must manage three fundamental types of financial priorities, as well as the balance between them. These priorities are profit, position, and cash. Collectively, these priorities are known as the financial imperatives of Senior managers. The goal of step 3 is to help you document what measures are of the most concern to your Senior managers and then help you translate those measures through the financial value chains of an organization directly to the value of your intervention.

Profit is calculated by taking the revenues of an organization and subtracting out the expenses required to run that organization. An organization tracks and reports its profit on its income statement. There are several ways to draw financial value chains based on the different profit lines or expense lines shown on the income statement.

Position is the amount of assets versus the amount of liabilities and owner's equity an organization maintains in order to make its profit. Position is tracked and reported in the organization's balance sheet. The organization needs to always maintain a solid position of being able to repay any debt that

Step 2 Checklist. *Research financial information.*

 If you prefer not to write in this book, or if you'd like to print out larger versions or multiple copies of exercises and forms, you can find a complete set of all forms on the CD or on the companion Website (www.astd.org/astd/publications).

			Yes	No
Information by Audience Level	1.	Do you have a copy of the most recent basic financial information for your organization: the income statement, balance sheet, and cash flow statement? Have you read them? *If not, update your copies and analyze them for changes.*	☐	☐
	2.	Have you double-checked the external and internal business intelligence lists (shown in chapter 7) to make sure you are gathering enough information for each level of your audience? *If not, try selecting at least one new type of business intelligence to gather to expand your knowledge base.*	☐	☐
	3.	Have you asked others for suggestions for sources for any other business intelligence that might be helpful to you? *If not, then check with others in your organization, with your manager, or with others in your industry.*	☐	☐
	4.	Have you created a list of business intelligence questions and scheduled informal networking meetings or phone calls to find answers? *If not, take the time now write down some of the questions that you cannot find answers for, pick up the phone, and schedule a lunch date. Even if the person you ask to lunch cannot give you the answers, he or she can often introduce you to someone else who may have a powerful influence on your career.*	☐	☐
Gathering Information with Minimal Effort	5.	Do you have a regular schedule for collecting and updating your information once a month or once a quarter? *If not, then schedule some time in advance on your calendar. This can go a long way to keeping your value proactive instead of reactive.*	☐	☐
	6.	Have you gotten yourself on regular distribution lists or subscribed to useful industry reports so that information automatically comes to you? *If not, consider automating some of your intelligence gathering.*	☐	☐
Confidentiality	7.	Are you scrupulous in maintaining the confidentiality of the information you receive? *If not, people may be withholding information from you because they are unsure how, when, or with whom you will share sensitive information.*	☐	☐

it may have incurred to earn its revenues. Too much debt, or leverage, places the organization in a risky financial position that could collapse under adverse business conditions. There are also multiple financial value chains that can be connected to assets, liabilities, or owner's equity.

Senior managers must manage the relative size of each asset, liability, or owner's equity item to ensure they maintain an optimal balance and enough return for their efforts. Balance is calculated by using ratios—the comparison of one item of profit, expense, assets, liabilities, or equity to another. Operating ratios tell a Senior manager if the organization's day-to-day activities are staying within acceptable boundaries. Financial ratios tell a Senior manager if the organization is maintaining the appropriate returns for its efforts. Financial value chains can use a ratio as the Senior manager measure in a financial value chain.

Maintaining cash on hand is the third financial imperative of Senior managers. It is important to understand that profit does not equal cash. Profit can be tied up in non-liquid assets or, in other words, in forms like accounts receivable that are not necessarily easy to collect and spend. Cash is analogous to the oil in a car's engine. If an engine ever runs out of oil, even for an instant, the engine can be heavily damaged or destroyed. Running out of cash can damage or destroy the organization. Senior managers must ensure that the organization generates enough cash from ongoing revenues to sustain the organization long-term. Cash is tracked and reported on the cash flow statement. Financial value chains can use cash or another cash measure as the senior management starting point for financial value chains.

This book uses a fictitious company, ABC MediCompany to demonstrate basic concepts for profit, position, cash, and balance.

Exercise and Examples. Examples of financial measures and financial value chains for profit, position, and cash can be found in chapters 4, 5, and 6. The exercises and forms for this step are at the end of each chapter in exercises 4-1, 5-1, and 6-1. If you prefer not to write in this book, or if you'd like

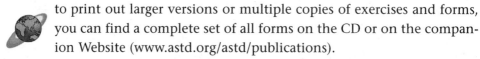 to print out larger versions or multiple copies of exercises and forms, you can find a complete set of all forms on the CD or on the companion Website (www.astd.org/astd/publications).

Checklist. Use the step 3 checklist to see if there are any ways that you can improve your knowledge of your organization's financial imperatives or improve the financial value chains you create to translate your value into the measures that each level of your audience cares most about. If you need help to complete any of the questions on this checklist, please see concepts and figures in chapter 3, 4, 5, or 6.

Step 3 Checklist. Identify financial imperatives

 If you prefer not to write in this book, or if you'd like to print out larger versions or multiple copies of exercises and forms, you can find a complete set of all forms on the CD or on the companion Website (www.astd.org/astd/publications).

			Yes	No
Profit/Position/Cash	1.	Have you verified that you are focused on the most important measures for your organization? *If not and you are internal to an organization, sit down with your manager, someone in the line organization that you support, or someone from the finance department to discuss what is important to your organization.* *If not and you are external to your target organization, either invite someone from that organization or industry to lunch with you or at least have a colleague review your logic as you show him or her how you arrived at your conclusions.*	☐	☐
	2.	Have you considered whether your intervention helps multiple profit, position, or cash measures? *If not, perhaps you can add more power to your value communication by creating more financial value chains for your intervention.*	☐	☐
	3.	Have you continued to learn more beyond the basic financial measures described in this book? *If not, ask someone in your finance department what he or she would recommend that you know. Or, spend more time on stock investment or industry Websites to pick up the financial terms that might be common in your industry, but unfamiliar to you.*	☐	☐
	4.	If you cannot find profit, position, or cash information for your target organization, have you created potential profit, position, or cash value chains for comparable organizations? *If not, try looking up information on your target organization's competitors and analyzing their organizations. The information may help you show your target organization how to beat its competition with help from your services.*	☐	☐
Balance	5.	Have you calculated operating or financial ratios for your organization? *If not, try calculating a few. It may give you fresh insights that you can use when communicating financial value.*	☐	☐
	6.	Have you calculated operating or financial ratios for the organizations considered best in class in your industry? *If not, these ratios may give you ideas about the standards your Senior management must live up to in order to stay competitive.*	☐	☐

Step 4: Identify Intervention and Step 5: Clarify Perceptions

It is assumed that WLP professionals will use the best industry methods available to select, design, and produce interventions that bring the most value to the organization at every opportunity. Step 4 is not about how to select or design the intervention you wish to deliver. It is about *focusing your communication* on a chosen intervention. Step 4 asks you to choose an intervention to apply the remainder of the financial value process toward in your communication plan.

Now that you have chosen the intervention for which you will apply the remainder of the financial value process, step 5 asks you to examine the perception of your chosen intervention from the perspective of your audience. The perception of your intervention will be somewhere on a continuum of an unknown expectation (a surprise), a conscious expectation (a negotiable), or an unconscious expectation (a given). When your audience estimates the value you bring to an organization, they are often so delighted with the surprise that they rate the value very highly. They are less enthusiastic about negotiables because their value is already expected. Your audience is often extremely harsh in their estimate of the value of a given because the value is no longer apparent. The perception of your audience affects how easily they accept your claim of value.

Interventions will always slide from surprise to negotiable to given if their value is left unmanaged. Many WLP professionals work with a large majority of what they do in an invisible or given state. Because WLP expenses are easier to cut than many fixed expenses, you need to work diligently to keep the majority of your interventions in surprise or negotiable status.

Exercise and Examples. A more complete discussion of these steps as well as the introduction to a case study about an internal WLP professional working at ABC MediCompany can be found in chapter 8. The exercise and form for this step are at the end of that chapter in exercise 8-1. If you prefer not to write in this book, or if you'd like to print out larger versions or multiple copies of 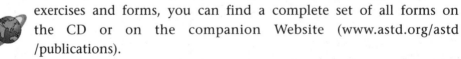 exercises and forms, you can find a complete set of all forms on the CD or on the companion Website (www.astd.org/astd /publications).

Checklist. Use the steps 4 and 5 checklist to check the intervention you have chosen and your audience's perceptions about it. If you need help to complete any of the questions on this checklist, please see concepts and exercise in chapter 8.

Step 4 and 5 Checklist. Identify intervention and clarify perceptions.

 If you prefer not to write in this book, or if you'd like to print out larger versions or multiple copies of exercises and forms, you can find a complete set of all forms on the CD or on the companion Website (www.astd.org/astd/publications).

			Yes	No
Identify Intervention	1.	If you have a choice about the intervention you are communicating value for, have you chosen one that will create surprise and delight, or is most closely aligned with Senior management's top priorities? *If not, consider focusing on a different intervention or adding another intervention to your communication plans.*	☐	☐
	2.	Do you feel you will be able to reasonably forecast (estimate) numbers for the value of your intervention and reasonably measure (evaluate) the impact of the intervention later? *If you do not feel you can estimate or gather good enough numbers, seriously consider another intervention.*	☐	☐
	3.	Is the timing right for this intervention? Will you be able to begin work or show value in the needed timeframe? *If not, is there a way to change your schedule or choose another intervention?*	☐	☐
	4.	Have you checked others' opinions about the suitability of this intervention? *If not, take the time to include others in your plans. It will gain support for you later.*	☐	☐
Clarify Perceptions	5.	Perceptions shift over time. Have you checked the perception of your intervention with each level of your audience lately? *If not, then make some time to talk informally with your clients or line managers about how you can increase the perception of your intervention in their department or organization.*	☐	☐
	6.	Has there been a significant change in your audience? *If yes, then check the perceptions of your new audience members and adjust your timing, message, or delivery to accommodate them.*	☐	☐
	7.	Are you prepared to work harder to defend what would happen if you didn't have an intervention that is perceived as being in the given state? *If not, consider choosing another intervention that is perceived as a surprise or negotiable.*	☐	☐

Step 6: Develop Scorecard

To be able to state the amount of value you will bring or have already brought to an organization with your intervention, you will need to keep track of your numbers in a consistent, easy-to-read fashion. The scorecard you develop during step 6 can help you with this task.

Chapter 9 introduces the financial imperatives scorecard. The format consists of some basic scorecard heading information, plus benefits, costs, and totals. The names of the benefits on your scorecard are transferred directly from your financial value chains. Each time you change or improve your intervention is an opportunity to add more value to your organization. Each significant change on your scorecard is tracked with a set of columns called a value add. Your costs for each value add are tracked along with your benefits. You'll calculate totals for each value add that you create.

When working with scorecards, never present costs without corresponding benefits, keep your scorecards up-to-date, capture the data right away, be ethical by tracking the obvious and being consistent, and be conservative with your numbers. These rules will make the process easier and maintain a precious thing—your credibility.

Exercise and Examples. A more complete discussion of how to complete a scorecard, as well as a detailed walkthrough of a completed scorecard for our fictitious character Marcella can be found in chapter 9. The exercise and form for this step are at the end of that chapter in exercise 9-1. If you prefer not to write in this book, or if you'd like to print out larger versions or multiple copies of exercises and forms, you can find a complete set of all forms on the CD or on the companion Website (www.astd.org/astd /publications).

Checklist. Use the step 6 checklist to review your financial imperatives scorecard. If you need help to complete any of the questions on this checklist, please review the concepts and exercise in chapter 9.

Step 7: Deliver Intervention and Step 8: Evaluate Results

Step 7 is a step that many WLP professionals are very comfortable with. It is assumed that the WLP professional will use the best industry methods available to make sure his or her intervention is delivered to the highest standards. Step 7 exists to mark the point where a critical threshold is crossed in the minds of your audience. Up to this point, you could talk about the value that you were planning for. Now you must talk about what you actually accomplished. From this point forward, you must invest the effort to evaluate your results.

Step 6 Checklist. Develop scorecard.

 If you prefer not to write in this book, or if you'd like to print out larger versions or multiple copies of exercises and forms, you can find a complete set of all forms on the CD or on the companion Website (www.astd.org/astd/publications).

			Yes	No
Top of Scorecard	1.	Have you used monetary, intervention, and time units that your audience will understand? *If not, how can you change your units or describe the units you are using so that your audience will quickly understand that what you are tracking matters to it?*	☐	☐
Benefits	2.	Have you included all of the benefits that you can reasonably claim your intervention brings to the organization? *If not, consider adding them to your scorecard. Even small increments can add up over time.*	☐	☐
	3.	Are you updating your benefits frequently enough? *If not, schedule the time to make sure your numbers are always up-to-date. Ask your manager for help if you are tracking something for his or her department.*	☐	☐
	4.	Are you using a conservative, documented, industry-standard approach for your estimation, evaluation, and measurement? *If not, repair your numbers now. Conservative numbers maintain your credibility. Once gone, credibility is very difficult to get back.*	☐	☐
	5.	Are you keeping detailed notes of any assumptions or extra data you used to calculate your numbers? *If not, write down your notes. This information is very hard to remember or re-create later.*	☐	☐
Costs	6.	Have you consistently and conservatively included all costs that your intervention creates for the organization? *If not, do so now. This is much better than having anyone in your audience ask you about a cost you have not considered. If this happens, expect at least some damage to your credibility.*	☐	☐
	7.	Are you updating your costs frequently enough? *If not, schedule the time to make sure your numbers are always up-to-date. Ask your manager for help if you are tracking something for his or her department.*	☐	☐

(continued on page 220)

Step 6 Checklist. Develop scorecard (continued).

			Yes	No
Totals	8.	Are you keeping detailed notes of any assumptions or extra data you used to calculate your costs? *If not, take down some notes. This information is very hard to remember accurately later.*	☐	☐
	9.	Have you calculated your total net benefit, benefit-to-cost ratio, and ROI correctly? *If not, double-check. Some members of your audience will check your calculations to verify your claims to value.*	☐	☐

It is also assumed that as a WLP professional, you will use the most appropriate, industry-standard evaluation techniques to verify the value that you have brought to the organization. Because this book is about communication, step 8 focuses on mapping types of evaluation data to the types of data each level of your audience needs to hear. In this book, the mapping of evaluation data to the levels of your audience is based on the evaluation models of Kirkpatrick and Phillips.

Individuals need levels 1 and 2 evaluation data. 1st/Ops needs level 3 data, and Mid needs levels 4 and 5 evaluation data. Senior managers need level 5 data until they are satisfied that ROI can be reliably proven. At that point, level 5 data becomes a given for them, and they are most interested in knowing how you will optimize performance in terms of penetration, sustainability, and speed.

Exercise and Examples. For a discussion of crossing the threshold and for a full explanation of matching value and the levels of evaluation, please see chapter 10. The exercise and form for step 8 appear at the end of that chapter in exercise 8-1. (There is no exercise for step 7.) If you prefer not to write in this book, or if you'd like to print out larger versions or multiple copies of exercises and forms, you can find a complete set of all forms on the CD or on the companion Website (www.astd.org/astd/publications).

Checklist. Use the steps 7 and 8 checklist to document any special circumstances about your delivery and to ensure you have the appropriate levels of evaluation data for each level of your audience. If you need help to complete this checklist, please look back at the concepts and exercise in chapter 10.

Steps 7 and 8 Checklist. Deliver intervention and evaluate results.

 If you prefer not to write in this book, or if you'd like to print out larger versions or multiple copies of exercises and forms, you can find a complete set of all forms on the CD or on the companion Website (www.astd.org/astd/publications).

			Yes	No
Deliver Intervention	1.	Did you have any special circumstances during your delivery that will positively or negatively affect your ability to provide value? *If yes, document what happened. It may help you explain any numbers that are different from what you originally expected.*	☐	☐
Evaluating Your Interventions	2.	Level 1 (smile sheet) data is easy to gather. Do you know how to gather level 2, 3, 4, or 5 evaluation data? *If not, then grab some books or schedule a class. Knowing how to get the necessary types of evaluation data, and then doing it, is critical to your career success.*	☐	☐
	3.	Are you gathering and using the appropriate level of evaluation for each level of your audience? *If not, then step back and adjust the types of data you are using to avoid either leaving out necessary information or creating the too-much-information syndrome.*	☐	☐
Strategic Planning	4.	Do you know where you want to optimize the impact from your interventions? Have you created a strategic plan to enhance penetration, sustainability, or speed? *If not, remember that your Senior managers want you to think strategically. Now is the time to dream, brainstorm, get creative, and get it down on paper so you'll have your goals ready when the time comes to make your value statements.*	☐	☐

Step 9: Plan Quarterly Context

The goal of step 9 is to make sure that you not only communicate value, but that your audience wants to pay attention to that value right now. That is accomplished by tying your value to an urgent and important, or relevant context of today.

What is urgent and important for today follows a predictable pattern. That pattern is driven primarily by the quarterly fiscal lifecycle. The behavior of your audience is predictable within the implementation, validation, vision-setting, and budgeting quarters of the year. Urgent and important activities can also be driven by the new product introduction lifecycle and seasonal sales lifecycles of an organization.

Communicating value is even more effective when others communicate your value for you. By mapping your quarterly context to specific dates, you can plan to have your value statements in front of the right people at the right time to show how you have helped them do an even better job. This is news they'll want to share with others, because it helps them look good too.

Exercise and Example. To read more about relevant context and fiscal, new product, and seasonal sales lifecycles, please see chapter 11. The exercise and form for step 9 is in exercise 11-1. If you prefer not to write in this book, or if you'd 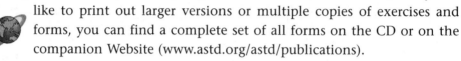 like to print out larger versions or multiple copies of exercises and forms, you can find a complete set of all forms on the CD or on the companion Website (www.astd.org/astd/publications).

Checklist. Use the step 9 checklist to verify that you have taken full advantage of all relevant contexts for each level of your audience. If you need help to complete any of the questions on this checklist, please see the concepts and exercise presented in chapter 11.

Step 10: Create Value Themes and Step 11: Create Value Statements

The purpose of step 10 is to help you create concise, powerful communication about your value.

Value themes are a form of general value communication. Value statements give more detailed information about the value you bring to an organization. Both value themes and value statements translate from the language of performance to the language of finance by choosing a performance measure and a financial measure from a financial value chain. Value themes rely on either a specific performance measure or a generic base driver for the performance such as time, a count, or money. Value themes are used when a general value claim is appropriate as a descriptor in conversations, memos, brochures, or other media.

Value statements have four segments: performance value, financial value (*thereby*), relevant context (*which means*), and your goal. Value statements pull information from your financial value chains, financial imperatives scorecard, financial statements, evaluation data, and quarterly context plans. Value statements are customized to meet the needs of each level of your audience. In addition to communicating your value, the goal segment of your value statement is critical to helping to build your influence.

Exercise and Examples. For value theme and value statement examples and discussion, please see chapters 12 and 13. The exercise and form for step 10 is in exercise 12-1. The exercise and form for step 11 is in exercise 13-1. If you

---

Step 9 Checklist. Plan quarterly context.

 If you prefer not to write in this book, or if you'd like to print out larger versions or multiple copies of exercises and forms, you can find a complete set of all forms on the CD or on the companion Website (www.astd.org/astd/publications).

			Yes	No
Fiscal Context	1.	Are you stuck in the position of implementing someone else's initiative to improve the profit, position, or cash of the organization? It's easier to prove value if you are driving your own initiative. Have you proposed a separate WLP initiative that could stand on its own to improve a financial imperative? *If not, now's the time to do your research and lay out your plan on the fiscal calendar so that you'll be able to be at the right place at the right time to ask for what you want.*	☐	☐
	2.	Have you had someone else review your relevant context segments to give you coaching, hints, or feedback? *If not, get someone you trust to give you some honest feedback so that you make sure you have the most powerful connections possible.*	☐	☐
	3.	Have you adjusted your relevant context segments or dates to account for unexpected financial circumstances that may have arisen in your organization? *If not, take the time to write down a few context segments for your value statements and practice them.*	☐	☐
Product Context	4.	Have you estimated how much a new product introduction might be costing your organization in short-term revenue or in cash flow, and have you figured out a way to train salespeople, customer service engineers, or others to bring in revenues faster or cut costs more efficiently? *If not, then get your calculator out and spend some time making rough estimates of how much you could help revenues, costs, short-term liabilities, inventory, cash, or other financial items during a new product introduction.*	☐	☐
	5.	Are you able to increase revenues or cut costs for an existing product or product line? *If yes, then you can point out how you are helping the business stay healthy and competitive in other product areas while so much focus is on the new product introduction.*	☐	☐

(continued on page 224)

Step 9 Checklist. Plan quarterly context (continued).

			Yes	No
Seasonal Context	6.	Have you looked for new, more effective ways to handle perform-ance issues during seasonal highs or seasonal lows? *If not, do a little research so that you can make a proposal to influential members of your audience.*	☐	☐
	7.	Do you know if one of your organization's competitors implemented some best-in-class changes to pull ahead during the seasonal sales lifecycle in your organization's industry? *If not, think outside the box and examine how you can creatively use ideas from competitors or from other industries to maximize performance during seasonal highs or lows.*	☐	☐

 prefer not to write in this book, or if you'd like to print out larger versions or multiple copies of exercises and forms, you can find a complete set of all forms on the CD or on the companion Website (www.astd.org/astd/publications).

Checklist. Use the steps 10 and 11 checklist to help make sure you have the most powerful value themes and value statements possible. If you need help to complete any of the questions on this checklist, please see the concepts and exercises in chapters 12 and 13.

Step 12: Communicate and Refine Plan

In completing this chapter, you have reviewed and updated all of your key information about your value. You are in a great position to communicate your value. If you have created great value, your audience will want to know how you did it so that they can properly applaud your efforts and invite you to the table to tell them how you can do it again.

Steps 10 and 11 Checklist. Create value themes and create value statements.

 If you prefer not to write in this book, or if you'd like to print out larger versions or multiple copies of exercises and forms, you can find a complete set of all forms on the CD or on the companion Website (www.astd.org/astd/publications).

			Yes	No
Value Themes and Statements	1.	Would a change in either your performance measure or your financial measure reach more people in your audience or reach your audience more effectively? *If yes, change your message to capture more of your audience more effectively and efficiently.*	☐	☐
	2.	Are you using the most powerful direction verbs you can? *If not, use words that convey more movement, strength, and confidence.*	☐	☐
	3.	Have you pointed out your impact on multiple items of profit, position, or cash? Have you created some variety? *If not, perhaps you can take advantage of the impact your intervention creates on multiple financial statements.*	☐	☐
	4.	Are you using your value themes and statements creatively and in as many places as possible? *If not, consider various subtle marketing techniques to get your message across. For example, you may include a value theme in small letters at the bottom of every slide in a presentation, or you could include value themes and value statements inside your learning materials.*	☐	☐
Value Statements	5.	Are you using the highest level of evaluation data possible in your performance or financial amount of change? *If not, then give some thought to how you can improve the quality of the numbers that you are presenting so that your value statements carry more weight.*	☐	☐
	6.	Are your value statement and especially your goal segment stated as clearly as possible? *If you're not sure, ask a mentor or colleague for feedback. Practice pays off.*	☐	☐
	7.	Do you have a more detailed proposal ready to further explain your goal? *If not, then make sure you have one ready. You want to keep the interest of your audience when they ask you to tell them more about what you would like to do next.*	☐	☐

(continued on page 226)

Steps 10 and 11 Checklist. Create value themes and create value statements (continued).

			Yes	No
Value Statements	8.	Have you shown others in your organization or your client's how to use the same methods you've learned for communicating value? If not, then ask if they are interested. Teaching others ensures that you learn a subject better, plus having others who understand what you are trying to accomplish means more momentum for your flywheel.	☐	☐

 LET'S REVIEW: ────────────────

◆ This chapter contains a full set of checklists necessary for you to complete the 12th and final step in the financial value process: communicate and refine.

◆ Performing step 12 on a regular basis is good for your learning and helps you to think more strategically.

◆ To help you complete the checklists, this chapter contains pointers back to the appropriate chapters and to the CD and Website materials.

You've done it! You've gone from start to finish in the financial value process—one full turn of the flywheel.

One last note about what really is of value: You are in a unique profession that carries vast opportunities and profound responsibilities as a steward for your people. As a WLP professional, you are working with the most precious asset an organization can have to fulfill its quest to become successful, vibrant, and meaningful in the world. That asset is its people. As a WLP professional, you are privileged to be able to make deep and powerful changes in the lives of every individual that your interventions touch because learning and performance improvement always carries the potential for creating profound goodness in the lives of others. In the next and last chapter of this book, you'll find one final reminder of the importance of your effort to communicate your value.

15

---→

Conclusion:
The Courage to Begin

With knowledge as the driver for economic success, the people who have the best knowledge and who perform most effectively with that knowledge create huge competitive advantage. One cannot simply hope that the WLP interventions for an organization's people will be valuable. And, one cannot hope that the value of these interventions is obvious. Too much is at stake.

As WLP professionals we tend to focus on the *goal of the job*—excellence in performance at specific tasks. Behind every job, however, is the reason for its existence. As stewards of their organizations, executives focus on the *goal behind the job*—excellence in financial performance. Many of us have grown up hoping that if we focus on the goal of our job, it will be valuable and the value will be obvious.

As a profession, we are learning slowly, sometimes painfully, that hope is not a strategy. Our executives are telling us more and more forcefully that it is not their job to find value for us or to tell us what our value is. Like general managers and salespeople, managing, understanding, and communicating value is our job. We must do more than hope if we want a seat at the table with the stewards of our organizations.

It is out of character for WLP professionals to rely on mere hope. As WLP professionals, we know that one of the most difficult undertakings for anyone in any profession is to get people to adopt and apply learning and change. We don't hope that when we apply a WLP intervention that the intervention will be what the performance problem needs. As professionals, we have invested countless hours in performance analysis to ensure that we know exactly what we are doing and why we are doing it. We don't hope that our interventions will be designed with the most advanced performance and instructional theory and delivered to exacting standards.

We have invested the genius of our best in developing methodologies, tools, and techniques to ensure that we aren't just hoping that what we do will be acceptable. We are a profession that works with pride and honor. We strive for excellence. As a group, we do not accept that the best we can do is to throw something out there and . . . hope.

George Bernard Shaw wrote, "The reasonable man adapts himself to the world; the unreasonable one persists in trying to adapt the world to himself. Therefore all progress depends on the unreasonable man." There was a time when conventional wisdom said that ROI measurement for workplace learning or performance could not be done. I am grateful for the courage of the unreasonable men and women who stepped forward and refused to accept conventional wisdom about WLP measurement and evaluation. Because of their courage and example, the profession as a whole moved forward again, not with hope but with knowledge and assurance.

Yet, ROI measurement is not enough. For many in our profession, ROI measurement is applied as a one-time reaction to executives' demands to demonstrate our value. What our executives are really looking for is a keen awareness and a proactive, continuous approach to value management.

The Information Age has sped up life for all of us. By the time the results of many ROI studies are known, the gains are already factored into the financial statements and have become a given. To be sure, we must validate our results. Validation earns us trust, credibility, and insight into how we can do even better next time. But, to communicate value, the WLP professional needs something more. He or she needs the ability to continuously scan the financial horizon, the courage to propose new initiatives in terms of their contribution to the bottom line, and the tenacity to drive that contribution to reality.

There may be those who believe that keeping up with the financial issues of an organization, figuring out how to create and update a financial imperatives scorecard, staying mindful of organizational perceptions and context, and creating 30-second value statements is unreasonable. Perhaps they think, "Who has the time? You'd never get any real work done!" Or possibly, "I've tried this and it didn't work. All this talk must be for someone else, not me."

To those who think this way, I offer the following: First, it is your executives who are telling you to make the time. Translation from the language of performance to the language of finance is your job, not theirs. Second, even for the most successful salespeople who use similar concepts, this approach is not a magic potion that suddenly caused them to win every deal every time. But, with persistence and consistency, every one of them had the opportunity to win bigger and better than before.

Finally, it matters how much you are willing to fight for what you want. We all have personal stories of courage and determination. For example, I nearly died after childbirth and knew that the doctors did not give me much chance of survival. I am here today to write this book, so obviously I was determined to prove everyone in the hospital wrong. So fight for it if not for yourself, then for the ones you love. When it comes to communicating your value in terms that your audience appreciates and applauds, hope is not a strategy. Workplace learning and performance is a profession of pride, honor, and determination; it is not a profession that merely hopes.

The people in your organizations depend on you to get the support *you* need so you can equip *them* with what they need not just for performance on the job, but also for performance and satisfaction in every aspect of their lives. As a steward of your people, I call you and compel you to accept the same challenge as your peers at the table. Accept the challenge of leadership and change. Lead others to an understanding of the power of developing people. Change their understanding of the numbers to an understanding of the immense potential in performance. For this, courage is essential. As Goethe said, "What you can do, or dream you can do, begin it; boldness has genius, power, and magic in it."

All that is left is for you to begin. Enjoy your journey. Let it call to your soul as you communicate the genius, power, and magic of your people. May such courage bring you a life well spent in the service of others.

Glossary of Terms

A

Accounts Payable: Payments owed by a business to its vendors or suppliers for goods and services purchased.

Accounts Receivable: Payments owed to a business by its customers for goods and services purchased.

Accounts Receivable Collection Period: The average amount of time it takes to collect the money owed to a business from its customers.

Accrued Expenses: Expenses that accumulate at regular intervals, such as each day, but which will be paid at a future date.

Accumulated Depreciation: The cumulative amount of depreciation for the assets listed under property, plant, and equipment (PPE).

Asset Intensity: The amount of assets required to generate an organization's income.

Assets: The items on a balance sheet showing the value of the property an organization owns that are expected to be used to generate future income.

B

Balance Sheet: A written statement of the financial condition of an organization at a specific point in time and specifying all of the organization's assets and liabilities.

Balanced Scorecard Movement: A management strategy pioneered by Robert Kaplan and David Norton designed to give a complete picture of an organization by focusing on finances, customers, internal processes, and learning and growth.

Base Driver: A more detailed, lower-level performance measure on a financial value chain that is used to explain the movement in a higher, more broad financial measure.

Benchmarking: The practice of comparing one's own processes or services against the best practices of other highly regarded organizations with the goal of learning what others do that can be transferred into improving the processes of one's own organization.

Benefit-to-Cost Ratio: A ratio that shows how many dollars (or other monetary unit) of benefit were created for every one dollar of cost spent. Benefit-to-cost ratio is calculated by dividing the total gross benefits by the total costs of an intervention.

Bottom Line: Gross sales minus cost of goods sold/cost of services, other sales-driven expenses, fixed expenses, taxes, interest, depreciation, and other one-time or special expenses. Also called net profit (or loss).

C

Calendar Year: A 12-month period beginning on January 1 and ending on December 31. May or may not correspond with the fiscal year.

Capital: Funds, or other forms of assets and liabilities, used to generate income for an organization.

Cash: An asset of an organization that is held in the form of coins, currency, checks, or money orders or the amount representing these items held in a bank account.

Cash Flow Statement: A statement specifying sources and uses of cash over a particular period of time.

Change Management: A proactive, systematic, and planned approach to changing an organization so that it will achieve its organizational vision and goals, with minimal disruption to the individuals within the organization and to the organization as a whole.

Contribution Profit Margin: Equals the sales revenue minus cost of goods sold (COGS), revenue-driven expenses, and volume-driven expenses.

Contribution Profit Margin Ratio: Ratio of contribution profit margin to sales revenue.

Cost of Capital: The finance charges, or the cost of borrowing funds, to pay for an investment in a major new project for a business or to pay for other seasonal or extraordinary items.

Cost of Goods Sold (COGS): The sum of material costs, labor costs, and direct overhead costs.

Cost per Order Dollar (CPOD): Gross sales divided by sales-driven expenses. Provides a way to track if sales-driven expenses are dropping, holding steady, or rising to obtain the same level of gross revenue from customer orders.

Current Assets: Assets that will be converted to cash within 1 year.

Current Liabilities: Liabilities that will paid within 1 year.

Current Ratio: Current assets divided by current liabilities.

D

Days Inventory Supply: The average number of days inventory is held before it is sold.

Depreciation: The process of expensing the cost of a fixed asset over a useful life. The amount of the asset expensed is determined using one of several defined depreciation methods.

E

Earnings Before Income Taxes: Net sales (or revenue) minus all expenses except income taxes, specifically COGS, other revenue-driven expenses, fixed operating expenses, and interest expenses.

Earnings Before Interest, Taxes, Depreciation, and Amortization (EBITDA): Calculated by looking at earnings after COGS, other sales-driven expenses, and fixed operating expenses have been removed from revenue, but before interest, taxes, depreciation, and amortization are taken into account.

Effectiveness: Creating new or additional impact on an organization's financial measures or financial statements such that the impact makes a significant or sizable difference to the success of the organization.

Efficiency: Delivering the same level of benefit as before but at a lower intervention cost.

F

Financial Imperatives Scorecard: A format for tracking the benefits and costs of workplace learning and prevention interventions.

Financial Metrics or Measures: Measures of value that are based strictly on financial or monetary considerations, such as COGS.

Financial Ratios: Measures describing whether an organization is making enough return for its efforts. Ratios describe balance.

Financial Statements: Written statements detailing an organization's finances, including balance sheets, income statements, and cash flow statements. Together these statements give a presentation of the organization's financial condition for a specific time period.

Financial Value: The worth of a workplace learning and performance intervention as expressed in financial terms.

Financial Value Chain: A cascading, linked set of measures where the leftmost measure is a broad, financially based measure of a Senior executive and the rightmost measure is a specific, performance-based measure of an Individual contributor.

Financial Value Process: A process for connecting the merit or value of a workplace learning and performance intervention directly to the financial measures and goals of an organization.

Financing Activities: A section on the cash flow statement that displays all of the changes in cash flow caused by management's decisions to obtain or pay back debt. Transactions with owner's equity, such as issuing or purchasing stock, also go in this section of the cash flow statement.

Fiscal Year: A 12-month accounting period adopted by an organization starting on the first day of a specified month and ending on the last day of the twelfth month. May or may not correspond with the calendar year.

Fixed Operating Expenses: Expenses that are incurred regardless of the level of production. An example would be the cost to pay a monthly lease on a building that houses a production plant. The monthly lease must be paid, even if the plant is shut down and not producing anything. Also referred to as fixed expenses.

G

Generally Accepted Accounting Principles (GAAP): In the United States, the Financial Accounting Standards Board (FASB) issues and regularly updates a huge set of statements that define acceptable accounting practices.

Gross Profit: Net sales minus COGS.

H

Hoshin Process: A strategy based on identifying vital key issues in an organization and focusing on these issues at all levels of the organization.

Human Performance Technology (HPT): A methodology that uses performance analysis, cause analysis, and intervention selection for solving problems or enabling new opportunities based on the improved performance of people. People may be classified in any combination of individuals, small groups, or large organizations.

I

Income Statement: A written financial statement showing details of revenues, costs, expenses, losses, and profits for a specific time period.

Indicators: Measures where changes could imply that an intervention is or is not having the desired effect on the workplace. For example, if the goal of a stress management program is to reduce errors as a result of reduced stress, then a reduction in the error rate may mean that stress has indeed been reduced.

Intervention: A systematic, planned response to an identified gap between current performance and desired performance. Can take many forms depending on the business conditions and allowable time frame for implementation. Also commonly referred to as programs, solutions, or strategies in workplace learning and performance literature.

Inventory: The monetary value of the product a company has on hand but has not yet sold in the normal course of operating its business. Inventory may be referred to by its various states, such as raw materials, work in process, or finished goods.

Investing Activities: A section on the cash flow statement that displays all of the changes in cash flow caused by investments made by the management of the organization. A common investment is the purchase of new property, plant, or equipment (PPE).

J

Just-in-Time (JIT) Inventory Management: A strategy in which raw materials and components that meet pre-specified quality levels are produced, or delivered from a supplier, immediately before they are needed in the manufacturing process. The underlying goal is to reduce waste from several areas of the production process such as waste from overproduction, transportation, processing methods, production defects, or production waiting or idle time.

K

Kano Model of Product Quality: A theory developed by Noriaki Kano describing levels of value perception.

L

Leverage: The amount of debt or borrowed money an organization is using to fund its operations. Leverage is not good or bad. If it is used wisely, it can have tax advantages or other beneficial impacts. Organizations that are highly leveraged (that is, carrying too much debt versus their assets) may be at great risk if any adverse business conditions arise that would cause them to be unable to pay their expenses. They may not be able to get any additional loans in an emergency. Such organizations may be forced into bankruptcy or driven out of business.

Leverage Ratio: Total liabilities divided by owner's equity.

Liabilities: Debts and other financial obligations that an organization has at a particular point in time.

Liquidity: A measure of the ease that a non-cash asset (such as real estate) can be converted into cash assets.

Liquidity Ratio: See quick ratio.

Long-Term Assets: Assets that will be held by an organization for more than 1 year from the date of the balance sheet.

Long-Term Liabilities: Liabilities that will come due for an organization more than 1 year from the date of the balance sheet.

M

Managing Position: Maintaining the appropriate mix of the assets, liabilities, and owner's equity of the organization.

Market: A defined group of buying customers. Examples are: Eastern European small business owners, adults over age 50 in the United States, worldwide automobile consumers.

Market Share: The percentage of sales for a type of product or service, made to a specific market, by a given company. For example, if Company X sold 15 percent of all scuba diving gear to consumers in Florida, Company X would have a 15 percent market share for this type of product, in this market.

Material Costs: Also known as direct materials. Direct materials are all materials that become a part of the finished product of a manufacturing operation.

Measures: See Financial Metrics or Measures; Performance Metrics or Measures.

Metrics: See Financial Metrics or Measures; Performance Metrics or Measures.

N

Net Profit (or Loss): Gross sales minus cost of goods sold/cost of services, other sales-driven expenses, fixed expenses, taxes, interest, depreciation, and other one-time or special expenses. This is the proverbial bottom line.

O

Operating Activities: A section on the cash flow statement that displays all of the changes in cash flow caused by the normal day-to-day operation of the business. Increases or decreases in accounts receivable would be an example of changes from an operating activity.

Operating Earnings: Contribution profit margin minus fixed expenses.

Operating Expenses: See Fixed Operating Expenses.

Operating Margin: The percentage difference between gross revenue (R) and operating costs (C), or $(R - C) \div R$.

Operating Ratios: Measures of the relationships and balance between revenue and expenses and their corresponding assets and liabilities.

Organizational Chain: The management structure of an organization expressed in broad layers or terms.

Overhead: Costs that are not directly attributable to a specific product.

Owner's Equity: Total assets minus total liabilities.

P

Penetration: The total number of intervention attendees or intervention participants who successfully applied the intervention on the job.

Performance Metrics or Measures: Measures of value that are based on an individual or organization's performance, for example, an outstanding appraisal or the number of individuals trained in a particular area.

Position: The financial condition of an organization. Positions can be fairly secure (healthy) or highly at risk (unhealthy) due to situations such as too much liabilities versus assets.

Prepaid Expenses: Expenses that must be paid for before they are used.

Profit: The amount of revenue or gain left over for a business after all expenses have been subtracted from revenue. Always a positive number. (The opposite of loss, which is always a negative number.)

Profit and Loss Statement: Another name for income statement.

Profit Line: One of several lines in an income statement detailing contribution profit margin, operating earnings, earnings before income tax, or net profit (or loss).

Profit Ratio: The ratio of one of the profit lines to the net sales (revenue).

Q

Quick Ratio: Total amount of current assets less inventory, divided by current liabilities.

R

Ratio: The result of dividing one value by another. In financial terms, ratios are indicators of the amount of balance between different factors. Examples include the amount of assets versus liabilities or the amount of a line of profit versus revenue.

Return-on-Assets (ROA): Net income divided by net operating assets, expressed as a percentage.

Return-on-Equity (ROE): Net income divided by owner's equity, expressed as a percentage.

Return-on-Investment (ROI): Net return divided by investment, expressed as a percentage. The return may refer to earnings, income, profit, gain, or appreciation in value. Investment means the amount of capital used to generate the return. Frequently refers to the return gained and the investment made in a 1-year period. Specifically, ROI equals $[(R - I) \div I] \times 100$, where R is the total return and I is the total investment cost.

Rework Rate: Percentage of goods or actions that are defective or of low quality that they must have additional work added to them before they can be sold or accepted.

S

Sales Mix: The balance of products and services sold as related to their price and volume.

Seasonality: The naturally occurring cycles of variations in sales levels or other measures during the course of the year.

Shareholder's Equity: The equivalent of owner's equity in a corporation.

Source and Application of Funds: Another name for cash flow statement.

Speed: How quickly the benefits of the intervention can be obtained.

Statement of Operations: Another name for income statement.

Statement of Utilization of Funds: Another name for cash flow statement.

Succession Plans: Plans created within an organization to identify and then develop one or more potential successors for key positions within the organization.

Sustainability: The length of time participants who apply the WLP intervention continue to do so.

T

Total Quality Management: An organizational management approach to managing the process, culture, innovation cycle, and customer satisfaction goals of an organization through a focus on continuous improvements in quality and value.

V

Value: The relative worth, importance, utility, or degree of excellence of something or someone.

Value Add: A column on the financial imperatives scorecard describing the amount of financial change an intervention has, or is expected to create for an organization.

Value Communication: Clearly and succinctly describing the value of your interventions in terms of the measures that your audience is judged by.

Value Connection: The connection between the employee's contribution and its benefit to his or her target audience.

Value Lifecycle: A set of urgent and important activities corresponding to the annual budget and planning cycle, product development cycle, or seasonal sales cycle of an organization.

Value Statement: A concise description of value that translates performance improvement into financial improvement relevant to the listener's current priorities. The value is linked to a goal that the person making the statement would like to achieve next to add even more value to an organization.

Value Theme: A statement of a specific intervention to an organizational problem or an activity that will have a positive effect on a financial measure, in terms of how and why that problem or measure will be affected.

W

White Paper: Documents of 10–20 pages that can be read in 30–60 minutes. White papers summarize the position, approach, framework, issues, strategies, trends, and/or conclusions about a particular topic from the group producing the white paper. White papers may be produced internally to an organization and remain confidential or may be publicly distributed by government agencies, special interest groups, marketing organizations, technology groups, or research committees.

Workplace Learning and Performance (WLP): Professional activity focused on improving productivity in the workplace through learning, training, or other performance improvement processes, programs, and interventions.

References

Beginnersinvest.about.com. (2003a). "Return on Assets (ROA): Investing Lesson 4: Analyzing an Income Statement." http://beginnersinvest.about.com/cs/investinglessons/l/blreturnonasset.htm.

Beginnersinvest.about.com. (2003b). "Return on Equity (ROE): Investing Lesson 4: Analyzing an Income Statement." http://beginnersinvest.about.com/library/lessons/bl-returnonequity.htm.

Bing, G. (2002). *Selecting Your Employer: A Guide to an Informed Pursuit of the Best Career for You.* Boston: Butterworth-Heinemann.

Cialdini, R. (1998). *Influence: The Psychology of Persuasion* (revised edition). New York: Quill.

Collins, J. (2001). *Good to Great: Why Some Companies Make the Leap...and Others Don't.* New York: HarperCollins.

Drake, S.M., and R.G. Dingler. (2001). *The Practical Guide to Finance and Accounting: A Plain-Language, Non-Technical Explanation of All Key Concepts, Terms, Practices, and Procedures That Anyone Can Use.* Paramus, NJ: Prentice Hall Press.

Gardner, D., and T. Gardner. (1996). *The Motley Fool Investment Guide: How the Fool Beats Wall Street's Wise Men and How You Can Too.* New York: Fireside.

Hunter, J.E., Schmidt, F.L., and M.K. Judiesch. (1990). "Individual Differences in Output Variability as a Function of Job Complexity." *Journal of Applied Psychology, 75*(1) 28–42.

Investorwords.com. (1997–2003). "EBITDA." http://www.investorwords.com/cgi-bin/getword.cgi?1632.

Kano, N. (1984). Translated by G. Mazur. "Attractive Quality and Must-Be Quality." *Japan Society for Quality Control, 14*(2), 39–48.

Kaplan, R.S., and D.P. Norton. (1996). *The Balanced Scorecard: Translating Strategy into Action.* Boston: Harvard Business School Press.

Kenyon, D.A. (1997, May). "Strategic Planning With the Hoshin Process." *Quality Digest.* http://www.qualitydigest.com/may97/html/hoshin.html.

Kindley, R.W. (2001, November). "Human Asset Professionals and the Quest for Leadership Status." HR.com. http://www.hr.com/hrcom/index.cfm/3/65ED3C5A-C494-4A8A-842DE654D0A8BC47.

Kirkpatrick, D.L. (1994). *Evaluating Training Programs: The Four Levels.* San Francisco: Berrett-Koehler Publishers.

Kruse, K. (2002). "Introduction to Instructional Design and the ADDIE Model." E-LearningGuru.com. www.e-learningguru.com/articles/art2_1.htm.

Phillips, J.J. (1997). *Return on Investment in Training and Performance Improvement Programs: A Step-by-Step Manual for Calculating the Financial Return.* Houston: Gulf Publishing Company.

Robinson, D.G., and J.C. Robinson. (1995). *Performance Consulting: Moving Beyond Training.* San Francisco: Berrett-Koehler Publishers.

Seagraves, T. (2003). "The Competitive Weapon: Using ROI to Drive Results." In: Schmidt, L. (editor). *In Action: Implement Training Scorecards.* Alexandria, VA: ASTD.

Stolovitch, H.D., and E.J. Keeps (editors). (1999). *Handbook of Human Performance Technology: Improving Individual and Organizational Performance Worldwide.* San Francisco: Jossey-Bass Pfeiffer.

Sugrue, B. (2003). *2003 State of the Industry: ASTD's Annual Review of U.S. and International Trends in Workplace Learning and Performance.* Alexandria, VA: ASTD.

Tracy, J.A. (1996). *Budgeting à la Carte: Essential Tools for Harried Business Managers.* New York: John Wiley & Sons.

United Kingdom Department of Trade and Industry. (1998). Untitled paper. http://www.dti.gov.uk/comp/competitive/pdfs/ap_pdf1.pdf.

U.S. Department of Labor. (2003). *Occupational Outlook Handbook.* Washington, DC: Bureau of Labor Statistics, U.S. Department of Labor.

Additional Resources

Business Finance

Myriad books and references are on the market to help you understand business finance. Just a few are listed here. A visit to your local bookstore or a browse online will help you find many, many more.

Books

How to Use Financial Statements: A Guide to Understanding the Numbers. Bandler, J. (1994). New York: McGraw-Hill.

> In this short book (147 pages), Bandler does an outstanding job of explaining the basic relationships among financial statements. Bandler uses excellent pictures to demonstrate the makeup of financial statements and to show how a single financial transaction can affect statements. This is an excellent reference for people who want to know more and have no previous exposure to understanding basic financial statements.

Budgeting à La Carte: Essential Tools for Harried Business Managers. Tracy, J.A. (1996). New York: John Wiley & Sons.

> Tracy is a very popular financial author who specializes in writing books to help nonfinancial people understand accounting and finance. A browse through the business book section of your local bookstore will turn up several of his books. *Budgeting à La Carte* utilizes an extra-wide layout that allows the author to use well-drawn examples to show the connections between financial statements. Tracy has also written easy-to-read explanations of why different budgeting decisions can have dramatic impacts on these statements. These explanations should help you be able to speak more knowledgeably with Senior managers about why your solutions will help their profit, position, and cash.

Modern Cost Management and Analysis (2d edition). Shim, J.K, and J.G. Siegel. (2000). Hauppauge, NY: Barron's Educational Series.

> This book provides a wealth of detail about different types of costs and financial scenarios for many types of businesses. This is a great book to browse through if you are having trouble creating value chains to fit the expense situations in your target organization. It can help give you

additional financial terms to use in translating from the language of performance to the language of finance.

The Portable MBA in Finance and Accounting (3d edition). Livingstone, J.L, and T. Grossman (eds.). (2002). Hauppauge, NY: John Wiley & Sons.

The *Portable MBA* is actually rather thick so don't plan to put it in your back pocket! You'll find 18 different authors discussing common financial budgeting and management issues. The book uses case studies, pictures, and examples that you can use in making the case for your contribution to the bottom line. Like *Modern Cost Management and Analysis,* this book gives you additional financial terms and value examples to use in translating from the language of performance to the language of finance.

Websites

The Internet can provide a world of information about companies and their financial status. Websites tend to disappear over time and are often replaced by others that are even better. Here are some Websites that were available when this book was written that can help you research financial information:

The glossary available at Investorwords.com (www.investorwords.com) is a goldmine for all those hard-to-understand terms that you may hear in financial discussions. It's a quick way to find well-written definitions for words, ratios, and terms. Most items are cross-referenced to related topics.

The U.S. Securities and Exchange Commission's Website (www.sec.gov) is a source for annual reports and other statements for publicly held companies.

Forbes, Inc. maintains a Website (www.forbes.com) with information on the 500 top private companies. Other valuable business sites include Dun & Bradstreet (www.dnb.com), the Brandow Company (www.bizminer.com), Zacks (www.zacks.com/research), and Hoover's Online (www.hoovers.com). They all specialize in information for investors and business people. You can find information on companies and industries at these sites.

www.monster.com is a job search site that can give information about where the company is hiring and what types of measures and responsibilities are expected of the applicants.

Don't overlook general search engines, such as www.google.com, for searching for a company name alone or together with other words or phrases such as "annual report" or "press release."

Management and Organization Analysis

Knowing how to look for potential management issues when analyzing an organization is a fundamental skill in proposing value. Many basic investing books and Websites will explain how to analyze an organization. Here are a few that go beyond the norm to help you gain broader insights:

The Turnaround Prescription: Repositioning Troubled Companies. Goldston, M.R. (1992). New York: The Free Press.

> Goldston built a reputation in the early 1990s as a company-turnaround expert. In this book, he lays out the symptoms to look for in troubled companies and recommends actions to take to get a company back on track. Although the book is very marketing-oriented, the symptom and transformation blueprints are applicable in a wide range of settings. The descriptions in this book can help anyone trying to discern the real value of potential solutions from a maze of financial statements, industry data, press releases, internal memos, and hearsay.

Selecting Your Employer: A Guide to an Informed Pursuit of the Best Career for You. Bing, G. (2002). Boston: Butterworth-Heinemann.

> This book is the only one I have found that walks a job seeker through the appropriate financial, company ownership, and management issues that affect the decision of whether a company is a good one to want to join. This is an excellent perspective for many consultants and vendors as well, not to mention people within an organization who are evaluating how much of themselves to continue to invest in that organization. Bing does an excellent job of describing what traits to look for and questions to ask to uncover strengths and trouble signs in an organization.

Workplace Learning and Performance ROI

Publications

There are a number of excellent authors writing about how to measure ROI for WLP interventions. Some of my favorites include:

How to Measure Training Results: A Practical Guide to Tracking the Six Key Indicators. Phillips, J.J., and R.D. Stone. (2002). New York: McGraw-Hill.

> Phillips is one of the premier authors on calculating training ROI. He has written and edited several books on the subject. This book is written in very straightforward terms with plenty of forms and examples. Pages 54 and 55 give excellent examples of hard and soft data that can be used in value chains. Once you've targeted the value you want to provide, Phillips' process is very helpful in proving that you actually provided it.

Linking Learning and Performance: A Practical Guide to Measuring Learning and On-the-Job Performance. Hodges, T.K. (2002). Boston: Butterworth-Heinemann.

> This book outlines the links between the language of finance and the language of performance. In *Linking Learning and Performance,* Hodges has done a masterful job of describing how to design learning and performance so that they can be consistently accomplished and measured within an organization. This book is an excellent reference to help you ensure that the value you are claiming you will create is actually accomplished on the job.

Performance Consulting: Moving Beyond Training. Robinson, D.G., and J.C. Robinson. (1995). San Francisco: Berrett-Koehler Publishers.

> The Robinsons' book is a classic in the field, focusing on the need to connect to the business concerns and describe the performance that must be delivered, and then suggesting ways that the WLP professional can meet the business and performance need. Their performance relationship maps and step-by-step instructions help both the members of our profession and the managers we work with in understanding the difference between training and performance.

Handbook of Human Performance Technology: Improving Individual and Organizational Performance Worldwide (2d edition). Stolovitch, H.D., and E.J. Keeps (editors). (1999). San Francisco: Jossey-Bass Pfeiffer.

> This comprehensive volume has chapters by more than 65 distinguished WLP authors. The chapters offer a wide range of insights into a full range of performance challenges.

In Action: Measuring Return-on-Investment (volumes 1, 2, 3). Phillips, J.J. (series editor). (1994, 1997, 2001). Alexandria, VA: ASTD.

> The case studies in these books describe how WLP practitioners have accounted for costs, benefits, and ROI. They are excellent references to see how others have handled making the case for their value.

Websites and Organizations

ASTD's ROI Network is an organization that hosts its own focused conferences on training, performance, and ROI measurement. This is a great place to get additional information, hear about leading-edge research, and meet other ROI practitioners. You can learn more at www.roi.astd.org.

The author maintains a Website (www.drive-roi.com) dedicated to WLP ROI measurement and ways to rapidly communicate the value of WLP interventions.

Yahoo ROInet is a moderated discussion group with lively chat threads covering different viewpoints about training and ROI measurement for WLP interventions. Members are very helpful in answering questions. A wealth of information can be found by searching the discussion logs for the last several years.

Sales and Communicating Value

Your executives want you to act more like salespeople. There are a number of excellent books about selling on the market. Here are some that explicitly address the issue of communicating value with executives.

Books

Hope is Not a Strategy: The 6 Keys to Winning the Complex Sale. Page, R. (2002). New York: McGraw-Hill.

> In this book you'll find a very important discussion of what business developers do to uncover the real pain, tie it to the financial future of a company, and put themselves in a much more strategic position with their clients. This is exactly what WLP professionals need to do to gain a seat at the table and fulfill their duties as the true stewards for their people, their organizations, and their clients. This is a book for WLP professionals who want to know more about why senior executives want you to act more like salespeople.

Selling to VITO: The Very Important Top Officer. Parinello, A. (1999). Holbrook, MA: Adams Media Corporation.

> Parinello spends a great deal of time sorting out who in an organization makes decisions and who does not. Using this information, you can figure out how to spend your time on the right kind of people. As a WLP professional and not a pure salesperson, you need to continuously communicate and deliver value at all levels of your organization. What you will find interesting in Parinello's book are his examples of how to use what he calls opening statements in phone calls, letters, memos, and other forms of communication. Parinello has done an excellent job of providing a wealth of examples to describe the objections that executives often raise. He then shows you how to handle those objections.

What's Keeping Your Customers Up at Night?: Close More Deals by Selling to Your Client's Pain. Cody, S., and R. Harte. (2003). New York: McGraw-Hill.

> When you venture into discussions of how to make a difference on financial statements, you'll inevitably touch on sensitive subjects. It may take some time for your executives to open up to you. It's possible to inadvertently make a situation worse instead of better by not knowing how to recognize and diffuse sensitivity and distrust. Cody and Harte describe how to approach difficult subjects with executives or decision makers. Their book gives examples of body language and samples of actual conversations.

About the Author

With more than 18 years of experience working in workforce development, career development, total quality management, information systems, and high technology, Theresa Seagraves became a recognized leader at Hewlett-Packard for creating innovative, world-class data and people-development systems.

In 2001, Theresa established her own consulting company, Theresa L. Seagraves & Associates (TLSA). Theresa works full time consulting with clients on ROI evaluations, conducting ROI studies, and coaching organizations and individuals in aligning and communicating their financial value. Theresa has filed for a U.S. patent for software that tracks ROI, penetration, sustainability, and best practices gained from workplace learning and performance initiatives.

Theresa has written newsletters on personal success as well as case studies on ROI and creation of training scorecards.

Theresa lives near Denver, Colorado. She is married to her high school sweetheart. They have two wonderful children. In her spare time, she attends her daughter's marching band competitions, her son's baseball and basketball games, takes classes in her community, keeps up with extended family, and finds ways to bring laughter to each day.

Theresa may be contacted at tseagraves@drive-roi.com. Her Website is www.drive-roi.com.